Psychology,
Theology,
and Spirituality
in Christian
Counseling

OTHER BOOKS TO BE RELEASED IN THE AACC COUNSELING LIBRARY

Counseling Children through the World of Play
   by Daniel Sweeney, Ph.D.

Treating Sex Offenders
   by Dan Henderson, Ph.D.

Counseling through the Maze of Divorce
   by George Ohlschlager, J.D., L.C.S.W.

Treating Victims of Sexual Abuse
   by Diane Langberg. Ph.D.

Counseling in Trauma Situations
   by H. Norman Wright, D.D., and Tim Thompson, D. Min.

Brief Counseling
   by Gary J. Oliver, Ph.D.

AACC
COUNSELING
LIBRARY

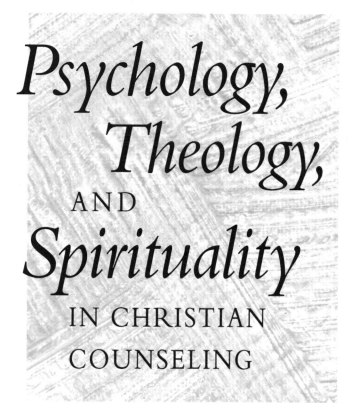

Psychology,
Theology,
AND
Spirituality
IN CHRISTIAN
COUNSELING

MARK R. MCMINN, PH.D.

 Tyndale House Publishers, Inc.
CAROL STREAM, ILLINOIS

The American Association of Christian Counselors is an organization of professional, pastoral, and lay counselors committed to the promotion of excellence and unity in Christian counseling. The AACC provides conferences, software, video and audio resources, two professional journals, a resource review, as well as other publications and resources. Membership is open to anyone who writes for information: AACC, P.O. Box 739, Forest, VA 24551.

Visit Tyndale's exciting Web site at www.tyndale.com

TYNDALE is a registered trademark of Tyndale House Publishers, Inc.

Tyndale's inkwell logo is a registered trademark of Tyndale House Publishers, Inc.

Psychology, Theology, and Spirituality in Christian Counseling

Copyright © 1996 by Mark R. McMinn

Designed by Beth Sparkman
Edited by Lynn Vanderzalm

Library of Congress Cataloging-in-Publication Data

McMinn, Mark R.
   Psychology, theology, and spirituality in Christian counseling / Mark R. McMinn.
      p.   cm.
   Includes bibliographical references.
   ISBN-13: 978-0-8423-5252-9 (alk. paper)
   ISBN-10: 0-8423-5252-X (alk. paper)
      1. Pastoral counseling.   2. Psychology and religion.   I. Title.
   BV4012.2.M26   1996
   253.5é2—dc20   96-12604

Printed in the United States of America

12   11   10   09   08   07   06
15   14   13   12   11   10   9   8

Dedicated to Christian counselors
May we grow in depth as we grow in numbers.

CONTENTS

ACKNOWLEDGMENTS

The idea for this book started when I could not find a text for a Religious Issues in Psychotherapy class I was teaching at George Fox College. Students in that class helped me develop and refine many of the ideas written here. Similarly, my current students at Wheaton College have helped me think carefully about the integration tasks we confront in the counseling office. I am particularly grateful for the help of my two graduate student assistants, John D. Scanish and Katheryn Rhoads Meek. They each spent many hours helping me collect materials for this book. In addition to helping with background research, Kathy's conceptual and literary contributions to chapter 7 were especially helpful and important.[1]

Several have helped with my relatively recent interest in spiritual formation. Dr. Jim Wilhoit made many important contributions to chapter 1 and taught the spirituality class at Wheaton College that changed my life in 1993.[2] My wife, Dr. Lisa McMinn, has encouraged me in the spiritual disciplines by her example and words of support. A number of contemporary authors, especially Richard Foster and Dallas Willard, have ushered me along this spiritual journey with their insightful books.

Dr. Gary Collins, president of the American Association of Christian Counselors, has encouraged my writing in recent years. More important, he models Christian integrity with his quiet commitment to serving others, usually in ways that bring no recognition or credit. Ms. Joyce Farrell, my literary agent, shares her gift of encouragement and the expertise that comes from many years of working in publishing. Finally, Lynn Vanderzalm and others on the editorial staff at Tyndale House Publishers have been wonderful in every way: technically excellent, pleasant, encouraging, and ministry focused.

INTRODUCTION

This is a book about two secret places in counselors' lives. First, it is a book about what happens behind the closed doors of counseling offices. Over the past few decades, Christian psychologists and counselors have made great progress in reuniting the disciplines of theology and psychology after they were torn apart by antireligion psychologists and antipsychology religious leaders early in the twentieth century, but this progress is often difficult to translate into specific counseling strategies. Too often the best academic books and articles about integration are filled with intriguing ideas and models but do not practically address how we ought to be integrating them in the counseling office. Though I also do some theoretical pondering and model building (chapters 1 and 2) in order to provide a context for subsequent chapters, I have devoted the largest portion of this book (chapters 3–8) to the questions we confront when sitting face-to-face with our clients. Is it wise to pray with this client? Under what circumstances should I use Scripture memory as part of counseling? What is the proper role of confession in the therapy process? Is forgiveness a reasonable goal in this situation? These are the kinds of practical questions I have pondered in developing this book.

Second, this is a book about the secret spiritual life of Christian counselors. Throughout my years of professional work, I have become increasingly convinced that the value of counseling interventions is found less in one's technical training and theoretical orientation than in one's character. At first this may seem discouraging because most of us struggle with nagging character flaws and because we are unsure how to train ourselves in matters of character.

But as we are drawn deeper into the spiritual life, we recognize that it is not merely our flawed character that we bring into interactions with others; it is divine character revealed through us. Furthermore, we learn training methods and spiritual disciplines that gradually transform us and make us more likely to reflect the humility, compassion, forgiveness, and redemptive capacity that we find in Christ.

I also need to offer a disclaimer in introducing this book. The methodology of this book is integration, not exhaustive review. Even if I were qualified to write a comprehensive book about theology or spirituality, I would be left with the questions of which theology and which spirituality to review. The ambitious title of this book is meant to reflect the *integration* task I am undertaking by bringing spirituality, as well as psychology and theology, into the Christian counseling office. Thus, my chapters reflect a relatively thin slice of theology in the Reformed tradition, an even thinner slice of spirituality that is consistent with evangelical Christianity, and a somewhat broader look at psychology. The goal of each chapter is to bring these three together for Christian counselors.

I hope you find value in these pages and that you will take time to communicate your ideas and responses to me. Integration is a community process that calls Christian counselors from all over the world to work together.

Mark R. McMinn
Wheaton, Illinois

1/ RELIGION
in the
COUNSELING OFFICE

written with James C. Wilhoit

After lying awake in bed for several hours, as she does most mornings, Jill drags her tired body downstairs, starts the coffee-maker, plops the Yellow Pages on the kitchen counter, and "lets her fingers do the walking" to *Counselors*. Jill knows she is depressed, overwhelmed with feelings of guilt and inadequacy, and she knows she needs help. But she worries about finding the right counselor, recognizing that her choice could have profound implications on her spiritual life.

Counselor A might tell Jill that her depression is worsened by her silly religious ideas. What she really needs, according to this counselor, is to think clearly and logically about the world, relax her neurotic demands for perfection, and begin finding ways to enjoy life. Counselor A tells Jill that as soon as she grows beyond her religious faith, she will be well.

Counselor B is more interested in listening than in telling Jill what to do. Jill's religious values have meaning for her, so Counselor B listens and responds to Jill empathetically: "Your religious values seem very important to you. It sounds as if you want to do the right thing, but you're not always sure what the right thing is. What I hear you saying is that you want God to help you through this difficult time in your life." This counselor assumes that Jill needs a supportive companion or a transitional object to help her learn new ways of relating to others and herself. Religion can be discussed in therapy, but the power of change is found in the therapeutic relationship.

Counselor C tells Jill that depression results from personal sin. She feels guilty because God has given us all the gift of guilt so that we remember to confess our sins and depend more on him. By looking carefully at Scripture, the counselor helps Jill find areas of sin in her life, admit her fallenness, and ask God for forgiveness.

These are just a few of the possible counseling approaches hidden behind block ads and telephone numbers in Jill's Yellow Pages. How will she decide? Will Jill reach out to the right counselor for help? Will she find someone to help her toward greater emotional and spiritual health?

Jill is not alone in her search for spiritually sensitive counseling. In a survey of Florida residents randomly selected from telephone listings, a greater number of respondents preferred help from a pastor than from a psychologist, social worker, psychiatrist, or community mental health center.[1] Similarly, in an analog study with middle-aged adults, participants found religiously sensitive counselors more trustworthy, likable, and approachable than agnostic or atheistic counselors.[2]

COUNSELORS ARE CONFUSED TOO

Religion and religious values have become a frequent topic of discussion for many counselors in recent years, and most counselors have thought a great deal about the confusion their clients face in choosing a good therapist.[3] But when it comes to religious values in the counseling office, our clients are not alone. Many counselors feel confused too.

Counselor A sounds confident in rejecting religion but is having problems finding evidence to support such a view. Strident atheists, such as Albert Ellis, have argued for years that religion causes illness.[4] But as their claims have been contradicted by research evidence, they have become more cautious in their rejection of religion.[5] Ellis, for example, now says it is fanatical and rigid religious beliefs, not religion per se, that cause problems. Ellis even endorsed the Bible as a useful self-help book in a 1993 article: "I think that I can safely say that the Judeo-Christian Bible is a self-help book that has probably enabled more people to make more extensive and intensive personality and behavioral changes than all professional therapists combined."[6]

Counselor B has always been open-minded and willing to accept any widely accepted religious belief as an important aspect of mental health. But some of the recent critiques of postmodernism have Counselor B wondering: If we accept any belief as valid, then do any beliefs have merit? If all truth is constructed by one's own values and beliefs, then can't truth also be deconstructed, so that nothing is ultimately true?[7]

Counselor C is a biblical counselor who rejects all secular theories of counseling in favor of using Scripture as the source of all knowledge. But every now and then Counselor C reads about the integration movement in psychology and theology and privately wonders if some psychological techniques may help resolve some emotional problems. What about the finding that panic attacks can be effectively treated with twelve sessions of breathing training and cognitive therapy?[8] Or what about the list of empirically validated treatment procedures being developed by the Clinical Psychology Division of the American Psychological Association (APA)? Each procedure on the list has been verified effective by at least two double-blind controlled-outcome studies.[9] Can biblical counselors continue to say that psychotherapy and counseling don't work when there is so much evidence to the contrary?

It is good we have a group of religious counseling specialists—those who have spent many hours preparing to transcend the confusion faced by clients and most counselors. These specialists integrate Christian theology and psychological techniques and help their clients with both spiritual and emotional growth. They cling to the truth of Christ as revealed in Scripture and deliberately allow their beliefs to saturate their counseling methods. They respect and honor people's Christian values while helping them understand and change their emotional pain. They help people like Jill. Surely they never feel confused when people like Jill come for help. Right?

Wrong. Even those involved in the Christian counseling movement often face feelings of confusion in the counseling office. The counseling office is where the integration of Christian beliefs and counseling techniques becomes most practical, and it is often where we feel most bombarded with unanswered questions. When should we pray with clients? Is forgiveness reasonable for a survivor of sexual abuse? Should we confront sin or wait for our clients to recognize it on their own? Is reconciliation always a reasonable goal? Are there times when divorce is acceptable? Do I have any evidence that this religiously oriented counseling approach is effective? Are the spiritual disciplines a necessary part of emotional healing? Is one theoretical approach to counseling more compatible with Christianity than another? Can Scripture memory contribute to denial and unhealthy defenses? Are positive self-talk and self-esteem contrary to Scripture?

What seems clear in the latest scientific journal or latest professional book somehow seems fuzzy in the counseling office. Even biblical principles, which we hold to be true and authoritative, sometimes seem difficult to apply as we work with our clients.

This is a book about counseling process and techniques. Although I will review a number of surveys, scientific studies, Scripture passages, and theoretical models, my primary purpose is to focus on the problems we face in the counseling office. I don't have all the answers, and I cannot promise that those who read this book will never again feel confused and uncertain about religious issues in the counseling office. But perhaps this book will help Christian counselors and researchers unite around certain key questions and perspectives so that our interventions become increasingly relevant and effective.

THE FRONTIER OF INTEGRATION

When Jill finally finds a Christian counselor, she schedules an appointment, rehearses what she will say, and shows up ten minutes early for her first appointment. Her counselor, Dr. N. T. Gration, ushers Jill into the office and listens to her story. Jill begins by describing how distant she feels from everyone, including God. Now in her early thirties, Jill does not feel satisfied in her career as an accountant. None of her dating relationships has turned into a stable, long-term commitment. She has stopped communicating with her parents because a former counselor told her to. Jill's parents, she says with an emotionless face, never took the time to figure out that her older brother sexually abused her for five childhood years. Jill's intellect tells her that God loves her, but her emotions scream out that she is abandoned, drifting all alone in a cruel world.

Fortunately, Dr. Gration is an expert in integrating Christianity and psychology. She graduated from a psychology doctoral program at a Christian institution; she has read hundreds of books and articles about integration; and she has even written a few articles herself. Jill made a good choice in deciding to see Dr. Gration.

But Dr. Gration isn't always sure how the articles and books she has read help her with the struggles her clients face. Is it wise for Jill to isolate herself from her parents? Is it reasonable for Jill to forgive her parents, or even her brother? What counseling approaches might help Jill feel closer to God? Dr. Gration can go to the local university library or to her old course notes from graduate school, but she probably won't find answers to these questions.

Dr. Gration's dilemma illustrates the slow evolution of the integration movement in psychology and Christianity—an evolution outlined by Everett Worthington, Jr., in a 1994 article in *Journal of Psychology and Theology*.[10] Worthington describes three stages of interdisciplinary integration—blending psychology and theology into a framework for Christian counseling. In the first stage, before 1975, a variety of articles introduced rudimentary concepts that were mostly unrelated to one another. In the second stage, between 1975 and 1982, integration models flourished. Integration journals were filled with schematic drawings of how Christianity and psychology can be related. Following this period of model madness, since 1982 the integration movement has become increasingly relevant and practical. We have considered how our theories of counseling can and should be enhanced or modified by Christian values, and we have started reporting empirical studies that help build a scientific base for our claims.

Thus, it appears we are making good progress in what Worthington calls interdisciplinary integration. But what about Dr. Gration's questions about Jill? These pertain more to *intra*disciplinary integration—that which occurs *within* the disciplines of counseling and psychotherapy. In other words, how do I implement religious values and beliefs into my treatment of this client? In this regard, the journals and professional books are less helpful. In 1983 Gary Collins wrote this about the *Journal of Psychology and Theology:*

> The *Journal of Psychology and Theology* does publish practical articles and the "publications policy" clearly indicates that applied papers are welcome. Nevertheless the major emphasis in the *Journal* appears to be theoretical. I suspect that relatively few pastors or full-time professional care givers find the articles to be of practical help in their counseling work. It would be helpful to see more of an applied perspective in this publication. . . . We must give more attention to the previously mentioned issue of integration methodology. How do we do integration? What skills and methods are involved?[11]

Worthington concludes, and I agree, that Collins's call for practical integration methods has not produced much change: "Practice-focused, training-oriented articles have been scarce to non-existent." [12]

But things may be starting to change. The International Congresses on Christian Counseling in 1988 and 1992 have brought together Christian counselors from around the world to discuss counseling techniques and methods. The American Association of Christian Counselors (AACC) publishes *Christian Counseling Today,* a popular periodical with many practical counseling suggestions. Integrative counseling methods may be the next frontier for Christian counselors and researchers to explore. This is a book for those wanting to investigate the frontier of intradisciplinary integration.

LIFE ON THE FRONTIER

A number of personal and professional challenges face Christian counselors as we confront this new frontier of intradisciplinary integration.

Challenge 1: Moving from Two Areas of Competence to Three

Dr. Gration has a master's degree in theology and a doctorate in psychology. She is well prepared for interdisciplinary integration. But she feels unprepared for many of the practical questions Jill brings to the counseling office. What more does she need?

For Christian counselors doing interdisciplinary integration, two areas of competence are necessary and sufficient: psychology and theology. When psychologists without theological training attempt to do integration, they often minimize the importance of doctrine, psychologize Christian beliefs, and overlook the historical and sociological context of today's psychology. Orthodox Christian theology keeps counselors grounded in the midst of a profession easily swayed by new theories, fads, and sensationalistic claims. When theologians without psychological training attempt to do integration, they often misrepresent the nuances of psychological science and misunderstand the complexities of clinical applications. So the best interdisciplinary integration work usually comes from those who have formal or informal preparation in both psychology and theology. Even the titles of our integration journals demonstrate these two essential ingredients: the *Journal of Psychology and Theology* and the *Journal of Psychology and Christianity.*

Intradisciplinary integration introduces a need for a *third* area of competence. If we are to bring religious issues out of the scholarly journals and into the Christian counseling office, we must understand spirituality and the process of spiritual formation. The importance of spirituality in emotional healing has been known for centuries in the Catholic Church and is particularly evident in monastic life and spiritual direction. But contemporary Protestant counselors have often overlooked spiritual disciplines. Those attending seminaries for counseling degrees receive training in psychological theory and techniques and in theological theory and techniques. What are the techniques of spiritual formation? How does one learn spiritual passion and devotion? These questions are often overlooked, even in the best training programs, leaving counselors with only two of the three essential components of training. Just as a tripod with one leg missing is of little value, a Christian counselor who lacks understanding of spirituality will be handicapped in bringing religious issues into the counseling office.

WHAT IF THIS HAPPENED?

Your client, Jim, places his head between his palms, sighs deeply, and begins describing the spiritual darkness he feels. A Christian for many years, Jim has viewed his spiritual life as a pilgrimage. Many times he has felt overwhelmed with God's gracious presence and kindness. At other times he has felt distant from God. He understands what Saint John of the Cross called the "dark night of the soul." But this time, the night seems darker and deeper than ever before. He feels alone, sad, confused, and empty. He comes to you, a Christian counselor, for help.

This is a multiple-choice question. Which would you do?

1. Diagnose Jim with depression, arrange for antidepressant medication to be prescribed, and begin a regimen of cognitive therapy for depression.
2. Encourage Jim by reminding him that his feelings do not

determine his faith. Even though God seems far away, nothing can separate Jim from God's love revealed in Christ (e.g., Rom. 8:35-39).
3. Explore Jim's inner spiritual longings, and allow him to grieve about his feelings of distance from God.
4. Consider all of the above possibilities.

The first option reflects the approach that might be taken by many psychologists who have no religious training or experience. The second choice might be added by counselors with theological understanding. The third requires an understanding of spiritual formation. Those who yearn for God and take the spiritual life most seriously always experience periods of spiritual darkness and loneliness; it is part of the spiritual quest for Christians. Only those counselors aware of psychological symptoms, theological principles, and spiritual formation will be able to discern the best treatment for Jim.

Unlike competence in psychology and theology, understanding spirituality does not lend itself to credentials. In *The Spirit of the Disciplines,* Dallas Willard writes that a spiritual life "consists in that range of activities in which people cooperatively interact with God—and with the spiritual order deriving from God's personality and action."[13] Spiritual training is experiential and often private. It is rarely found in the classroom or represented by graduate degrees, but it is found in private hours of prayer and devotional reflection, in church sanctuaries where Christian communities worship, in quiet disciplines of fasting and solitude.

There is another reason that spiritual competence cannot be represented as a credential on a curriculum vitae: those with the richest spiritual life recognize that spiritual competence is, in one sense, an oxymoron. We can become more or less competent in the spiritual disciplines, training ourselves to experience God more fully, but we can never be spiritually competent. Christian doctrine teaches that we are spiritually incompetent, in need of a Redeemer.

The spiritual life directs us away from illusions of competence and causes us to confront our utter helplessness and dependence on our gracious God. When we recognize our weakness, then Christ's strength can work through us (2 Cor. 12:10).

Balancing Christian theology, psychology, and spiritual formation is important in a time when so many conflicting and confusing messages bombard us. If we drift away from Christian theology, we find ourselves in the strange world of spiritualism.[14] Many writers speak of a spiritual quest that is born out of insatiable human curiosity about the world. The quest at times seems quite narcissistic, its goal and focus involve personal well-being, and some writers applaud those who have sacrificed families and other relational responsibilities in their search for meaning. Christian spirituality does not begin merely in our quest for understanding. It begins in our understanding that something is deeply wrong with us—a realization that can lead to a renewed dedication to the values of the gospel.

If the spiritual life of the Christian counselor is important for intradisciplinary integration, then the distinction between professional life and personal life becomes difficult to define because the Christian counselor's piety and personal practices affect the counseling process and outcome.

Challenge 2: Blurred Personal-Professional Distinctions

Though most professional-ethics codes make a distinction between the personal and professional life of the counselor, this distinction is blurred for the spiritually sensitive Christian counselor. If a Christian counselor gets up early in the morning and prays for a client, is this an illustration of the counselor's personal life or professional life? If counselors train themselves, through practicing spiritual disciplines, to remain kind and calm in the presence of angry, provocative circumstances, is it personal or professional when they apply those skills with difficult clients? The professionalization of counseling has led to the myth that all that is relevant are those things that clients observe, such as a counselor's demeanor, affective response, and display of empathy. I disagree: the kind of therapeutic relationships that foster healing are not formed merely from well-chosen techniques but grow out of the person's inner life.[15] In this sense, counseling is both professional and personal.

To justify a clearly defined division between a counselor's personal and professional life, we must view the counselor as a dispenser of healing technology—one who treats specific symptoms with specific techniques that make a person feel better. To some extent this is true—certain counseling techniques work better than others with certain disorders. But ideally a Christian counselor is also a healing agent—one whose spiritual life spills over in interactions with everyone, including clients.

It is now clear that counseling is effective.[16] It is also clear that the effects of counseling cannot be solely attributed to the techniques used by the counselor. A number of other ingredients, called "nonspecific factors," affect the outcome of counseling.[17] The most important of these nonspecific factors appears to be the counseling relationship. In a 1993 review of the counseling literature, psychologists Susan Whiston and Thomas Sexton reported that a strong therapeutic relationship is one of the best indicators of success in psychotherapy.[18] Most people seeking counseling are not looking for a specific set of techniques but for a relationship with someone who has values they respect.[19] They seek this relationship because they are wounded, driven to sorrow by the natural consequences of living in a fallen world. In the midst of a Christian counseling relationship they often move from brokenness and sorrow to hope and restoration.

Is this therapeutic bond personal or professional? It is both. A counseling relationship is professional in many ways: it occurs at a specified time and place; a fee is often charged; the client discloses much more than the counselor; and the relationship is terminated at a specified time. A Christian counseling relationship is also personal: both counselor and client invest energy and emotion in the relationship; both use words that emerge from their personal histories and ways of understanding the world; both pray outside of the counseling sessions that the relationship might help the client; and both are brothers or sisters in Christ.

This blending of personal and professional can be seen in the increasing interest in *values* and psychotherapy.[20] The myth of value-neutral counseling has been shattered, and now researchers and clinicians are trying to understand the place of values in counseling. Two psychologists started a recent journal article with, "It is now an accepted fact that psychotherapy is a value-laden enterprise. . . . [Values] are inextricably woven into the counseling process."[21] If this is true, then how can counseling ever be reduced to a set of professional behaviors? Professional behaviors are important, but a value-laden process must also rely on personal qualities and perspectives.

Thus, the Christian counselors best prepared to help people are those who are not only highly trained in counseling theory and techniques and in theology but also personally trained to reflect Christian character inside and outside of the counseling office. This character cannot be credentialed with graduate degrees or learned in the classroom; it comes from years of faithful training in the spiritual disciplines—prayer, studying Scripture, solitude, fasting, corporate worship, and so on.[22] On this new frontier of intradisciplinary integration, the personal life of the counselor is an essential ingredient for productive professional work.

Challenge 3: Expanded Definitions of Training

If intradisciplinary integration requires an awareness of spirituality in addition to theology and psychology, how are we doing at preparing ourselves for intradisciplinary integration? To answer this, we must consider both professional and personal training.

Moon, Bailey, Kwasny, and Willis surveyed eighty-seven religiously oriented graduate training programs to determine the coverage of Christian disciplines in their training programs.[23] Unfortunately, only twenty program directors provided usable data, despite two mailings from the authors. Although many of the disciplines—including various forms of meditation and prayer, confession, worship, forgiveness, fasting, and simplicity—were seen as having scriptural support and therapeutic utility, they were not emphasized in the graduate curricula. The authors conclude, "The results of this study generally support the hypothesis that instruction in the Christian disciplines is a rarity."[24] Despite the low rate of training in Christian disciplines, the authors go on to note the increasing receptivity to religion and religious issues among mental health professionals. They conclude, "Christian counseling can legitimately make more use of explicitly Christian techniques that arise from within the Christian tradition."[25] Thus, it appears that professional training in spiritual-guidance techniques is lacking, even in religiously oriented training programs.

If the distinction between personal and professional life blurs for the spiritually sensitive Christian counselor, then it is important not to leave this discussion of training at the professional level. Adams surveyed 450 members of the Christian Association for Psychological Studies (CAPS), received 340 completed surveys, and found that the best predictors of using spiritual-guidance techniques in professional work were personal factors.[26] Two of the three strongest predictors were the spiritual well-being of the counselor and the practice of personal devotions. The personal life of counselors appears to be revealed in their professional work.

Just as professional training is essential for competent counselors, personal training is important for those who see the spiritual life as an essential component of effective Christian counseling. As Dallas Willard suggests in *The Spirit of the Disciplines*, whether playing a piano or performing surgery, it is disciplined preparation and not just an exertion of willpower at the moment of performance that produces masterful results. A counselor cannot simply walk into the office and "put on" an effective counseling demeanor, even if the counselor uses prayer, Scripture, and other religious interventions during the session. The substance of spiritually sensitive counseling goes deeper than technique; the care, disciplined objectivity, trustworthiness, empathy, wisdom, and insight must come from within.

The spiritual disciplines provide a way for deep internal change that mere willpower can never bring about. The disciplines are God's provision for enabling us to become what we could never become through human effort. Christian therapists who are sensitive to the spiritual life recognize the importance of personal training in developing habits of holiness. They are, as Eugene Peterson (borrowing from Nietzsche) tells us, the product of a "long obedience in the same direction."[27]

This does not mean that the spiritual disciplines themselves are spiritual. When we assume that having a personal devotional time defines our spirituality, we miss the point of the disciplines and risk an externalized faith that is disturbingly similar to the outward form of righteousness displayed by the hypocritical religious leaders who plotted to kill Jesus. The disciplines are not spiritual, but they provide opportunities to experience God. They are vehicles of spirituality that bring us face-to-face with God's grace. God transforms us as we invite change through using the spiritual disciplines.

Challenge 4: Confronting Dominant Views of Mental Health

Conversations about Christian counseling methods often focus on techniques and specific interventions. Many practical techniques will be considered throughout this book. However, spiritually sensitive counseling is not merely a matter of implementing a set of techniques in the counseling office.

Beneath every technique is a counseling theory, and beneath every theory is a worldview. Because we are sometimes too eager to import psychological techniques into Christian counseling, we overlook the troubling theoretical and worldview implications of the techniques we use. As Christian counselors face this new frontier of intradisciplinary integration, we must deliberately look at the worldview assumptions that underlie our theories and techniques.[28]

Most contemporary forms of Christian counseling are religious adaptations of mainstream counseling techniques. For example, many Christian writers and therapists have adapted techniques from

Albert Ellis's Rational-Emotive Therapy (RET) to Christian counseling.[29] Though Ellis is an outspoken atheist, many Christians have accepted his techniques as legitimate. One has even described RET as "perhaps the most compatible with biblical teaching of all current major psychotherapeutic systems."[30] But can we really accept RET without critically evaluating the underlying hedonistic, relativistic worldview?[31] We can bend Christian assumptions to conform to existing techniques, but at some point our belief system snaps, and we are left with only theistic scraps saturated by atheistic definitions of mental health. Intradisciplinary integration—bringing the Christian faith into the counseling office—requires us to evaluate carefully the goals of therapy and to challenge the views of healing that surround us in the mental health professions.

WHAT IF THIS HAPPENED?

Chris is a bright, motivated Christian, intent on serving Christ and others. After college Chris applies to graduate school in clinical psychology and is readily admitted to a top program. He arrives on campus, meets his new adviser, pays his tuition, and begins attending classes. Chris is immediately overwhelmed with the quantity of work required: he learns psychometrics, test administration, counseling theory, counseling techniques, basic science areas in psychology, professional ethics, and so on. Because he is busily involved in research and studying, he doesn't stop to ask questions about the goals of professional interventions.

Five years later, doctoral degree in hand, Chris is ready to begin his work as a Christian psychologist. He is armed with an arsenal of therapeutic concepts and techniques: systematic desensitization, progressive relaxation, cognitive restructuring, analysis of resistance, projective identification, unconditional positive regard, daily record of automatic thoughts, and many more. Here's the irony: Chris has never been taught and never

stopped to question why he is using these techniques. What is
the goal of therapy? How do we define healing?

One example of the worldview challenges facing Christian
counselors is seen in the widespread assumption that mental health
requires us to feel good about who we are. In 1967, when Dr.
Thomas Harris set out to convince a culture that "I'm OK—you're
OK," he probably didn't realize the impact his words would have.[32]
Now, by the time people are willing to seek help from a counselor,
pastor, or friend, most have already formulated the problem. It goes
something like this: "I have problems because people have hurt me,
and I have spent my life trying to please them. Well, I'm tired of
being hurt by others. Now I realize that I am okay, and it's time to
take care of myself. So please help me learn how."

In other words, "Help me look out for myself and feel good
about who I am so that I can be happy." We're bombarded with
similar messages every day:

"You have to look out for yourself; no one else will."

"Go ahead, you deserve it."

"No one else can tell you what's right and wrong for you."

"You're a good person. You need to believe in yourself."

"Assert your rights."

"Speak your mind."

Counselors often accept these definitions of mental health un-
critically and shape their clinical work accordingly.

These contemporary messages of mental health are not all
wrong. People really are hurt by others, and the scars that remain
can be devastating. Some emotional problems are almost purely
the result of past wounds, prior conditioning, and faulty self-
image, and they can be effectively treated with counseling techniques. Although the contemporary messages of mental health are
not *all wrong,* they are not *all right* either. They tell us we are not
sick but are victims of our genetics, life circumstances, and neuro-

chemicals. After all, we're okay. So contemporary pop psychologists instruct their readers to look out for their own needs, give up silly ideas of altruism or forgiveness, and get out of relationships that are not fulfilling. Their message is clear: happiness comes by avoiding discomfort, sacrifice, and pain. Psychologist Albert Ellis wrote, "The emotionally healthy individual should primarily be true to himself and not masochistically sacrifice himself for others."[33] This type of hedonistic, individualistic ethic is not compatible with Christian spirituality. In Scripture we are instructed to look out for the interests of others (Phil. 2:4) and to prefer one another in honor (Rom. 12:10). Those who see hedonism and shallow independence as the goal of counseling deny the spiritual life and the role of brokenness in healing.

Christian doctrine teaches us to view ourselves as participants in sin rather than as innocent victims, that sickness is a part of our nature, and that recognizing our spiritual condition is a prerequisite to healing. Every Christian must be a broken person. To enter the kingdom, we must acknowledge that the inner peace we yearn for can never come by our own efforts but only by admitting we are powerless to conquer our self-centeredness and by turning over the rule of our life to Christ. Our sinful hearts show themselves through what we do and what we fail to do. We end up broken not only because we are victims but also because we have hearts of rebellion and stubborn independence.

The Christian gospel gives hope for broken people, but only after they recognize their brokenness. Brokenness was the experience of the Bible heroes: Abraham, Moses, David, Elijah, Paul. Our society may tell us to avoid brokenness by looking out for ourselves, but the heroes of our faith, who really knew what it was to live, were all people who had been broken.

From a Christian worldview, a client might describe a problem more like this: "I have problems. It's tempting to believe I have spent my life trying to please others, but I suppose I have done that to cover my faults, to hide the parts of me that I don't like. I say I've been pleasing others, but really I've been trying to please myself. I'm left with a sense of despair. I feel that there is something terribly wrong with me (and everyone else, too). And I can't fix it on my own."

In our sickness and pain, we grope for answers, for better understanding, for meaningful relationships. Our sickness leads us to God. God can restore and use broken vessels for divine purposes. David wrote:

> I waited patiently for the Lord;
> he inclined to me and heard my cry.
> He drew me up from the desolate pit,
> out of the miry bog,
> and set my feet upon a rock,
> making my steps secure.
> He put a new song in my mouth,
> a song of praise to our God.
> Many will see and fear,
> and put their trust in the Lord.
> Psalm 40:1–3

The good news of Christianity is that God brings us out of our brokenness and draws us into relationship. The Christian message is one of hope. We have been restored to God through the work of Christ.

So what does the Christian counselor do when sitting with sobbing clients who feel a deep sense of inadequacy and neediness? Is the best treatment to convince these clients that they are wrong, that they are actually wonderful people who have misinterpreted the world? Or is it more reasonable to reflect on the role of brokenness in healing and to recognize that inadequacy and neediness are prerequisites to restoration and hope? Counseling, when practiced by those who respect brokenness as part of healing, is a reflection of redemption. Those who enter therapy in the midst of their pain experience a restorative counseling relationship that brings acceptance, hope, and meaning into their broken lives. In this sense, counseling mimics the gospel—people are broken, and broken people are restored in the context of a healing relationship.

Challenge 5: Establishing a Scientific Base

Of course, one can err in either direction. We can become so intent on avoiding a "secular" worldview that we end up rejecting all that psychology and counseling theory have to offer. Sometimes our zeal for Christian counseling starts to look like excessive confidence, or even pride. Sometimes we act as if our methods have been scientifically validated or as if they do not need to be scientifically validated because we have found a more direct route to truth. These are dangerous views that sometimes alienate us from our colleagues in various mental health fields.

Thus, we also face scientific challenges. Christian counselors who wish to be accurately understood among mental health professionals must use the language of science that is common among these professions. This poses a challenge for Christian counselors, especially those in academic and research settings, to demonstrate scientifically the unique interventions Christian counselors use in the counseling office and their effectiveness.

With regard to the first question, What do Christian counselors do in the counseling office? it is important to remember that Christian counselors are a diverse group with varying backgrounds and perspectives on the use of Christian disciplines in counseling. Worthington, Dupont, Berry, and Duncan evaluated ninety-two counseling sessions led by seven Christian counselors.[34] Religious homework, quoting from Scripture, discussing the Christian faith, and prayer were frequently used techniques, but all techniques were used in fewer than half of the sessions, and Christian counselors varied considerably in their use of spiritual-guidance techniques. As expected, counselors were more likely to use religious techniques with highly religious clients than with marginally religious clients, but the number of religious guidance techniques used was not a good predictor of counseling outcome, even with religious clients. The authors conclude: "For the Christian psychotherapist, it is not the mere number of spiritual-guidance techniques used that is important in influencing clients' perceptions of effective therapy. Rather, the choice of *which* techniques to use at what time is more important."[35]

Ball and Goodyear found that prayer is the most commonly used spiritual intervention among CAPS members, accounting for approximately one-fourth of the spiritual interventions reported.[36] Referring to Scripture and teaching religious concepts were frequently reported on a paper-and-pencil questionnaire but infrequently reported when some of the same respondents were interviewed and asked to describe five critical incidents in treating Christian clients. Conversely, techniques that had no religious foundation were infrequently reported on the pencil-and-paper questionnaire but frequently reported during interviews. Thus, it seems likely that what Christian counselors want to do in counseling sometimes varies from what they actually do.

What can we conclude from these studies? The most obvious conclusion is that research evidence regarding spiritual-guidance techniques in counseling is sparse and needs to be a high priority for the Christian counseling movement. Many Christian counselors are using spiritual techniques in therapy, including prayer, religiously oriented homework, Scripture, and faith-related discussions, but perhaps not as often as they would like.

How effective are religiously oriented therapies in counseling? Five outcome studies that attempt to answer this question are reviewed by psychologist W. Brad Johnson.[37] It is striking that three of the five studies demonstrated significant methodological inadequacies. It is even more striking that among the many hundreds of psychotherapy outcome studies, only five studies have investigated religiously oriented therapies. Three of the studies indicated no difference in effectiveness between religious and nonreligious forms of therapy for depression.[38] The two remaining studies demonstrated an advantage for religiously oriented therapies with religious depressed clients.[39] However, in the most comprehensive study reported to date, Rebecca Propst and her colleagues found that a religious form of cognitive therapy was most effective if delivered by a nonreligious therapist.[40] This is an intriguing finding that will require more research to be understood.

It is important to recognize that all reported outcome studies of religiously oriented interventions compare religious and nonreligious versions of well-established cognitive interventions for depression. We can only speculate on the effectiveness of Christian counseling interventions that are built on different worldview and theoretical assumptions. Much more research is needed as Christian counselors continue to articulate intradisciplinary integration.

Challenge 6: Defining Relevant Ethical Standards

This new frontier of intradisciplinary integration introduces new ethical challenges as well. Only those treatments that have been effective in two independent double-blind studies with adequate control groups are included on the APA's list of empirically validated psychological procedures. In the near future, insurance companies may require counseling to be conducted according to an approved treatment protocol. Because no religiously oriented interventions have been evaluated in two independent double-blind studies, none are on the list. This is both a scientific challenge, as described previously, and an ethical challenge. Will Christian counselors continue to thrive if their techniques are not endorsed by third-party payers? What ethical principles must be followed in such a dilemma?

WHAT IF THIS HAPPENED?

As you begin your first session with a distressed couple, Will and Patty, Will looks you in the eye and says, "We're doing some research on the best counseling approach. We figure this will take some time and cost some money, and we want to be sure to get the best help available."

Patty quickly adds, "We're wondering what you mean when you say you're a Christian counselor. How does Christian counseling differ from other counseling? And how confident can we be that our relationship will get better?"

At the heart of Will and Patty's questions is the ethical principle of *informed consent*. When people come to a counselor for help, they should be given thorough and accurate information about the proposed counseling procedures, should be informed of alternative treatment approaches, and should sign a written consent form.[41] With each client, we must ask ourselves several questions. Was this person freely given a choice to participate based on a full understanding of the counseling procedures and the alternatives available? Does he or she know the nature of the counseling services and the likelihood of success? Giving a standard answer to these questions is impossible because Christian counselors are a diverse group, offering many different approaches to counseling. It's not just that we use different techniques or styles; we don't agree on what Christian counseling is.

When Worthington reviewed the research on religious counseling, he found three types of assumptions.[42] First, some people assume religious counseling is any type of counseling delivered by a religious person. This assumes that the counselor's availability as an agent of God's grace will have a healing effect on a client, even if no religiously oriented techniques are used. From this perspective, a discussion of Christian counseling techniques misses the point because the relational aspects of counseling are valued above techniques. This view is partly right; a great deal of evidence suggests that the relational aspects of therapy are essential for good outcome.[43] However, it is not clear what is Christian about this counseling, and Propst and her colleagues found no advantage for religious therapists using nonreligious therapy in treating depressed clients.[44]

The informed-consent procedure for Christian counselors in this group is not particularly difficult because their counseling services do not differ significantly from non-Christian counseling. These counselors can develop informed-consent forms that look like the industry standard. There is one problem though: the relational therapies are not well represented on the APA's list of empirically validated procedures. Thus, when describing alternative treatments, the form should include a description of treatment approaches that are quicker, less expensive, and effective.

Second, some people believe that religious counseling is applying counseling techniques within formal religious practice. Biblical counselors and Christian counselors who use spiritual-guidance techniques as their primary means of intervention are operating from this view of counseling. Although these counselors are often criticized as being "too religious," it is interesting to note that those receiving pastoral counseling in the Propst et al. study showed as much progress as those in the religious cognitive-therapy condition, and they maintained their gains during the two-year follow-up period.[45]

Often Christian counselors in this category are practicing not within the mainstream mental health community but as extensions of church and parachurch ministries. Usually they are not seeking insurance reimbursement for their services and often do not consider informed consent an important part of their work. Nonetheless, informed consent is becoming an important obligation for all counselors because those seeking our services are often unaware of the options available. Informed-consent procedures will play a prominent part in the AACC code of ethics currently being developed.

Third, some see religious counseling as "supercharged" secular counseling, adding religious elements to well-established counseling models. Propst et al. found that standard cognitive therapy enhanced with religious imagery and religious arguments to counter irrational thoughts was superior to standard cognitive therapy in relieving depression.[46] However, this view perpetuates the problem mentioned earlier, that a Christianized form of therapy can be built on flawed, misleading, and damaging worldview assumptions.

Counselors working from this perspective are sometimes inclined to use standard informed-consent forms and then "throw in" the religious interventions as an extra part of treatment. This is probably not wise, because Propst reported two separate studies that suggest religious elements change the effectiveness of treatment.[47] Thus, Christian counselors from this third perspective should attempt to describe both their therapeutic model and their religious adaptations of the model.

For many Christian counselors, none of these three approaches to counseling seems satisfying. Perhaps we need a fourth option—an empirically validated Christian counseling model of personality, mental health, and therapy. Many questions would need to be answered: What is human personality? What motivates humans? What goes wrong to create mental health problems? What should the competent counselor do in the counseling office to restore clients to mental and spiritual health? Developing this fourth option will require philosophers, theologians, researchers, and clinicians to collaborate in building a scientifically respected and theologically sound model for Christian counseling; this task probably will require several decades of work. If we build our counseling models prematurely, they will not be taken seriously—even by those within the Christian counseling movement.

This discussion of ethical challenges has been limited to informed consent, but many more ethical tensions arise when considering intradisciplinary integration. These will be explored throughout the remaining chapters.

SUMMARY

Intradisciplinary integration is a recently emerging frontier for Christian counselors. The question is not how we understand the relationship between psychology and theology but how we practically use the Christian faith in our counseling. Change brings challenge, and Christian counselors face several significant challenges as they bring religion into their counseling offices. Religious interventions require us to understand spiritual forma-

tion, place priority on personal spiritual training as well as professional development, challenge prevailing models of mental health,
work toward a stronger scientific base, and sensitively recognize
ethical issues.

2/ TOWARD PSYCHOLOGICAL and SPIRITUAL HEALTH

With their minivan fully loaded, cartop carrier securely fastened, dog safely kenneled, and the iron turned off, the Johnson family pulls out of the driveway for their family vacation. Wendall Johnson is behind the wheel, humming a tune, when family members start asking questions.

"Are we almost there?" his six-year-old asks.

Chuckling to himself, Wendall answers calmly, "You must be looking forward to getting there, Brian."

Scowling at Brian and feeling a bit smug about her twelve-year-old sophistication, Monica rephrases the question. "Dad, about how long does it take to drive where we are headed?"

"Yeah," Brian adds, "are we almost there yet?"

Wendall stops humming his tune just long enough to reply, "I'm not sure, Monica, but we'll all know when we arrive. Brian, this could be a long trip or a short trip. It's just too early to tell."

From the passenger seat, Rhonda Johnson gasps and exclaims, "Honey, we forgot to bring the road map!" The kids join the panic and ask a flurry of new questions.

"Calm down, Rhonda! Kids, don't worry so much. I've come on many vacations before, and I know what I'm doing. We all just need to trust the process. Everything will turn out fine."

The Johnson family is not relieved.

Neither are many of our clients when we explain the counseling process to them. Sometimes I try to picture the anxiety of a first-time counseling client. After trying for many weeks or months to cope without counseling, the potential client finally sets an appointment and shows up for that first interview. The concerns, which are quite normal, are seen in the questions. What type of counselor are you? Have you worked with others who have had these problems? How long will this take? What has caused my problems? These are the same questions Wendall Johnson's family members were asking him. Do you know how to get where we are going? How long will it take?

Sometimes our answers are just as frustrating as Wendall Johnson's. We look empathically at our anxious clients and say, "This must be a difficult step for you to come to counseling, and you're feeling anxious about how long it might take." Or we assure them that counseling is complex and that it is impossible to tell how long it will take until the journey is underway. We tell ourselves not to be anxious about where things are headed in counseling with the tired words, "Just trust the process."

On one hand we are wise to believe in the process of counseling. A confiding, trusting relationship with a counselor helps people get better.[1] But we are also wise to believe in road maps. Process alone helps, and most people eventually get better, but a road map helps make the process efficient. If the Johnsons have a basic understanding of geography, they will eventually get to their destination, even without a map, through trial and error. But that's not what Brian or Monica or Rhonda wants! They want to get there as soon as possible. Similarly, our clients want to reach their destination as soon as possible, and they want a counselor who knows how to help them reach their destination.

My theoretical road map for counseling is cognitive therapy.[2] I like having a map. It helps me give direct answers to my clients' questions. After a few sessions, I can usually predict with reasonable accuracy how long counseling will take and what we will be doing in the sessions. A strong therapeutic relationship and trust in the counseling process are essential ingredients of effective counseling, but a theoretical map helps, too.

Sometimes I feel a nagging dissatisfaction with my theoretical map. I wonder, for example, if teaching my clients positive self-talk sometimes feels trite and superficial, as if I am trying to put a Band-Aid on a gaping wound. How should a cognitive therapist interpret a recent study that suggests the reason cognitive therapy works is that good cognitive therapists employ the same relational and affective sensitivity in counseling that good psychodynamic therapists employ?[3] And how do I make sense of the many clients for whom standard cognitive therapy simply doesn't work? Those who come with chronic personality-adjustment problems often don't respond to cognitive therapy unless the therapeutic methods are substantially altered.[4] And then there is the biggest concern of all: most forms of cognitive therapy are silent about the spiritual life, and the few Christianized versions of cognitive therapy seem simplistic and naive, as if a cognitive therapy worldview has been unquestionably accepted and then cloaked with a few strategic Bible verses and religious-imagery exercises.

This is not to say that we should give up the theoretical maps that counselors and psychologists have spent decades developing and researching. The maps we have borrowed from psychology have been helpful and have led us to this new frontier of intradisciplinary integration. But can they lead us further? At the frontier, we need better maps.

MAPPING SPIRITUAL AND PSYCHOLOGICAL HEALTH

Christian counseling is more complex than other forms of counseling because our goals are multifaceted. Whereas the behaviorist can focus on symptom reduction and the psychoanalyst on ego strength, Christian counselors are concerned with spiritual growth as well as mental health. Yet most of the maps we use for therapy are based only on mental health and have been developed with the assumption that mental health can be separated from the spiritual life—an assumption that most Christian counselors do not share.

We need a map for spiritual growth. This map must be true to Scripture and theologically sound yet completely relevant to the various mental health problems we see. Furthermore, it must be a practical map, not one of those complex figures that can be understood only by philosophers and theologians and has limited use in the counseling office. And ideally it should be a map that we can superimpose on the standard theoretical maps of counseling. Most of us do not want to replace our theoretical commitments to behavioral, cognitive, psychodynamic, family systems, and other forms of therapy, but we want a deeper understanding of the spiritual life and spiritual wisdom to see ourselves, our clients, and our counseling relationships more accurately. Finally, it should be a map that assumes neither a one-to-one correspondence between spiritual and psychological health nor complete separation between the two.

The map I begin with is simple, almost embarrassingly simple, but it provides an important starting point for discussions about religious issues and interventions in subsequent chapters.

A PATTERN OF HEALING
The healing motif woven throughout the narrative of human history reflects a common pattern to healing and health. We see this pattern in good literature, in Scripture, in the church calendar, in one another's lives. Figure 1 demonstrates the pattern graphically.

FIGURE 1

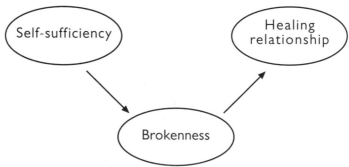

This pattern begins with our distorting what is good into something evil. God created humans with volition, a capacity for agency and selfhood. This capacity for self is good; it allows us to choose to be loving and kind, to enter into meaningful relationships with God and others, to exercise creative energy in our work and play, to set and reach goals. But we, like Adam and Eve, are prone to take our freedom too far, asserting our self-sufficiency and freedom without considering the consequences.

The consequences of unbounded independence are woundedness, brokenness, and pain. The adult who asserts willful independence by abusing a child causes great pain in many lives. The young child who overestimates his or her capacity to handle the demands of a busy shopping mall ends up lost and alone, crying for a loving parent. The husband or wife who cares more about freedom and independence than about sacrificial love and mutual submission ultimately faces great pain. And, as we see throughout the Old Testament, a nation that turns away from God faces pain and loss.

Eventually the myth of self-sufficiency sours, and we are left staring at our neediness, confronted with the brokenness and pain that have shadowed independence throughout human history. Sometimes pain is caused by personal rebellion; other times deep wounds result from the rebellion and sin of others.

We often think of brokenness and neediness as bad, but the gift of pain draws us into community with God and one another. In the midst of deep pain and brokenness, an adult abused as a child reaches to a counselor for help. A child lost in the mall instinctively wails until Mom and Dad come running. A couple in crisis learns how to listen to one another, to understand what sacrificial love means. The Old Testament nation of Israel, though repeatedly rebellious against God, also repeatedly repented and experienced God's rich blessings.

At the heart of Christian spirituality is a healing relationship with God. We were broken and dead in our life of sin when "God, who is rich in mercy, out of the great love with which he loved us even when we were dead through our trespasses, made us alive together with Christ" (Eph. 2:4-5). Brokenness is a prerequisite to understanding God's grace, but the Christian gospel does not leave us in a state of broken despair. Easter follows Lent. The apostle Paul was blinded so he could receive true sight. Jonah, Esther, Elijah, Moses, Peter, Elizabeth, David, Joseph, Anna, and virtually every other Bible hero knew the joy of God's grace because they endured difficult circumstances and times of suffering. Redemption gives hope and meaning to fallen humans. "Weeping may linger for the night, but joy comes with the morning" (Ps. 30:5).

This simple pattern can be seen all around us. Consider these examples from three areas: human development, spiritual growth, and psychological change.

Example 1: Human Development

From the perspective of human development, we see this pattern emerging as children learn to distinguish themselves from the rest of their world. They explore, become autonomous, and often grow stubborn.[5] Parents complain of the terrible twos, but it would be even more terrible if a two-year-old sat passively staring into space all day. The energetic, exploring, ambitious two-year-old exemplifies the human quest for understanding and adventure. Although this drive for autonomy is an essential good in human development, there is a natural limit to autonomy, and that limit is defined by pain. As children encounter the trials of hunger, injury, or loneliness, they naturally turn to their caregiver for help and comfort.

Example 2: Spiritual Growth

The same pattern can be seen in the spiritual life. In order to draw close to God, to understand his grace and love, we must also understand our need for God. James writes, "'God opposes the proud, but gives grace to the humble.' Submit yourselves therefore to God. . . . Humble yourselves before the Lord, and he will exalt you" (James 4:6-10). The apostle Paul reflects on this pattern when he describes his fallenness and his struggle with excessive independence in Romans 7 and then reflects on God's immense grace in the next chapter. Paul could not find God's healing love until he acknowledged his broken, needy condition.

Spiritual transformation, from a Christian perspective, always involves an awareness of neediness, as illustrated on Wheaton College's campus in 1995. Students sensed the stirring of the Holy Spirit for revival on campus, and hundreds corporately confessed the limits of their abilities to handle the stresses and temptations of college life in their own power. Each evening for almost a week, more than a thousand students met for prayer and confession until the early morning hours. After the week of corporate confession, small accountability groups were formed, and students continued to meet together, confess their sins, and seek spiritual and emotional restoration. This spiritual revival was a beautiful reflection of this simple pattern of healing. College students value independence—breaking away from family and developing one's own identity is the crisis of early adulthood, according to Erik Erikson.[6] But college students, like the rest of us, sometimes overadjust and assert too much independence. In the midst of campus revival, students acknowledged their brokenness and their need. Men and women waited in line, sometimes for hours, to get to the microphone and publicly confess their fallen condition. They brought their symbols of excessive independence—CDs, magazines, and books that caused them to stumble spiritually—and voluntarily handed them over to be destroyed. Perhaps the most moving and powerful part of the revival process was not watching students confess in a crowded auditorium but what happened next. Each time someone left the microphone, he or she was immediately surrounded by a group of concerned students, faculty, and staff. They knelt on the floor and prayed for one another. Healing relationships with God and others were established when brokenness and need were openly acknowledged.[7]

Example 3: Psychological Change

A third example of this pattern of healing can sometimes be seen in psychological growth. The proliferating recovery movement is based on the assumption that people must acknowledge their powerless, broken condition before they can improve. By attending twelve-step meetings frequently, recovering addicts repeatedly acknowledge their brokenness and draw together with others in a healing community. This same process is sometimes seen in the counseling office.

WHAT IF THIS HAPPENED?

When Karen and Bill arrive for their first counseling session, anger is painted all over their faces. Bill describes his feelings of betrayal and hurt over Karen's recent affair. Karen feels justified, blaming Bill's emotional distance and lack of affection. As the weeks go by, each begins to take more responsibility. Eventually they both confront their personal selfishness and sinfulness and express sorrow and remorse to one another. With time, their relationship heals, and they draw close to one another.

Karen and Bill started counseling in a state of stubborn self-suffi-ciency. Each had transgressed, valuing self above other, avoiding blame by accusing each other. But with time they each accepted their fallen, needy, broken condition. From their point of brokenness they could reach out to one another and establish a healing bond.

All these examples demonstrate this simple pattern of healing: our independence goes too far; we acknowledge our brokenness and our need; and we are welcomed into loving relationship with God or others. Unfortunately, life doesn't always work as neatly as these examples might imply. As they grow, some children continue to assert excessive independence and seem unable to recognize their need for others. Sometimes spiritual brokenness turns into chronic helplessness and despair. Some couples never acknowledge their responsibilities in counseling, and they end up bitter and divorced. Many people in recovery end up sinking back into patterns of addiction. Thus, this simple pattern of healing is not an adequate road map to understand the complexities of psychological and spiritual health.

PROBLEMS WITH THE MAP

Maps only represent reality, and simple maps omit many complexities for the sake of making reality easily understood. If the Johnson family ends up buying a simple map on their family vacation, they might find the freeways that take them close to their destination. But the complexities—the back roads leading to the mountain cabin—will be omitted. The simple map isn't wrong; it just leaves out details.

The pattern of healing discussed thus far captures and helps simplify much about spiritual and psychological health, but it leaves out many details. There are several valid criticisms of this simple model of health.

Problem 1

First, this pattern of healing implies a linear progression that is not true in every situation. Sometimes we enter a state of brokenness not because of our own stubborn independence but because we are wounded by others' sins. Sometimes we see our brokenness only after experiencing a healing relationship. Sometimes a healing relationship enhances our capacity for a healthy sense of self. Sometimes brokenness has a different effect and leads us away from healthy relationships rather than toward them.

Problem 2

Second, this model of health assumes insight and self-awareness, an assumption that does not hold true for everyone. It assumes the capacity to assert one's will, but many people have learned to be passive and helpless in life, rarely exerting their will. It assumes an ability to see value in brokenness, but many people retreat into a victim stance or maladaptive defenses in the presence of pain. It assumes that people have the social skills to enter into healthy human relationships, an assumption that does not apply equally well to all people. When counselors assume their clients are insightful and have self-awareness, they risk oversimplifying complex and difficult psychological problems.

WHAT IF THIS HAPPENED?

Jill comes for her first counseling session complaining of how badly people treat her at work, how her love relationships have not worked out well, and how difficult other people are. She describes her emotions with intensity. In fact, intense is a good way to describe her life. She pursues relationships intensely, experiences anger, love, joy, and fear intensely, and even talks intensely. By the end of the first session you can tell that she likes you intensely and looks forward to your next meeting. As the weeks pass, you find her unpredictable and difficult. Her moods are volatile and intense. She calls you at home frequently, and she accuses you of saying things you don't remember saying.

You think about this simple road map of health and decide she needs to understand her sin and brokenness before she can find a healing relationship with a therapist or anyone else. You suggest that Jill memorize certain Bible passages and confess her past sins against God and others. But as you start narrowing in on her weaknesses and problems, she decompensates. She starts cutting her wrists at home, calling you in the middle of the night with suicidal plans, showing up at your office at unscheduled times, demanding to see you. Jill has become worse rather than better.

Jill's pattern of behavior, consistent with the condition known as borderline personality disorder, needs to be considered before applying this (or any) model of health. She is unable to cope with her sense of brokenness because she has not yet learned a capacity for understanding and placing appropriate value on herself. In a psychological sense, Jill invalidates her own experience, looking to others to understand what she should be thinking and feeling.[8] Thus, her fragile emotional resources and her mechanisms of self-protection keep her from looking insightfully at her own brokenness. She will decompensate if a counselor pushes her toward confessing personal sin. There is hope for Jill, and she may eventually be strong enough to see herself more clearly, but only after the therapeutic relationship is safe and consistent enough that she begins to understand and value her own experiences as distinct from others'.

Problem 3

A third problem with this simple model of health is the difficulty of properly understanding a healthy state of brokenness. This is like walking a tightrope. If we lean too far in one direction—the direction counselors have typically leaned—then we view all human discomfort as problematic and may try to excuse our clients prematurely from their healthy sorrow. Discomfort often motivates insight, and when we use clinical tricks to erase misery prematurely from our clients' lives, we short-circuit their opportunities for emotional and spiritual growth. Throughout Scripture and throughout the history of the Christian church, God has used pain to bring people to maturity. What if Job had gone for cognitive therapy and learned to talk to himself in different ways?

> "It's not awful that my family died, I can always have another family."

> "My friends are saying some tough things, but it doesn't really matter what they think anyway."

Or what if David had learned "healthy" self-talk after Nathan confronted him about adultery and murder?

> "This was a bad thing to do, but other people do bad things all the time, too. I don't have to upset myself about this."

> "I have learned from my mistakes, and there is no point in blaming myself or thinking of myself as a bad person."

But God *used* pain to shape Job's and David's characters. Here is what Job and David really said:

> [Job said,] "I had heard of you by the hearing of the ear, but now my eye sees you; therefore I despise myself, and repent in dust and ashes." (Job 42:5-6)

> [David said,] "For I know my transgressions, and my sin is ever before me. Against you, you alone, have I sinned, and done what is evil in your sight, so that you are justified in your sentence and blameless when you pass judgment. Indeed, I was born guilty, a sinner when my mother conceived me." (Ps. 51:3-5)

As we sensitively allow our clients to feel pain and brokenness, they are able to see themselves, others, and God more accurately.

We face the danger of idealizing pain if we lean too far in the other direction on this tightrope. Some forms of pain are almost always destructive and should not be seen as a gateway to insight. When we confuse a healthy awareness of human fallenness with unhealthy experiences, such as helplessness and clinical depression, we risk hurting those seeking our help. In the midst of clinical depression, people are not sad simply because of the human condition; they are surrounded by unrealistic feelings of worthlessness and hopelessness. A healthy awareness of human fallenness enhances our relationship with God by getting our eyes off ourselves and onto God's magnificent character. Clinical depression does just the opposite, trapping people in a cycle of self-absorption and sapping spiritual and psychological insight.

Problem 4

Fourth, this simple map implies that health is tantamount to close relationships. This is true only in our relationship with God. Other relationships sometimes disappoint and devastate and evoke our self-sufficiency and sinfulness in ways that are far from healthy. Many close relationships do more damage than good.

Even a counseling relationship, though a significant part of effective treatment, is prone to self-serving distortion, manipulation, and abuse.[9] When the counseling relationship works well, it is because it mimics the redemptive relationship Christians experience with God through Jesus Christ. Unfortunately, we counselors sometimes forget that our best work is only a poor imitation of God's redemptive nature, and we start seeing ourselves as powerful saviors.

"The closer, the better" is a good motto for our relationship with God, but because of our human capacity to distort and serve ourselves, it is not a good motto for a counseling relationship. Effective counseling requires us to scrutinize the counseling relationship, looking for indications of excessive dependency, monitoring and understanding feelings of transference and countertransference, always keeping the client's welfare our first priority. Closeness in itself does not produce health, but a counseling relationship carefully modeled after Christ's redemptive relationship with humankind can draw people toward greater spiritual and psychological health.

Problem 5

Fifth, this simple model of healing implies that our human sense of self is bad because it leads to rebellion and self-sufficiency. This is only partly true. It is correct that we are in a lifelong struggle to keep our independence, our will, within the boundaries of God's will. John the Baptist, after a time of high-visibility ministry, said, "He [Jesus] must increase, but I must decrease" (John 3:30). We face the same task today—a challenging task in the midst of a culture that values self-determination and independence. But self, as defined by psychologists throughout the past century, is not all bad. When clinicians and personality theorists speak of self, they do not refer to reckless independence but to a capacity to distinguish one's own identity from others in the environment.[10] The capacity to make decisions, to function when a loved one is absent, to have preferences, to set goals, and to discuss feelings requires an awareness of self.

Thus, the simple model of healing described here may be a helpful way to conceptualize spiritual and psychological health under many circumstances, but it can be dangerous if improperly applied in a counseling relationship. We need a map with more sophistication to guide us through the many nuances of counseling.

A MORE DETAILED MAP

A more comprehensive perspective on psychological and spiritual health requires us to consider self, brokenness, and healing relationships as interactive rather than linear, as shown in figure 2.

All three parts of the triangle contribute to health. An accurate sense of self allows us to recognize our responsibility to God, others, and ourselves. Having a healthy awareness of brokenness keeps us

FIGURE 2

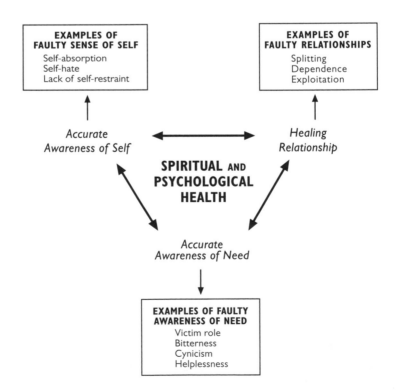

humble and helps us fight our natural propensity toward self-centeredness. Healing relationships allow us to experience grace and hope in the midst of life's trials.

Some forms of therapy focus more on one component than others. Behavioral treatment, for example, teaches new skills to compensate for previous maladaptive learning. Behaviorists teach clients to have a healthier, more confident sense of self. Psychologist Albert Bandura calls this self-efficacy.[11] Traditionally, cognitive therapists have focused on an accurate sense of self, but more current forms consider the importance of relationships as well.[12] Psychodynamic therapists focus on the therapeutic relationship as essential, while looking for growth in the client's self-awareness.[13] Biblical counselors focus on the state of brokenness and to some extent on the therapeutic relationship.[14] Though different approaches emphasize different parts of this model, all three components are important for spiritual and psychological health.

In a state of spiritual and psychological health, the three components interact and contribute to the others. We become increasingly willing to discuss our brokenness as we feel secure in close relationships, and our relationships become closer as we honestly admit our faults. An accurate understanding of self helps us admit our needs and allows us to be full partners in meaningful relationships, and recognizing our needs contributes to our awareness of ourselves. We are able to draw close to God as we humble ourselves, and we are able to humble ourselves as we draw close to God.

A balanced sense of self, brokenness, and close relationships with God and others bring maturity and health. Unfortunately, the converse is also true: a misunderstanding or deprivation of any part can lead away from health.

Accurate Sense of Self

Those who have an accurate understanding and acceptance of themselves are freed to experience greater emotional or spiritual health.

This is not the same as saying that we should all love ourselves more. In many ways, we love ourselves too much.[15] Rather, I am suggesting that we should understand ourselves accurately enough that we can stop worrying about whether we are bad or good. To be healthy, we need to move beyond a preoccupation with self.

Psychologist Abraham Maslow studied and wrote about the concept of self for many years. Though Maslow would not agree that the Christian faith can help lead people to emotional health, his reports of the characteristics and desires of healthy people who have moved beyond preoccupation with self (he called them self-actualizers) are remarkably similar to the fruit of the Spirit described by the apostle Paul in Galatians 5:22-23.[16]

PAUL and MASLOW

Fruit of the Spirit	Characteristics of Self-Actualizers	Desires of Self-Actualizers
Love	Profound relationships	Unity, Beauty

Joy	Spontaneity
	  Peak experiences
	  Continued freshness
	   of appreciation
		Aliveness, Playfulness

Peace	Fellowship with humanity
	  Acceptance of self
	   and others
		Simplicity

Patience		Individuality, Richness
Kindness	Unhostile sense of humor	Justice

Goodness	Efficient perception
	  of reality
		Goodness, Values,
		  Truth

Faithfulness		Completion
Gentleness		Balance, Harmony
Self-control	Autonomy, Task-Centeredness	

The fruit of the Spirit described by Paul do not correspond perfectly with the characteristics of emotional health described by Maslow. And emotional health is not exactly the same as spiritual well-being. However, we see substantial overlap. The more accurately we understand ourselves, the more freedom we have for emotional and spiritual health.

Faulty Sense of Self

When a healthy sense of self has not been established, people easily slip into a variety of psychological and spiritual problems.

WHAT IF THIS HAPPENED?

Jeff is a twenty-six-year-old single male who is still living with his devout Christian parents. As a child, he was given a clear sense of right and wrong, and he worked hard to please his parents. Because his home lacked affection, Jeff learned to equate his worth with his outward display of piety. During his years at a Christian college, feeling lonely and isolated, Jeff became obsessed with pornographic magazines and videos. After graduating, he became a missionary. During his missionary work, he continued to view pornography frequently and secretly. In the midst of his shame and confusion, Jeff became more withdrawn and isolated. He eventually had a brief psychotic episode that resulted in the loss of his missionary position. Since returning to his hometown, he has renounced his religious faith. Jeff now works in a fast-food restaurant, is a heavy drinker, and thinks about killing himself almost every day.

Jeff's situation demonstrates what can happen without a healthy sense of self. During his childhood years, Jeff developed a belief that his value depended upon his ability to perform. When he was longing for a hug, he received interrogation about his personal quiet times. While other kids were going to the ballpark with their fathers,

Jeff was trying to please his father by sharing Campus Crusade's four spiritual laws with neighborhood children. When other children were being rocked to sleep on their mothers' laps, Jeff was sitting at the dining-room table, fighting back yawns during family devotions. Jeff's parents had the best intentions, and their spiritual passion is to be commended, but Jeff grew up without a healthy sense of self. He saw himself as an extension of his parents, a worker bee for the kingdom of God, but never as a choosing, autonomous, creative agent made in the image of God.

The results for Jeff were devastating. His unhealthy sense of self led to *self-absorption* (he spends hours thinking about himself and his lack of worth), *self-hate* (he wants to die and even plans ways to kill himself), and a *lack of self-restraint* (as seen in his pornography and alcohol-use patterns). In psychodynamic terms, he has poor ego strength, as seen in his difficulty in making responsible choices, his overwhelming feelings of shame, and his impulsive choices.

Jeff needs a counselor who will help him catch a glimpse of the warmth he longed for as a child, within the boundaries of an appropriate therapeutic relationship. Jeff needs to grow into an accurate understanding of himself as a person created in God's image.

Accurate Sense of Need

Just as an accurate sense of self leads to health and a distorted sense of self inhibits health, an accurate view of human fallenness fosters health, while a distorted view leads to denial and distortion. Richard Foster reminds us: "The closer we come to the heartbeat of God, the more we see our need and the more we desire to be conformed to Christ."[17]

The idea of admitting that one is needy is not popular in contemporary Western society. We see it as a sign of weakness and vulnerability. Some build persuasive arguments that emotional health comes with autonomy and individuality. But there is only one way to spiritual health, and that requires us to recognize that we need God. Spiritual leaders throughout history have written about their hunger and need for God. In the sixth century Benedict of Nursia described a ladder of humility—twelve steps that help us recognize our need for God: reverence for God, doing God's will, obedience to others, enduring affliction, confession, contentment, self-reproach, obeying the common rule, silence, seriousness, simple speech, humble appearance.[18] Though today's Protestants might challenge several of these steps, each of them points toward acknowledging need as a mechanism of spiritual growth.

Faulty Sense of Need

Unfortunately, many people have an unhealthy awareness of their need, which complicates counseling. Other times, counselors actually foster an unhealthy sense of need by confusing need with victimization.

WHAT IF THIS HAPPENED?

Jeff's therapist, Dr. Ura Vicktem, immediately recognizes Jeff's pain and his tendency to suppress emotions in order to avoid conflict. She encourages Jeff to explore his childhood pain, to talk to an empty chair as if his father were sitting in it. Eventually Jeff grows stronger, develops more confidence, and begins developing a healthy sense of self. Because Jeff is stronger now, Dr. Vicktem concludes that Jeff is ready to confront his parents. He does so, expressing his childhood pain and requesting that they not contact him until he has recovered fully from his childhood of "toxic faith."

The good news is that Dr. Vicktem has improved Jeff's sense of self and has provided a caring relationship for Jeff. In a psychological sense, Jeff may be healthier than he was before therapy started. The bad news is that Dr. Vicktem has perpetuated a problem that saturates the practice of psychotherapy by using Jeff's self-pity as a tool for building rapport. Rather than coming to a healthy sense of brokenness and an awareness of personal vulnerability, Jeff has become a *victim* of his past. With the help of Dr. Vicktem, he has become bitter and cynical about parents who loved him dearly but who did not know how to express their love.

Effective counseling often helps people identify pain from their past and sometimes requires people to confront parents, past abusers, and others. But when the pain, anger, confrontation, and therapy become a way of life, the counseling is no longer effective. In a spiritual sense, Jeff is no healthier than he was before therapy, and he may be further from understanding his personal need for God.

Like many situations counselors face, treating Jeff requires a careful balance of support and confrontation. With Dr. Vicktem, Jeff received high support and low confrontation. At the other extreme of high confrontation and low support, Jeff will find different perils.

WHAT IF THIS HAPPENED?

Jeff's therapist, Mr. U. R. Cinner, believes Jeff's pain results from his personal rebellion and choices that have drawn him away from God. His parents were not perfect, but they taught him right and wrong and provided him with an essential understanding of Christian doctrine.

Mr. Cinner confronts Jeff about his sinful choices. He has rebelled against God and others by obsessively viewing pornography, poorly controlling his use of alcohol, and deliberately disavowing his religious faith. Jeff needs to repent and to be drawn back into Christian community by joining a local church.

The good news is that Mr. Cinner has not overlooked the role of personal sin in Jeff's situation, as Dr. Vicktem had. The bad news is that Mr. Cinner's emphasis on personal sin and brokenness has further damaged Jeff's sense of self. Coming to a counselor was a bold act of self-care for Jeff, and in return he received the same judgmental advice he had been telling himself for years. Jeff may cancel his next counseling appointment and sink further into feelings of *helplessness.*

Somewhere between these extremes, Christian counselors need to create a nurturing, safe relationship in which clients can acknowledge and discuss their sin.[19] Nestled in this haven is permission to talk freely about human fallenness. Jeff is a fallen human, permeated by the effects of sin. So are his parents, siblings, childhood friends, peers at work, and counselor. In the midst of this haven, Jeff can safely explore his feelings of sadness, grief, and anger about past and present relationships. He can also explore his own broken, needy condition, a discovery that allows him to empathize with his parents and others who have hurt him. Just as Jeff has been hurt, he has hurt others. As he acknowledges true brokenness, he is able to draw close to God and others.

This is a difficult balance for Christian counselors to maintain. When we slip too far in one direction or another, we risk hurting our clients by damaging their often fragile sense of identity or by socializing them to blame others for their pain.

This difficult balance can be illustrated with a multiple-choice question. In the midst of a counseling session, Jeff says, "I feel so empty and ugly inside. I feel as if I'm a bad person. But I'm not a bad person, am I? When I think I am a bad person, then I get really depressed and start thinking about suicide and stuff."

How does the counselor respond? I see three possible options.

> Option 1: "You are not a bad person, Jeff."
> Option 2: "Let's consider some of the ways you feel you're a bad person."
> Option 3: "It seems important to you not to think of yourself as a bad person."

Although any of these responses might be appropriate under some circumstances, my preference is option 3. Option 1 tends to dismiss personal responsibility, build excessive dependency in the counseling relationship, and prevent Jeff from exploring his feelings and dealing with his internal sense of brokenness. Option 2 might lead Jeff to explore his sinfulness, but it detracts from the important emotions he is exploring. Also, Jeff might be less interested in really exploring his worth than he is in knowing how the counselor will respond to his provocative question, "I'm not a bad person, am I?" Option 3 allows Jeff to explore not only his feelings of inadequacy but also his sin. Furthermore, Option 3 is a less-affirming response, one that might prevent Jeff from becoming excessively dependent on his therapist's approval.

This example illustrates the sensitive balance Christian counselors must maintain to nurture a client's fragile identity while allowing for an honest discussion of personal fault and human fallenness. It also illustrates how the counseling relationship must be carefully monitored.

Accurate Understanding of Healing Relationships

Spiritual health, from a Christian perspective, is defined by the nature of one's relationship with Jesus Christ. Psychological health also requires a capacity for intimate relationships. Thus, the Christian who is psychologically and spiritually whole enjoys healthy, intimate relationships with Christ and others. This is not to say that relationships are tantamount to health. Many counseling clients already have good capacity for relationships but are struggling with faulty learning patterns or difficult life circumstances. But as their self-efficacy improves and their learning patterns change, they often experience even greater freedom for healthy, meaningful relationships.

In some forms of counseling, the therapeutic relationship is the prototype of a healthy relationship. Some clients have rarely experienced a confiding, intimate relationship with good boundaries until they come for counseling. They learn about trust, respect, care, and empathy by observing and interacting with the counselor. In this sense, a good counselor is a minister of God's grace, even to those who know nothing of a gracious God.

Though he does not claim to have a Christian perspective, leading psychotherapy researcher Dr. Hans Strupp is convinced that "therapists' skills contribute materially to the outcome of therapy and that these skills, rather than being specific techniques, are much more accurately described as the ability to manage the complex human relationship that is the essence of psychotherapy."[20] Counseling often involves applying specific techniques to specific problems, but the therapeutic relationship may be an even more important variable in good counseling.

Faulty Understanding of Healing Relationships

Sometimes the power of the counseling relationship is misunderstood or misused, and a healthy healing relationship gives way to a neutral or damaging relationship. What goes wrong in these counseling relationships?

The counselor sometimes enjoys the power of the healing relationship too much, resulting in a number of problems.

WHAT IF THIS HAPPENED?

Jeff finds a therapist, I. M. Savyer, and immediately likes him. Mr. Savyer is attentive, interested, respectful, and empathetic. In fact, Mr. Savyer is the nicest person Jeff has ever known. Together, Mr. Savyer and Jeff explore the pain of Jeff's childhood, concluding that his parents were rigid, unaffectionate people who cared more about the family's reputation than Jeff's welfare. They look at other important people in Jeff's life and come to equally cynical conclusions.

After every session, Jeff feels better. Something about being with Mr. Savyer just makes him feel better. He is thankful he found a good counselor.

Although Mr. Savyer has exercised good listening skills, he seems to be forgetting that he is participating in a transitional relationship for Jeff. Although Jeff feels better after each session, he still spends most of his week in his "real world," interacting with the people he is criticizing in Mr. Savyer's office. Without intending to do so, Mr. Savyer may be contributing to Jeff's tendency toward *splitting*—a phenomenon in which clients see some people as all good and others as all bad. The counselor in this case is seen as all good, and the rest of the world is all bad.

A related problem is that Jeff may become excessively dependent on his counselor. Some feelings of dependency are transferred onto a counselor by virtually all clients, but when the dependency becomes excessive, clients often are injured by being caught in an unrealistically long counseling relationship and by experiencing excessive pain when the counseling relationship is terminated.

In some extreme cases, the counselor uses the power of the healing relationship to meet his or her own needs. When a counselor begins perceiving the counseling relationship as a way to meet his or her own needs, an *exploitive* relationship often results.[21] Soon the counselor begins disclosing personal problems to the client. Sometimes sexual intimacies occur, and the relationship becomes emotionally or sexually damaging to the client.

Counselors are fallen humans, just as clients are. We need a keen sense of humility in the work we do, and we need to remember that we are only modeling healthy relationships with our clients. We are not saving them but pointing them toward a Savior and toward healthy earthly relationships that can be an ongoing part of their lives.

Counselors play three roles simultaneously. First, we are full participants in the interpersonal interactions that occur in counseling sessions. Second, counselors are observers, carefully noting the quality of the relationship and critically evaluating what is and is not going well in the relationship. Third, we are engineers of the counseling relationship, adjusting the relationship by becoming more compassionate and understanding when a client feels alienated and isolated, becoming more distant and guarded when a client becomes too dependent, and asserting appropriate boundaries throughout the counseling relationship. The relationship we establish with clients is an important part of the healing process.

Assessment as the Rate-Limiting Step

When chemists compute the rate of chain reactions, they refer to the slowest reaction in the chain as the rate-limiting step. The entire process can go no faster than the rate-limiting step. Commuters find the same thing during rush hour, as their travel time is defined by the freeway bottleneck where four lanes merge into two. In counseling, good assessment is similar to a rate-limiting step. The effectiveness of counseling is limited by the accuracy of the counselor's ongoing assessment. A theoretical map, such as the one presented in this chapter, promotes competent assessment by providing a gauge by which we can measure our clients' needs and progress.

I was on a television show recently in which a leading figure in biblical counseling announced that students in psychology, including students in the Wheaton College doctoral program, were taught not to pray with their clients. As quickly as I could jump into the conversation, I denied the claim. Many students in Christian psychology programs, including those at Wheaton, are encouraged to pray with clients under many circumstances. However, before using any counseling intervention, including prayer and other religious interventions, it is wise to anticipate the possible effects. Sometimes it is best not to pray with clients in a session, and other times it can be a valuable part of Christian counseling.

Should a counselor have clients memorize Scripture? Is it wise to pray with clients during a counseling session? Should a counselor confront sin in a client's life? Should clients be encouraged to forgive those who have hurt them? The answers to these questions, which will be considered in detail throughout the remainder of this book, will vary from one client and one situation to the next. Just as a good basketball coach is able to watch several players at once and call the best play for the moment, an effective counselor watches these three components of psychological and spiritual health—healthy sense of self, awareness of personal brokenness, and confiding relationships—and adjusts the treatment accordingly.

Effective counseling requires an ongoing assessment of treatment goals and the client, as well as an accurate self-assessment of the counselor.

ONGOING ASSESSMENT OF GOALS

Maggie comes for counseling because of her recurrent stress-related tension headaches. Kristin comes for counseling because she has been suicidally depressed for several months. Maggie is happily married, successfully employed, and spiritually vital. Kristin lives alone, drifts from job to job, and feels God could never love her. Clearly, the goals for treating Maggie and Kristin will be different.

Current standards of care suggest that counselors should define goals and the nature of the counseling with their clients at the beginning of the counseling relationship.[22] It is wise to review these goals every session or two so the counseling can remain effectively focused. Maggie and her counselor set two goals: reducing the frequency of her headaches to no more than twice per week and experiencing greater satisfaction with her career. Kristin and her counselor set four goals: reducing her levels of depression, finding and maintaining at least one meaningful relationship, finding secure employment, and deepening her understanding of God's love.

These goals will need to be reviewed frequently throughout treatment. Whatever religious interventions are selected can be evaluated in light of these goals.

ONGOING ASSESSMENT OF THE CLIENT

At first glance, it may appear that Kristin needs religious interventions much more than Maggie. After all, Maggie just needs some relief from her headaches, and Kristin needs radical life transformation. But a closer look tells a different story.

Maggie enters into counseling in a relatively healthy state. She has an accurate awareness of herself; she is aware of her strengths and skills, including her tendency to worry too much about unimportant things at work. She recognizes she needs help, which reflects her awareness of human brokenness and need. And she has healthy relationships in her life. Maggie is in a position of strength and will probably not slip into a state of self-hate, begin seeing herself as a hopeless victim, or become excessively dependent on her counselor. Her counselor can use spiritual interventions with confidence. In fact, a published study has demonstrated Christian forms of devotional meditation to be an effective way of releasing muscle tension.[23] This type of spiritual intervention might be ideal for Maggie.

Spiritual interventions might also be appropriate for Kristin, but her counselor should be careful to consider the possible implications before using the interventions. Kristin and her counselor might find it helpful to pray together at the end of each session, but the counselor should remember that prayer is an intimate activity, and Kristin might easily become excessively dependent on her counselor. Believing in the power of prayer, the counselor might choose instead to pray for Kristin privately, outside of the counseling sessions. Similarly, Kristin and her counselor might consider using forgiveness of a past abuser as a treatment strategy. But it will be important for the counselor to recognize Kristin's weak sense of self-identity. Does she really understand the implications of forgiveness before she understands the toll exacted on her life by her abuser? Can she understand the act of forgiveness before she better understands that God has forgiven her? These are important questions for her counselor to consider before using religious interventions.

ONGOING ASSESSMENT OF THE COUNSELOR

Making decisions about treating Kristin and Maggie is made challenging enough by their different personalities and different treatment goals, but it becomes even more challenging when we remember that counselors also bring styles and personalities into the counseling process. Some counselors are naturally confrontive and work to help their clients quickly see personal sin and begin making better choices. Other counselors are naturally supportive and work to make therapy a safe place to explore a variety of feelings. Some are primarily trained in psychology, some in theology, some in counseling, and some in pastoral care. Some are Reformed, some charismatic, some Anabaptist, and some from other denominations. Some experience a profound spiritual life, and others struggle with spiritual disciplines and personal piety. Some are professionally trained, and some are peer counselors. Some are psychodynamic, some humanistic, some behavioral, some cognitive, and some come from a myriad of other theoretical perspectives. All these differences affect our choices in using spiritual interventions.

The naturally confrontive counselor may need to develop extra patience in order to wait for clients to grow strong enough to benefit from prayer, Scripture memory, personal confession, and so on. The psychodynamic therapist may have to work hard to recognize the simple beauty of Christian humility and not confuse it with masochism or a defense against grandiosity. The naturally supportive counselor may need to develop both distancing skills to prevent excessive dependency and confronting skills to keep clients out of chronic victim roles. The behavior therapist may need to exert extra effort to evaluate the therapeutic relationship. The professionally trained counselor may need to remember Christ's transforming power, which is rarely taught in the classroom.

Good assessment, and good counseling, starts and ends with a simple Socratic admonition: Counselor, know yourself. To this we must also add: know your client, know your goals, and know your theoretical road map.

SUMMARY

Throughout Scripture and history we see a healing pattern that requires humans to recognize limits to their self-sufficiency and reach out in their state of need to a gracious God. This same pattern can help us understand emotional health, but we must be cautious not to apply such a simple model in a haphazard or perfunctory way.

A more careful look suggests that spiritual and psychological health require a confident (but not inflated) sense of self, an awareness of human need and limitations, and confiding interpersonal relationships with God and others. Effective Christian counseling strengthens all three of these areas. Unfortunately, there are many difficulties in the process of counseling, and a faulty understanding of self, brokenness, or counseling relationships can increase the client's concerns and problems. From the basis of this theoretical map, we can begin to consider the potential value and dangers of using religious interventions in counseling.

The remainder of this book will use the foundation established in these first two chapters as a framework to consider a variety of religious interventions such as prayer, use of Scripture in counseling, forgiveness, and so on. Each chapter will have three main sections, as illustrated in figure 3.

FIGURE 3

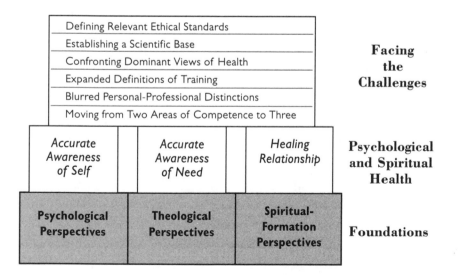

Defining Relevant Ethical Standards			Facing the Challenges
Establishing a Scientific Base			
Confronting Dominant Views of Health			
Expanded Definitions of Training			
Blurred Personal-Professional Distinctions			
Moving from Two Areas of Competence to Three			
Accurate Awareness of Self	*Accurate Awareness of Need*	*Healing Relationship*	**Psychological and Spiritual Health**
Psychological Perspectives	**Theological Perspectives**	**Spiritual-Formation Perspectives**	**Foundations**

First, each chapter will consider a few relevant issues from the existing literature in psychology, Christian theology, and spirituality in order to provide a foundation on which to build an accurate understanding of the religious intervention. Volumes have been written from each of these three perspectives, and I am not so grandiose as to presume competence or time for a thorough review of any of this book's topics from psychological, theological, and spiritual-formation perspectives. Rather, my goal in each remaining chapter will be to highlight one or more themes from these three foundational perspectives and discuss its relevance to Christian counseling.

Second, each chapter will evaluate each religious intervention according to the model of *psychological and spiritual health* described in this chapter. Each chapter will evaluate the interventions by asking three questions: Will this help establish a healthy sense of self? Will this help establish a healthy sense of need? Will this help establish a healing relationship?

Third, each chapter will discuss the six *challenges for intradisciplinary integration,* as described in chapter 1.

3 / PRAYER

Is it okay if we pray together before ending today's session?" Christians answer this question in different ways. Some always say yes, insisting that prayer is an essential part of all Christian experience and should routinely be included in Christian counseling. Others say no, asserting that counseling should remain distinct from spiritual-guidance or pastoral interventions. Either answer oversimplifies the complexities counselors face.

WHAT IF THIS HAPPENED?

Ms. Henry is a counseling client whom you have been seeing for two months. Referred by her internist because of her excessive medical and physical complaints, she quickly displayed symptoms of somatization disorder. She avoids virtually all painful emotions and ends up having repeated physical problems as a result—stomach pain, irritable bowel syndrome, headaches, and so on.

During today's session, you have been trying to help Ms. Henry understand her feelings toward her unfaithful husband. She insists that she is not angry, that she is willing to forgive because she knows it is her Christian responsibility, and that she probably needs to be more attentive to his sexual needs at home. Throughout the session she sheds no tears, expresses no pain, and talks of how her Christian faith has allowed her to cope with

this, her husband's fourth extramarital affair. Near the end of the
session, she looks at you and asks, "Is it okay if we pray together
before ending today's session?"

How should the responsible Christian counselor respond to Ms.
Henry? Before answering this question, consider another situation.

WHAT IF THIS HAPPENED?

Ms. Thomas has been in counseling for six months, working on
her feelings of depression and fears of abandonment. She has
made excellent progress and until yesterday has felt hopeful
about the future and closer to God than ever before. Yesterday,
her mother died suddenly of a heart attack.

During today's session, Ms. Thomas cries freely, expresses her
pain, and reflects on her fears of being abandoned by those
closest to her. She stops crying near the end of the session, puts
her handkerchief in her purse, and begins to stand up to leave.
You stop her and ask, "Is it okay if we pray together before
ending today's session?"

Ms. Henry and Ms. Thomas are in different situations, and the
effects of praying with Ms. Henry will be different from the effects
of praying with Ms. Thomas. There is not a simple yes or no answer
to either scenario. On one hand, agreeing to pray with Ms. Henry
might encourage her to continue using her faith as a means of
denial rather than as a route to truth. On the other hand, refusing
her request to pray with her might hurt therapeutic rapport, and
prayer might be an avenue through which she could begin exploring her feelings. Praying with Ms. Thomas might lend a sense of
comfort and hope in the midst of her feelings of despair. However,
it could also contribute to feelings of dependency at a time when
terminating the counseling relationship is imminent. Praying with

her now might help bring her feelings of comfort and peace, or it might cause her greater feelings of abandonment later when the counseling relationship ends.

One of the common questions during my graduate school days in the early 1980s was, "Does psychotherapy work?" I remember a lecture in which Hans Strupp, Distinguished Professor of Psychology at Vanderbilt University, debunked the question. A more appropriate question, Strupp insisted, was, "Which types of psychotherapy work for which clients under which circumstances?" Similarly, "Should counselors pray with clients?" is the wrong question to ask. Instead we ought to ask, *"Which* forms of prayer should we use with *which* clients and under *which* circumstances?"

If we focus too intently on the question of praying with clients in sessions, we overlook other important questions about prayer in counseling. For example, how often do we pray silently for our clients during a counseling session? How often do we pray for our clients outside of the counseling session? What about devotional meditation as a spiritual and psychological tool for relaxation and anxiety management? By looking at the framework established in chapters 1 and 2, we can come to informed decisions about the questions.

FOUNDATIONS

Psychology

Though it is beyond the scope of this book to give a comprehensive literature review of prayer, it will survey the prominent themes in the psychological literature. The literature about prayer can be roughly divided into two categories: the effects of prayer and using prayer in counseling.

THE EFFECTS OF PRAYER

Prayer is a common human experience. Studies show that ninety percent of Americans pray.[1] However, studies about the effects of prayer are surprisingly sparse in the psychological literature, and most studies that have been reported are plagued with significant methodological problems. Dr. Michael McCullough has recently published a review of the psychological effects of prayer, including helpful discussions of the problems with previous studies and ideas for future research.[2]

McCullough identifies several themes regarding the psychological effects of prayer. First, prayer is associated with a subjective experience of well-being. Compared with those who do not pray, or who pray infrequently, those who pray often tend to experience more purpose in life, greater marital satisfaction, religious satisfaction, and a general sense of well-being. An even better predictor of well-being is the extent to which people experience a subjective sense of God's presence while praying. Those who experience prayer as a deeply significant, even mystical, experience have a greater sense of well-being than others. We must exercise caution in interpreting these results because most of the studies reviewed were correlational in nature. When two variables are correlated, as prayer and well-being are, it does not necessarily mean that one causes the other. It could be that people who pray are happier or that happier people pray more often. Alternatively, there could be some third variable that explains why prayer and well-being are related. For example, it may be that highly religious people are happier and that they also tend to pray more often than moderately religious or nonreligious people.[3]

Second, McCullough reviews the literature on using prayer as an aid in coping with physical pain and medical problems. A number of studies indicate that prayer is a helpful resource in coping with various medical problems. Other studies demonstrate that prayer is used often by those experiencing high levels of physical and emotional discomfort.

Third, several studies have considered the relationship between psychological symptoms and prayer. The few studies reported suffer from methodological problems and should be interpreted cautiously, but prayer appears to be positively related to abstinence for those in alcohol treatment and negatively related to fears of dying.

Fourth, one well-designed study demonstrated the effectiveness of intercessory prayer. Patients in a coronary care unit were randomly assigned to either the control group or the group that received intercessory prayer by a group that met outside the hospital on a regular basis. Neither the patients nor the researchers who assessed the outcome knew to which experimental condition the patients were assigned. On some (but not all) of the outcome measures, the recipients of intercessory prayer were healthier upon discharge from the hospital than the control group. The probability of some of the observed differences between groups occurring by coincidence or random chance is less than one in ten thousand!

These findings will come as no surprise to those who accept the Bible as authoritative. Nonetheless, the findings are important because they translate the effectiveness of prayer into the scientific language that is acceptable to those in mental health professions. Of course, these studies do not specifically address the focus of this book: What about the use of prayer in counseling?

PRAYER IN COUNSELING

Based on survey data, prayer appears to be a frequent but not routine part of Christian counseling and psychotherapy.[4] Prayer is used with some but not all counseling clients, depending on the theoretical orientation of the counselor and the diagnosis of the client.[5] Among those who view prayer as an important part of counseling, the methods of implementing prayer vary widely.

Some studies advocate praying aloud with clients during therapy sessions. In a recent survey of doctoral-level members of the Christian Association for Psychological Studies (CAPS), respondents reported using in-session prayer with approximately 30 percent of their clients.[6] There are multiple motives for including prayer in a counseling session. Some counselors pray in session because prayer can enhance clients' spiritual lives and clarify their perspectives. Craigie and Tan write from a cognitive-behavioral perspective: "Indeed, praying with clients that they may be liberated from resistant misbeliefs, that they may be empowered to do the truth, and that they may come into a deeper relationship with the truth can sometimes be a most powerful experience."[7] Others report using prayer because it models healthy interpersonal communication. Crocker advocates praying with couples in marital therapy because prayer models effective communication. "I believe that Christian pastors can use the traditional forms of prayer as a guide in teaching couples and individuals how to communicate well, and at the same time, can help the persons they work with come to a deeper understanding of the Christian life."[8] Still other counselors choose to pray with clients because their clients desire prayer to be part of the counseling relationship, and prayer enhances therapeutic rapport.[9]

It is important to note that none of these reasons for prayer is meant to undermine or dismiss the spiritual power of prayer. Prayer affects human interactions, but more important, it is a method of communicating with God. "It should be emphasized, particularly with prayer and imagery . . . that we take the position that it is the Holy Spirit who heals. The imagery and prayer approaches that have been described are not to be viewed as primarily psychological techniques or procedures. Rather, they should be viewed as vehicles to put clients, in the words of Foster, 'in the way of God.'"[10] Thus, for a variety of reasons many counselors choose to pray with clients during counseling sessions. To date, no empirical research has been reported on the effects of praying aloud during counseling sessions.

Others advocate using meditation, contemplative prayer, or imagery in counseling sessions, techniques that have received preliminary research support.[11] Carlson, Bacaseta, and Simantona demonstrated that meditating on Scripture and liturgical prayer helped reduce anger and anxiety more effectively than progressive relaxation training or no treatment.[12] Similarly, Propst found religious imagery, such as having clients picture Christ going with them into a difficult situation, helped reduce depression among religious clients.[13]

Although in-session prayer and meditation have received the most attention in the psychological literature, prayer can be integrated into counseling in other ways. Some counselors pray during sessions without disclosing their prayers to clients. Praying during pauses in the conversation is often a way not only to keep a spiritual focus in counseling but also to keep from impulsively filling the silence with unnecessary words.

WHAT IF THIS HAPPENED?

Theresa is a lay counselor working in individual and group therapy with survivors of sexual abuse. She has been a lay counselor for two years and feels good about her counseling skills, but she has one nagging problem: she feels uncomfortable with silence and compensates by changing the subject. Many times her clients begin exploring painful emotions, become quiet, and then Theresa changes the topic.

What if Theresa develops a new habit? In times of silence, she trains herself to silently pray for the client sitting across from her. *Lord, please embrace _____ with your love right now as she confronts this pain. Dear God, please help _____ see you clearly, even though there is such a cloud of evil in her past.* As Theresa develops this new skill, she will be introducing the power of prayer into her counseling work and breaking a bad habit at the same time.

Silent prayer during counseling can also be used to sustain the counselor through difficult and stressful work. Schneider and Kastenbaum surveyed hospice workers and found that prayer helped workers cope with the demands of their daily interactions.[14] Most often the workers used silent, private, spontaneous prayers and rarely prayed with the patients themselves.

Another way prayer can be used as part of therapy is by encouraging clients to pray outside of the counseling session. Finney and Malony found clients' contemplative prayer outside the counseling sessions to be a helpful addition to psychotherapy.[15] The nine adults participating in the study were trained in contemplative-prayer techniques after six weeks of psychotherapy, then kept records of their daily use of contemplative prayer throughout the remainder of therapy. The researchers used a time-series design to test the effects of psychotherapy alone versus psychotherapy plus contemplative prayer. The participants showed a striking decrease in subjective levels of discomfort as a result of psychotherapy plus prayer but little change on the scales used to measure personal spirituality. Because of the limits of the design (no control group), it is difficult to determine whether the overall benefits were due to psychotherapy, prayer, or a combination of both. Until more research is reported, we can only speculate that the use of prayer outside counseling sessions provides therapeutic benefit.

Finally, therapists can combine prayer and counseling by praying for clients outside of the counseling session. On the average, doctoral-level CAPS members report praying for 64 percent of their clients and view it as a valuable part of their clinical work.[16] The helpfulness of praying for clients outside of a counseling session is impossible to test scientifically in a double-blind study because counselors would always know which clients they prayed for and might inadvertently change the counseling process as a result. Even without scientific proof, we can assume that praying for clients outside of sessions helps counselors maintain a ministry focus and helps counseling clients in their spiritual and emotional healing. "The prayer of the righteous is powerful and effective" (James 5:16).

Christian Theology

Theologian J. C. Lambert notes that prayer has two meanings in Scripture. In the narrowest sense, prayer is petition, asking God for something. In the wider sense, prayer is worship, reflecting on God's character.[17]

PRAYER AS DIRECT PETITION

Prayer as direct petition is often used by people in need, including counselors and their clients. But this creates an interesting tension. On the one hand, if God is sovereign and already knows the future, then what difference does it make for us to pray? On the other hand, if prayer can change the future, then is God not really sovereign? This tension reflects the larger discussion of theological determinism versus free will, a discussion that has gone unresolved through centuries of debate. Though we must appeal to paradox and mystery rather than attempt a thorough resolution of the debate between determinism and free will, Millard Erickson helps by discussing our partnership with God in prayer.[18] When we pray, we humble ourselves and ask to become a partner in knowing and doing God's will. From this position of humility, we can see God's will more clearly, and God grants us our deepest desires. For example, only Peter walked on the water because only Peter asked (Matt. 14:22-33). By praying, we commit our will to partnership with God's will.

"May the force be with you" is not a good understanding of petitionary prayer. We are not harnessing a power that we control, and we are not simply creating a positive, expectant attitude for good things to come. Rather, petitionary prayer creates in us a longing for God's will. "Prayer is not so much getting God to do our will as it is demonstrating that we are as concerned as is God that his will be done."[19] Many prayers are not answered the way we would like, but we are to continue turning our hearts toward God and conforming our will to God's will in prayer. Eventually we change. "In prayer, real prayer, we begin to think God's thoughts after him: to desire the things he desires, to love the things he loves, to will the things he wills."[20]

We are told in Scripture to pray persistently because persistent prayer comes from a sense of compelling urgency (Luke 11:8-10). Prayer is not to be a casual encounter like a Christmas list for Santa Claus; prayer should be an extension of the passions of our heart. By praying persistently and consistently, we remind ourselves to seek God while telling God our deepest desires.

Using petitionary prayer in counseling, where the counselor prays for the client, can help model the qualities of effective prayer. However, it can also introduce problems.

WHAT IF THIS HAPPENED?

Mr. Baldwin prays at the end of each counseling session with Gene, his counseling client. Gene finds it reassuring and comforting to know his counselor prays for him. Gene also feels he can learn about prayer by observing his counselor. He has struggled with an inconsistent prayer life for years and feels relieved to know that God is now hearing his needs through his counselor's prayers.

The good news is that Gene is learning about prayer and that his counselor is praying for him. There is also bad news. First, Gene may believe his counselor's intercessory prayer removes his obligation to petition God directly. If prayer is partnering with God, then direct personal petition is an important element of effective prayer. Second, if prayer demonstrates a person's desire for God's will to be done, then it is an important personal discipline that should not be regularly delegated to another. Gene is losing an opportunity for shaping his character by relying on his counselor to pray for him. Third, the persistence of effective prayer might be compromised by the natural limits of weekly counseling sessions. The beauty of prayer is that we can approach God anytime: clients and counselors can pray outside of the office as frequently as they desire. Mr. Baldwin would be wise to teach Gene to petition God directly, both inside and outside of the counseling office.

PRAYER AS WORSHIP

Christian prayer goes far beyond petitioning God with our needs. In prayer we confess our sinful nature (Ps. 51:3-5), give thanks for

God's providence throughout history (Ps. 136) and in our personal lives (1 Sam. 2:1-10), and express adoration to God (Rom. 11:33-36). In this wider context of understanding prayer, many mystics and religious leaders have written about spiritual and emotional healing.[21]

As with petitionary prayer in counseling, there is good news and bad news. The good news is that contemplative prayer and worship can open our spiritual eyes at the same time that it can distract us from our human habits of egocentrism and self-absorption. Those who have mastered self-forgetfulness understand worship through prayer. Prayer is, as Richard Foster writes, "finding the heart's true home."[22] It is also good that Christian meditation appears to provide significant benefits in reducing anxiety and anger.[23] The bad news is that some people have not established careful theological boundaries for their understanding of prayer and meditation and have drifted toward heresy.[24] Thus, counselors who use devotional meditation and prayer in therapy should carefully evaluate their methods from theological as well as psychological perspectives.

Spirituality

The capacity to experience God through prayer is the center of Christian spirituality. Richard Foster begins his book on prayer with this invitation:

> God has graciously allowed me to catch a glimpse into his heart, and I want to share with you what I have seen. Today the heart of God is an open wound of love. He aches over our distance and preoccupation. He mourns that we do not draw near to him. He grieves that we have forgotten him. He weeps over our obsession with muchness and manyness. He longs for our presence.
>
> And he is inviting you—and me—to come home, to come home to where we belong, to come home to that for which

we were created. His arms are stretched out wide to receive us. His heart is enlarged to take us in.[25]

Foster's words welcome us to enter a place of rest, a place of wholesome spiritual renewal. Throughout the remainder of his book, Foster demonstrates that prayer is the door leading to such a place. Elsewhere Foster writes, "Of all the Spiritual Disciplines prayer is the most central because it ushers us into perpetual communion with the Father."[26] In his classic book, *Prayer,* Ole Hallesby comes to a similar conclusion: "Prayer is the breath of the soul, the organ by which we receive Christ into our parched and withered hearts. . . . As air enters in quietly when we breathe, and does its normal work in our lungs, so Jesus enters quietly into our hearts and does His blessed work there."[27]

This, of course, raises a nagging question for many Christians. If prayer is so powerful and if it ushers us into God's presence, why is it that we can fill our life full of prayer and yet so rarely experience God in deep ways? Many Christians pray before meals, pray throughout the day, pray in church, pray with children at bedtime, and still feel distant from God. How can this be?

Perhaps the spiritual power of prayer eludes us because we fail to have a balanced diet of prayer and other spiritual discipline in our lives. If prayer serves two functions in Scripture—petition and worship—we often overemphasize petition and neglect worship. "Lord, bless this meal to our bodies." "Dear God, grant us safe travel to our destination." "Heavenly Father, please restore my physical health." We keep prayer lists in which we describe our petitions and record the dates of answered prayers. These prayer activities are good; petition is an important part of prayer. But we must remember that prayer is also an act of worship, a way of celebrating God's character and gracious provision. Worship takes time.

Dallas Willard suggests that we cannot truly understand spiritually transforming prayer unless we are also practicing the disciplines of solitude and fasting.[28] Time-pressured prayer rarely allows us to enter into meaningful worship. It is difficult to worship God through prayer when the lasagna is getting cold or when the congregation is anxious to get home before the play-off game starts. Worship requires us to reflect deeply on our need and God's provision, insights that come most naturally in moments of quiet. Bill Hybels, in his book *Too Busy Not to Pray,* describes the importance of "RPM reduction," slowing down each day to worship and listen to God through prayer.[29]

To pray meaningfully, we must understand our deep thirst for God. Hallesby writes: "Listen, my friend! Your helplessness is your best prayer. It calls from your heart to the heart of God with greater effect than all your uttered pleas. He hears it from the very moment that you are seized with helplessness, and He becomes actively engaged at once in hearing and answering the prayer of your helplessness."[30]

We often cram our lives so full of activity that we fail to recognize our need for God. With solitude and fasting we are forced beyond our defenses of busyness, and we begin to see ourselves accurately as thirsty, needy people longing for a gracious Savior.

What are the implications for counseling? First, it seems clear that the transforming power of prayer cannot be fully experienced by praying at the beginning or end of a counseling session. Spiritually transforming prayer takes time and disciplined training. For prayer to be an active agent for change in a client's life, it must become part of a disciplined spiritual life outside the counseling office.

Second, spiritually sensitive counselors may sometimes need to teach clients about prayer. Counselors give homework for a variety of reasons, and prayer homework can be considered a legitimate assignment for many Christian clients. Bill Hybels outlines a series of behavioral steps that he uses each day to pray: journaling, writing out prayers, and listening to God.[31] Implementing these same steps can be a useful counseling assignment in many situations. Sometimes prayer training can begin in the counseling session, especially when devotional meditation is used as an intervention for anxiety-related problems. There are important ethical considerations for those using spiritual interventions, especially for those receiving insurance reimbursement for specified treatment protocols. These will be discussed later in this chapter and throughout the book.

Third, the insight people gain in counseling may often prove helpful in their personal prayer life. If effective Christian counseling brings people to a healthy sense of self-identity and greater awareness of their brokenness and the fallen human condition, then it also prepares people to reach out to God. Our sense of need propels us to meaningful prayer. Conversely, when counseling causes people to think of themselves as victims, their prayer life is hindered. Some people have been victimized and wounded by past events, and effective Christian counseling allows people to explore their pain, anger, and grief about past hurts. But deep inner healing requires more. Wounded people must recognize their personal need and their capacity to wound others before fully knowing God's healing grace.

PSYCHOLOGICAL AND SPIRITUAL HEALTH

From the preceding discussion, it seems clear that prayer is an important element of spiritual and psychological health. Prayer is at the heart of Christian piety, allowing us to humble ourselves and worship God and to bring our concerns directly to God. Preliminary scientific evidence, as reviewed earlier, supports the effectiveness of prayer in promoting health.

But we must also recognize that not all prayer is effective. In the Sermon on the Mount, for example, Jesus was critical of public prayers offered by those thinking more about the social impact of their prayers than about God (Matt. 6:5). Jesus taught, "Whenever you pray, go into your room and shut the door and pray to your Father who is in secret; and your Father who sees in secret will reward you" (Matt. 6:6). Jesus also condemned prayers of empty repetitious phrases and prayers of smugness (Matt. 6:7; Luke 18:9-14).

Because prayer is a good thing that can be misused, its use in counseling warrants careful monitoring. Some forms of prayer are always an important addition to effective counseling, and others can be easily misused and at times can work against the goals of Christian counseling. The amount of risk I associate with various forms of prayer is shown in figure 4.

FIGURE 4

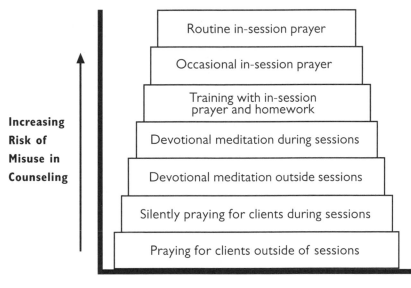

Increasing Risk of Misuse in Counseling

- Routine in-session prayer
- Occasional in-session prayer
- Training with in-session prayer and homework
- Devotional meditation during sessions
- Devotional meditation outside sessions
- Silently praying for clients during sessions
- Praying for clients outside of sessions

TYPES OF PRAYER

Some forms of prayer are almost always wise and productive. What case could possibly be made against a counselor's praying for clients outside of the counseling sessions? If, as Christian counselors, we are committed to the health of our clients and we believe in the power of prayer, then we have a spiritual obligation to pray faithfully for those in our care. These prayers of petition are to be persistent and regular, an essential part of the disciplines exercised by the spiritually vibrant counselor. It is encouraging to note that on the average, CAPS members report praying outside of sessions for the majority of their clients.[32] Praying outside of sessions provides spiritual resources for counseling clients, while reminding counselors of the importance of humbly seeking God's direction.

Similarly, praying for clients silently during pauses in the counseling dialogue is an excellent way to remind ourselves that we are imperfect ministers of God's grace and truth, seeking the Holy Spirit's guidance in each word and expression we use. Of course, if we are engaged in silent prayer too frequently or too actively during the counseling session, it could compromise our listening acuity, so the counselor needs to set some personal limits for silent in-session prayer.

Devotional-meditation assignments outside of sessions can also be helpful for many clients, especially those who are dealing with anxiety- or faith-related problems. Devotional meditation appears to be at least as effective as progressive relaxation in reducing anxiety and anger and should be considered a legitimate alternative for Christian counselors.[33] However, it is important to recognize that devotional meditation is not equally appropriate for all counseling problems. Also, some counselors have expressed concerns that imagery and meditation are spiritually dangerous interventions.[34]

Devotional meditation can also be effectively used as part of counseling sessions. This is sometimes effective in behavioral interventions when muscle tension needs to be reduced. Also, imagery and meditation can be used in reducing symptoms of depression among religious clients and in modifying faulty core beliefs in cognitive therapy.[35] The risk of in-session meditation is that the social demands of the situation might significantly change the worship experience. Clients might be concerned about being "spiritual enough" to please the counselor. Socially tense clients may find it threatening to close their eyes for a prolonged period during the session, wondering what the counselor is doing or thinking during those moments of silence. It is equally effective to make an audio recording of instructions and have clients do devotional meditation someplace where the social demands can be avoided.

For some clients, in-session prayer training might be an appropriate intervention. Just as some clients benefit from appropriate social skills or more accurate self-talk, others benefit from skills in spiritual disciplines. Clients can learn various types of prayer in sessions and then complete out-of-session homework assignments to strengthen their prayer life.

Prayer training holds potential but also introduces significant risk for several reasons. First, not all counseling is skills oriented. Those functioning from a client-centered or psychodynamic perspective may find that overt skills training detracts from the overall therapeutic process. Second, prayer training may pose ethical problems for counselors who are representing their techniques to insurance companies as mainstream interventions. This relates to a third problem—we have no scientific evidence for the effectiveness of prayer training. Although as Christians we may feel no need for such evidence (because we have experiential and scriptural evidence for prayer), we need to speak the scientific language of the mental health professions if our methods are to gain credibility.

Occasional in-session prayers of petition can be helpful under some circumstances. On the average, CAPS members use in-session prayer with approximately one-third of their clients.[36] However, as the cases at the beginning of this chapter illustrate, prayer can be more or less useful in various situations. In-session prayer for those facing acute stress and grief reactions may often be helpful, and a prayer of thanksgiving can be a spontaneous act of worship in the midst of a significant breakthrough in counseling. But praying in other situations can be harmful. For example, praying with an actively schizophrenic or manic patient could be destructive and harmful to the fragile psychological state of the patient and to the treatment relationship.[37]

Finally, though some competent Christian counselors will disagree with me, I believe routine in-session prayer introduces significant risk and minimal benefits to the counseling relationship. On the positive side, routine in-session prayer can model a commitment to spirituality, and it can remind both the counselor and client of their desire to follow God's leading. Some counselors advocate praying to invoke the Holy Spirit's power in counseling, but these prayers can be done privately and silently without introducing the therapeutic risks of praying aloud. On the negative side, there are many concerns to consider. First, although praying with clients may teach effective communication skills, it is this type of praying that Jesus condemned when he told the religious leaders of his time to stop praying for social effect.[38] Instead, Jesus taught that prayer should be an intimate part of a private relationship with God (Matt. 6:5-6). Second, counselors who pray routinely with most or all of their clients face a risk of praying words of meaningless repetition, as is common of prayers before meals. Prayer is not meant to be a ritual of special words that invoke God's blessing hour after hour but a way of humbling ourselves before our just and gracious God. When we give up the essence of prayer and rely instead on the empty symbols of language, we grieve God and deceive ourselves. Third, although counselors sometimes pray to meet their Christian clients' expectations, it is often more important to understand the origin of the clients' expectations than to placate them. Religious practices can be used as a defense against insight and self-understanding, as was the case for many of the religious leaders that Jesus criticized. Fourth, praying aloud in counseling sometimes weakens the clients' sense of direct accountability to God. "My counselor prays for me every week," is quite a different experience from praying without ceasing (1 Thess. 5:17)! Fifth, praying together introduces a form of interpersonal intimacy that may not be wise in every counseling situation. Sixth, praying together inhibits some from disclosing important information. Because routine prayer may elevate counselors to spiritual-giant status in clients' eyes, some will hesitate to discuss their struggles with sin, fearing a judgmental response.

Thus, some forms of prayer (e.g., praying for clients outside of sessions) are always helpful, and others (e.g., routine in-session prayers with clients) are sometimes helpful but pose significant risks.

My goal is not to identify a list of good types of prayers and bad types of prayers but to keep the question at the beginning of this chapter in the forefront: *"Which* forms of prayer should be used with *which* clients and under *which* circumstances?"* In answering this question for each specific counseling situation, it is important to remember the model of psychological and spiritual health described in chapter 2. Three specific questions can help counselors assess the appropriate use of prayer in a variety of clinical situations.

Will This Help Establish a Healthy Sense of Self?

In one sense, prayer may be a perfect illustration of getting beyond our human tendency to be self-focused to a state of self-forgetfulness. Those who are broken and weary find comfort in the presence of Christ (Matt. 11:28-30). Those who are self-absorbed must see beyond themselves to see Christ (Luke 18:9-14). Counselors can use prayer to help their clients gain perspective and a more accurate understanding of themselves.

WHAT IF THIS HAPPENED?

Sabrina suffers from self-hate and an impoverished self-image. Sexually and physically abused as a child, Sabrina believes that she will always be hurt, abandoned, and rejected. After being in a healthy counseling relationship for several months, Sabrina starts feeling better and expresses an interest in strengthening her spiritual life. Her counselor assigns a meditation exercise that she completes three times weekly outside of the counseling sessions. Sabrina pictures herself in Christ's presence. With a warm look of comfort on his face, Christ speaks to her, "Come to me, all you that are weary and are carrying heavy burdens, and I will give you rest. Take my yoke upon you, and learn from me; for I am gentle and humble in heart, and you will find rest for your souls" (Matt. 11:28-29). With time, Sabrina begins to experience an emotional warmth as she thinks of God's love. Prayer plays an important role in her healing process.

Though prayer is ideally suited to help us get our eyes off ourselves and onto a loving Savior, we are adept at distorting prayer and allowing it to distract from a healthy sense of self. For example, what if Sabrina's counselor has her do the same imagery exercise during a session? As she closes her eyes, trying to picture Christ, she instead is flooded with other distracting thoughts. *What is my counselor doing while my eyes are closed? Am I relaxed enough? Do I have the right expression on my face? Is he staring at my body?* In this context, prayer becomes a vehicle of greater self-focus and reinforces a faulty self-image.

Or what if Sabrina's counselor prays routinely at the beginning and end of each session? Sabrina begins counseling feeling angry at God and silently questions whether there is a benevolent God. She asks herself, *If God is so loving, then how could these awful things have happened to me in the past?* Each time her counselor prays in session, Sabrina feels unspiritual and increasingly committed to hiding her doubts from her counselor. As a result, she does not feel free to explore meaningful issues of faith in counseling.

When prayer helps a client establish a healthy, accurate sense of self, it can be a helpful part of treatment. When it is used insensitively or as a perfunctory part of treatment, it can be spiritually and emotionally harmful.

Will This Help Establish a Healthy Sense of Need?

Prayer assumes need. "Prayer and helplessness are inseparable."[39] Jesus described this in a parable of two churchgoers in Luke 18. One man, a religious leader, pronounced his self-sufficiency, "God, I thank you that I am not like other people: thieves, rogues, adulterers, or even like this tax collector. I fast twice a week; I give a tenth of all my income" (Luke 18:11-12).

The other, a tax collector, prayed a simpler prayer: "God, be merciful to me, a sinner!" (Luke 18:13). The tax collector knew more about prayer than the religious leader did. Prayer requires a humble awareness of our need for God.

In the mental health professions, we value autonomy and self-confidence more than brokenness and neediness. I believe both are important. A healthy sense of self allows us to exercise freedom, accept responsibility, and make good decisions. A healthy sense of need allows us to keep our humanness in perspective and to keep us looking to God for hope and direction.

The tax collector in Jesus' parable showed signs of both self-confidence and neediness. He had the confidence to come to the temple, though he knew he was a sinner, and to ask God for mercy, though he knew he was undeserving. He had the humility to admit his need and ask for help. Prayer that is used effectively in counseling is also based on both: enough self-confidence to ask for help and an accurate understanding of human need. God is found not by wallowing in shame or by feeling better about our human potential but by humbling ourselves and looking to a transcendent Creator for sustenance.

Today, the parable Jesus told might take a different form. Two counselors prayed with their clients. Counselor A prayed: "Dear God, help Sabrina recognize that she is a wonderful person created in your image. She is creative, energetic, fun, and caring. Help her see her value and stop being so critical of herself."

Was Counselor A talking to God or to Sabrina? This prayer may help Sabrina's self-image and self-confidence, but there are more direct ways to accomplish these goals. And more significant, this prayer may hurt Sabrina in her spiritual quest by communicating that God loves her because of her qualities rather than because of God's gracious character.

Counselor B teaches Sabrina to meditate on Psalm 40:17 ten minutes each day: "As for me, I am poor and needy, but the Lord takes thought for me. You are my help and my deliverer; do not delay, O my God."

Counselor B teaches Sabrina to recognize that God's love does not depend on her qualities. At the deepest emotional level, Sabrina does not want to be loved because she is good enough to be loved; she wants to be loved regardless of her strengths and weaknesses. God offers such a love, and Counselor B helps Sabrina see it.

Will This Help Establish a Healing Relationship?

Because effective counselors simultaneously observe and participate in counseling relationships, it is important to anticipate the relational effects of various forms of prayer in counseling. Counseling requires a close, confiding relationship, and in many cases, praying together draws two people closer together. In this sense, enhancing the human interaction can be a useful side effect of praying together in counseling. After an initial therapeutic bond is established, however, the counselor sometimes has to watch that the counseling relationship does not become excessively close. A counselor and client share a temporary, transitional relationship, and the counselor must maintain sole responsibility for keeping the relationship at an appropriate level of interpersonal intimacy. When the counseling relationship appears to be getting too close, praying together in a session is usually not a good idea.

Similarly, those who are inclined toward dependency may naturally look to their counselors for emotional and spiritual strength. As counseling progresses, it is important for the counselors to give clients progressively more responsibility for personal spiritual well-being.

Most important, effective Christian counselors recognize that counseling relationships often point clients toward a healthier view of God. The counseling relationship is helpful when it displays aspects of God's character; it is harmful when it becomes a means of personal power, grandiosity, or self-gratification. When prayer draws more attention to the counselor or the client than to God, it misses the mark. The beauty and changing power of effective prayer is accomplished as we humble ourselves and draw close to God.

FACING THE CHALLENGES

All the challenges of intradisciplinary integration discussed in chapter 1 can be seen in Christian counselors' understanding and use of prayer.

Challenge 1: Moving from Two Areas of Competence to Three

Many Christian counselors have training in theological perspectives on prayer, and many have thought in depth about the psychological implications of using prayer in counseling. The third area of competence, spiritual formation, is less familiar to most Christian counselors.

Here we must make a distinction between basic and advanced competence. When first trained, counselors have basic competence in counseling interventions. With time and experience, they become better counselors and often gain advanced competence in psychological theory and technique. Most counselors do not gain advanced competence in theology or spiritual formation; theologians and spiritual directors have advanced competence in their respective specialty areas. Nonetheless, counselors can aspire to basic competence by reading and studying the works of theologians and spiritual directors and by practicing their suggestions.

This distinction between basic and advanced competency is important because counselors must not confuse their roles with the roles of theologians and spiritual directors. Counseling is not the same as spiritual direction, and it should not replace spiritual direction.[40] In the same way, few Christian counselors are superb Bible expositors. Nonetheless, responsible Christian counseling is informed by a foundational understanding of theology and spiritual formation.

Those with basic competence in spiritual formation understand that prayer is an essential part of knowing God. Those with advanced competence view prayer as "the main business of their lives."[41] Prayer can never be captured by words in a counseling session or even by a weekly prayer journal. Prayer results from an awareness of being in God's presence continually, a natural part of the inner life of those who have learned the most about walking with God. Thus, as Dallas Willard writes, we cannot know the power of prayer until we understand and practice the other disciplines of the inner life.

When Dr. Gary Moon and his colleagues surveyed religiously oriented graduate programs in counseling and psychology, their respondents reported prayer to have scriptural support and subjective value in counseling. Despite the perceived value of prayer, respondents indicated that little attention was given to prayer in the curriculum.[42] Similarly, little emphasis was given to other disciplines of the inner life, including fasting, solitude, and meditation.

In the Wheaton College doctor of psychology program, we find it useful for students to take a spiritual formation course during their first semester of study. In addition to giving students an opportunity for focused study on the spiritual disciplines, it allows them to develop personal practices that enhance their spiritual development.

Challenge 2: Blurred Personal-Professional Distinctions

Virtually all mental health professions recognize the importance of the counselor's emotional health for effective counseling. A distressed counselor is a dangerous counselor.[43] The American Association of Marriage and Family Therapists (AAMFT) has addressed personal distress in its ethics code: "Marriage and family therapists seek appropriate professional assistance for their personal problems or conflicts that may impair work performance or clinical judgment."[44]

The National Association of Social Workers has a similar statement in its ethics code: "The social worker should not allow his or her own personal problems, psychosocial distress, substance abuse, or mental health difficulties to interfere with professional judgment and performance or jeopardize the best interests of those for whom the social worker has a professional responsibility."[45]

The American Psychological Association's (APA's) code of ethics requires that "psychologists recognize that their personal problems and conflicts may interfere with their effectiveness."[46] The American Counseling Association states that "the member avoids bringing personal issues into the counseling relationship, especially if the potential for harm is present."[47]

These guidelines limit the extent to which a counselor's life is personal, especially if personal issues affect professional work. In the same way, the personal prayer life of a Christian counselor—one who deals with the care of souls on a daily basis—is not private because the spiritual life of the counselor spills over into the counselor's understanding of problems, ways of relating, and therapeutic strategies. Though Christian counselors might like to define clear boundaries between personal, spiritual, and professional concerns, no such lines exist.

A Christian counselor's ability to understand the place of prayer in effective therapy is limited by the counselor's personal spiritual disciplines. The first step for counselors who want to increase the use of prayer in their counseling work is to evaluate their personal prayer patterns.

Challenge 3: Expanded Definitions of Training

Because effective prayer in counseling emerges from a counselor's inner life, the counselor's level of spiritual maturity will provide an upper limit for the potential impact of prayer in counseling. Thus, training is intensely personal.

Several excellent books on spiritual formation and spiritual disciplines are available. Richard Foster's books *Celebration of Discipline* and *Prayer* are inviting books with practical suggestions for personal training.[48] Dallas Willard, in *The Spirit of the Disciplines,* argues persuasively for the importance of personal discipline and training in spiritual formation.[49] Don Postema's *Space for God* provides appealing and practical examples for prayer and spiritual development.[50] Ole Hallesby's *Prayer* is a passionately written classic affirming the essential role of prayer for the growing Christian.[51] Reading is an important starting point, but practicing the inner disciplines, including prayer, is an essential part of spiritual formation. Each of these authors, and many others, describe helpful ideas for enriching one's prayer life. These ideas include taking courses in spiritual formation, enlisting the help of a spiritual director, getting away for a time of prolonged solitude and prayer, and participating in weekly prayer groups and special events such as concerts of prayer.

Challenge 4: Confronting Dominant Views of Mental Health

Though we are in the midst of an encouraging trend that leaves room for religious values in counseling, psychology and counseling have generally been overly concerned with self-determination and ego-istic goals.[52] In stark contrast, prayer moves one's eyes away from self and onto God. In this regard, Christianity and popular psychology often point in different directions: psychology toward greater self-determination and Christianity toward greater reliance on God.

Though some psychologists may pity those who deny personal freedom for the sake of religion, Christians believe that those who have journeyed far into self-forgetfulness by immersing themselves in the disciplined life of spiritual formation are not to be pitied. Rather, they are in the center of God's will, where they find peace and comfort and joy to sustain them through life's many challenges. Jesus put it succinctly: "For all who exalt themselves will be humbled, but all who humble themselves will be exalted" (Luke 18:14).

Challenge 5: Establishing a Scientific Base

Although psychologists once thought that religious ideas and prac-tices were inversely related to mental health, there is growing evidence that this is not the case. From a scientific perspective, people with a profound intrinsic commitment to their religious faith are at least as healthy, and probably more healthy, than their nonreligious counterparts.[53]

Despite these encouraging findings, a great deal of scientific work needs to be done. The few studies reviewed by McCullough, described earlier in this chapter, have left unanswered many questions about prayer. And most of the studies that have been reported are only remotely related to using prayer in counseling.

What are the effects of audible in-session prayer on therapeutic alliance, on the depth of disclosure, and on counseling effectiveness? How effective are devotional-meditation assignments in reducing stress when they are used as part of a counseling treatment? Does an active prayer life lower the occurrence or recurrence rates of various psychological disorders? These questions, and many more related to the emotional and spiritual effects of prayer, need to be explored through scientific inquiry in the future.

Challenge 6: Defining Relevant Ethical Standards

Using prayer in therapy raises several ethical problems that must be carefully considered. First, the principle of competence requires that counselors use only those interventions for which they are trained. Those with graduate degrees in counseling, even if from religiously oriented programs, receive little or no training in using prayer as part of counseling.[54]

This does not necessarily mean that we can never use prayer in counseling but that we must take extra precautions to avoid misusing prayer and hurting people as a result. As discussed earlier in the chapter, seemingly innocuous practices such as praying aloud with clients to begin counseling sessions may have a harmful effect on some clients. We must be aware of the potential harm of the techniques used in counseling, especially techniques that are not well established as part of counseling theory and practice. Psychologists, for example, are instructed in their ethics code: "In those emerging areas in which generally recognized standards for preparatory training do not yet exist, psychologists nevertheless take reasonable steps to ensure the competence of their work and to protect patients, clients, students, research participants, and others from harm."[55] For Christian counselors, this might involve meeting with peers for ongoing consultation about the appropriate use of prayer in counseling, obtaining supervision from a more experienced Christian counselor, and diligently working to develop personal patterns of prayer.

A second issue of concern is informed consent. A client who agrees to counseling with the assumption that standard counseling techniques will be used may be surprised and disillusioned when spiritual interventions are used. Spiritual interventions, per se, are not necessarily unethical, but promising one type of treatment and then delivering another is unethical. The best solution to this problem is to describe the nature of counseling in a written informed-consent form that is reviewed and signed by the client before beginning treatment. The consent form will be different for each client and should include a discussion of spiritual interventions that might be used in treatment.

A related problem is whether or not spiritual interventions should be reported to insurance companies who pay for counseling services. Many insurance companies, especially managed-care organizations, require that specific treatment plans be submitted before the counseling is authorized. If a counselor plans to use prayer as part of counseling, should prayer be included on the treatment plan? The answer depends on the type of prayer interventions employed. Counselors who privately pray for their clients while implementing a standard form of treatment (e.g., cognitive therapy for generalized anxiety, systematic desensitization for simple phobia, interpersonal therapy for depression) should feel no need to report prayer as part of their treatment. If, however, a counselor is using devotional meditation or another form of prayer as a central treatment technique, then it should be reported in the treatment plan along with a rationale for its use. Some forms of counseling that are based exclusively on spiritual interventions may not be recognized as legitimate counseling strategies by insurance companies, and counselors will need to reconsider their counseling strategies or their desire for insurance reimbursement.

Finally, charging fees for spiritually based counseling presents a quandary for many Christian counselors. Spiritual directors and pastors have generally not charged for spiritual guidance. If counselors use spiritual-guidance techniques as part of their counseling, should they continue to charge for their work? Some Christian counselors are pastors and lay counselors who do not personally confront this question. For the remainder of Christian counselors, whose livelihood often depends on generating fees, this is a relevant and difficult question. Although there may be many responsible ways to address this fee quandary, the easiest resolution to the problem is to inform clients of similar alternative services available. If a fee-for-service counselor is using spiritual interventions exclusively and if those same interventions are available elsewhere at little or no cost, the counselor should inform potential clients of the other options before beginning counseling. If a counselor uses prayer as an adjunct to a counseling approach that requires advanced training, such as time-limited psychodynamic therapy, then the counselor ought to inform clients of other possible professional counseling approaches (e.g., cognitive therapy) but can limit the discussion to the counseling approaches used by other professional counselors.

SUMMARY

Prayer is more than a counseling technique. It is the primary vehicle of growth in the spiritual life. Christian counselors who desire to use prayer as a vital part of their work must be committed to the spiritual disciplines of the inner life, including prayer, solitude, and fasting.

Despite the power and importance of prayer, bringing it into the counseling office is not a simple task. Counselors should carefully consider the potential effects of various forms of prayer before using them in counseling. Some forms of prayer, such as counselors privately praying for clients, are always useful; whereas other forms of prayer, such as routinely praying aloud in counseling sessions, introduce both potential benefits and risks to clients.

Initial studies of devotional meditation and religious imagery indicate that these forms of prayer can be useful in counseling, but most types of prayer have not yet been researched. In addition to the research task, Christian counselors need to define clear ethical guidelines for the use of prayer in counseling.

4/ SCRIPTURE

Karl returns home from his first counseling appointment, opens his Bible to Psalm 1, and begins reading. "Happy are those who do not follow the advice of the wicked, or take the path that sinners tread, or sit in the seat of scoffers."

Karl sets the Bible on his lap and reflects on the past ninety minutes. He thinks about the relief he felt telling Dr. Listner things he had never disclosed to anyone before. He thinks of her comforting smile and how genuinely concerned she seemed to be. But Karl also has nagging doubts. If Dr. Listner is really a Christian counselor as she claims, why didn't she mention God? Why didn't she have a Bible on her desk or in a visible spot on her bookshelf? Maybe the Christian antipsychology books Karl has read are correct; maybe Dr. Listner is a priest of a rival religion. Maybe he is following the "advice of the wicked" by going to a Christian counselor. Maybe he was sitting "in the seat of scoffers" while swaying in the swivel rocker in Dr. Listner's office.

Karl keeps reading: "But their delight is in the law of the Lord, and on his law they meditate day and night. They are like trees planted by streams of water, which yield their fruit in its season, and their leaves do not wither. In all that they do, they prosper."

Karl sets the Bible down again and reflects on a new set of questions. Does this mean that my depression will go away if I reflect more on the promises of Scripture? Am I looking for help in the wrong place? How can I learn to delight more in God's Word? Should I cancel next week's appointment with Dr. Listner? Karl's reflections on his first counseling appointment illustrate some questions Christian clients face when seeking help for their problems.

Dr. Listner has her own set of questions. In her personal times of studying and contemplating Scripture, she draws close to God and experiences a sense of comfort and purpose. She often memorizes Bible passages and recalls them in times of unusual stress. Why, she wonders, doesn't she use Scripture more in her counseling work? Then she remembers.

There are several reasons Dr. Listner does not use Scripture more actively in her work with clients like Karl. First, like most Christian psychologists, Dr. Listner was not trained to use Scripture in counseling. She hesitates to use the Bible with Christian clients because she might be taking a verse out of context or misapplying a fundamental theological concept. Second, Dr. Listner has seen many clients, like Karl, who are depressed about being depressed. Several people in Karl's church have told him that he would not be depressed if he took his spiritual life more seriously. Dr. Listner does not agree. She sees depression as resulting from a complex blend of interpersonal, biochemical, psychological, spiritual, and environmental factors. If she overuses Scripture with clients like Karl, she might communicate a simplistic view of depression that only makes her clients more depressed. Third, her theoretical orientation places her in the role of being a transitional object for Karl. If she introduces her own agenda by quoting or using Scripture, it might interfere with Karl's ability to project past emotional conflicts onto his new therapist. Fourth, when Dr. Listner has tried using Scripture in past counseling, it sometimes has evoked rigid defenses in her clients, as if the Bible gives an excuse not to look at feelings and inner experiences. Fifth, some people have used the Bible for selfish purposes. Dr. Listner recalls the time when a man used 1 Corinthians 7 to insist that his wife should have sex with him whenever he wanted, regardless of the fact that his wife had recently been raped by a stranger.

Many of Karl's questions about the absence of Scripture in his first Christian counseling experience seem valid. So do many of Dr. Listner's concerns about using Scripture in counseling. So what is the right answer? Should Christians use Scripture in counseling or not? This question, like the similar question about prayer posed at the beginning of chapter 3, is too general to be meaningful. A better question is, "In *what ways* should Scripture be used in counseling *which* clients and under *which* circumstances?" Though Christian counselors answer this question differently depending on professional, religious, and ideological assumptions, various methods of using Scripture in counseling deserve careful consideration and critical evaluation.

FOUNDATIONS

Psychology

Psychological journals and books include numerous references to Christian Scriptures, but few have direct relevance to Christian counseling, and even fewer are directly related to using the Bible in counseling. As with the previous chapter, my goal is not to provide a comprehensive literature review but rather a sampling of the types of articles and books that have implications for Christian counselors.

PSYCHOLOGICAL PERSPECTIVES ON SCRIPTURE

Many psychological critiques and evaluations of scriptural principles and characters are available. Between January 1990 and May 1995, the word *Bible* was included in 105 articles referenced in PsychLit, an electronic index of psychology journals. The majority of these articles pertain to a psychological evaluation of a biblical concept or person. This is not surprising. As interest in narrative psychology increases, the tools of literary criticism are more widely used in psychology journals. For example, a number of authors have produced psychoanalytic critiques of biblical characters in recent years.

Applying psychology's methods to understanding the Bible appears to be relatively rare among explicitly Christian authors, perhaps because we fear the diluting of scriptural truth with contemporary literary or social-scientific theories. However, some Christian authors cautiously advocate using psychology and careful biblical scholarship to understand the characters and stories of the Bible.[1]

SCRIPTURAL SUPPORT OF COUNSELING MODELS

Some authors have used Scripture as a foundation for developing responsible counseling strategies and techniques that share common features with traditional models of psychotherapy. For example, a number of authors have advocated models of Christian counseling that demonstrate a commitment to Scripture as well as psychological theory.[2]

Others have used Scripture to support existing counseling methods or models. For example, Daniel Sweeney and Garry Landreth describe scriptural support for using play therapy in treating children.[3] A number of authors use Scripture to support various forms of cognitive therapy, especially rational-emotive therapy.[4] One author concludes that "RET is based on a thoroughly biblical principle, the importance of what one thinks."[5] Using Scripture to support existing models of psychotherapy has generated some conflict and concern among many Christians. Some Christian antipsychologists see psychology as a competing faith, arguing that it is completely incompatible with Scripture.[6] Others have offered more measured criticism, suggesting that we must carefully evaluate worldview assumptions before importing and modifying a psychotherapy technique and calling it Christian counseling.[7]

USING SCRIPTURE IN COUNSELING

Some counselors advocate using Scripture as a therapeutic intervention. For example, various authors have suggested using Bible passages in church-based recovery groups to help confront themes of codependency, using Scripture in marital counseling to help couples recover from sexual affairs, using Bible stories in individual child therapy, using the Bible to confront irrational beliefs in RET, and using Scripture memory and meditation as homework in cognitive therapy.[8]

In one survey, almost half (43 percent) of the members of the Christian Association for Psychological Studies (CAPS) reported explicitly teaching biblical concepts to clients. Over two-thirds (71 percent) implicitly used biblical concepts in their counseling work.[9] While these survey results suggest a relatively frequent use of biblical concepts in counseling, they do not address the actual direct use of Scripture in counseling. In another survey of CAPS members, respondents were asked to describe Christian interventions they used in counseling.[10] Of the interventions reported, 13 percent involved the direct use of Scripture in counseling. When some of the same respondents were interviewed and asked to describe critical incidents they had faced in counseling and the interventions they used in response, only 3 percent of the interventions described involved the direct use of Scripture. Thus, it appears that directly using Scripture as part of counseling is relatively rare, even among Christian counselors.

THE BIBLE AS A SELF-HELP BOOK

Another use of Scripture in psychology is not limited to Christian counselors. Some have suggested using the Bible as a self-help book with religious clients. Even Albert Ellis, a self-proclaimed atheist and outspoken opponent of devout religious faith, had this to say about the Bible in a recent article: "I think that I can safely say that the Judeo-Christian Bible is a self-help book that has probably enabled more people to make more extensive and intensive personality and behavioral changes than all professional therapists combined."[11]

Although Christians may dislike the idea of reducing the Bible to a self-help book, it is heartening that some non-Christian therapists perceive an increasing need to work within the value systems of Christian clients.

Though the Bible offers much more than self-help, there are times when clients are searching for answers that can be readily found in Scripture. For example, counselors who use cognitive therapy often work with clients to modify faulty core beliefs that have contributed to poor self-awareness and unnecessarily painful emotional experiences. Meditating on Scripture can help Christian clients change these beliefs. Those who believe they are completely unloved and destined for rejection can meditate on Paul's words to Roman Christians: "But God proves his love for us in that while we still were sinners Christ died for us" (Rom. 5:8). Those who believe they are all alone, isolated and abandoned, can remember the psalmist's proclamation: "God is our refuge and strength, a very present help in trouble" (Ps. 46:1). Those who feel overwhelmed with life's burdens and God's apparent distance can recall the words of James: "Indeed we call blessed those who showed endurance. You have heard of the endurance of Job, and you have seen the purpose of the Lord, how the Lord is compassionate and merciful" (James 5:11).

UNTAPPED POTENTIAL?

The perspectives and studies reported here reflect the ways various authors have used Scripture in counseling. However, there may be many additional possibilities that have not yet been explored. Dr. Eric Johnson argues that the Bible belongs in psychological science and suggests eight ways Scripture can influence Christian counselors and psychologists.[12] First, the Bible plays an *experiential* role in our lives, providing a rich resource for wisdom and personal maturity. Second, Scripture plays a *foundational* role, providing a common starting point for understanding our basic assumptions and beliefs. Third, it plays a *contextual* role that allows us to understand human nature, meaning, and purpose in life. Fourth, Scripture plays an *axiological* role, giving us standards for what should be. Fifth, the Bible plays an *anthropological* role, providing us an awareness of the historical narrative of human sin and divine redemption. Sixth, it plays a *canonical* role, providing an unchanging standard of truth. Seventh, Scripture plays a *dialogical* role, providing rich resources for discussion and comparison between psychological knowledge and special revelation. Eighth, the Bible plays a *creative* role, allowing us to consider and explore concepts and ideas that might not be considered from a purely psychological worldview. These eight roles that Johnson outlines suggest that Christian counselors have only begun to explore the potential of integrating the Bible and psychology.

Christian Theology

Even if theologians agreed on the role of Scripture in theology, it would be impossible to summarize in a few pages. To complicate the task further, theologians do not agree. Traditionally, Scripture has been seen as the essential foundation for Christian theology. David Kelsey suggests that "virtually every contemporary Protestant theologian along the entire spectrum of opinion from the 'neo-evangelicals' through Karl Barth, Emil Brunner, to Anders Nygren, Rudolf Bultmann, Paul Tillich and even Fritz Buri, has acknowledged that any Christian theology worthy of the name 'Christian' must, in some sense of the phrase, be done 'in accord with Scripture.'"[13] But Kelsey goes on to point out that theology has changed in the past fifty years, and now a number of theologians argue that "Scripture does not, and indeed, some add, cannot serve as authority for theology."[14] Revisionist theology has risen to prominence with postmodernism, and Scripture is sometimes reduced to a literary construction of human attempts to understand God.

The few comments I make here are limited by my assumption that newer theology is not necessarily better theology; I begin with the belief, shared by Protestant theologians through the centuries, that Scripture is an essential tool for knowing God. Even with this assumption, there is considerable debate about the role of human reason in approaching Scripture. Because of the vastness of the topic, the lack of agreement among theologians, and my limited theological training, I make no attempt to survey the role of Scripture in Christian theology here. Rather, I will focus on one specific problem regarding Scripture and theology and discuss two implications for how Christian counselors understand Scripture.

THE PROBLEM: THE CHICKEN OR THE EGG?

Theological views of Scripture are plagued by the chicken-or-the-egg problem. Do we first know God through reason, as Thomas Aquinas believed, and then understand Scripture because we understand God? Or do we first know Scripture, which allows us to know God? In other words, is our knowledge of Scripture shaped by our prior knowledge of God, or does it work the other way around? Each view has been supported by reputable scholars. Theologian Millard Erickson proposes that this debate is unnecessary, that we can presuppose both a knowledge of God and a knowledge of Scripture as simultaneous and inseparable.[15] God cannot be known apart from Scripture, and Scripture cannot be properly understood without knowing God. Just as Scripture helps us know God, God helps us understand Scripture. Until we know God, our views and understanding of Scripture are clouded by our disbelief. But with salvation comes a cleaning of the lenses—a capacity to understand God's Word more clearly, though not perfectly.[16]

In the same way, we must know something about ourselves in order to know God. In the first of his *Institutes,* John Calvin argued that knowledge of self and knowledge of God are inseparable.[17] We cannot fully know ourselves without understanding God's character, righteousness, and love, and we cannot fully know God without understanding ourselves, including our capacity for sin, our human frailty, and our deep longing for someone transcendent.

Knowledge of self, God, and Scripture are intertwined. This is what scholars call the *hermeneutic circle*—the text cannot be separated from the perspectives of the reader, and the reader's perspectives are influenced by the text. The text affects our views of God and self: we see our need for God by understanding ourselves as revealed in

Scripture. God affects our capacity to understand the text, and so does our humanness: we understand Scripture because God has graciously granted us eyes to see, but even those eyes are affected by our fallen human nature.

These interconnections of human nature, God's character, and Scripture have at least two important implications for Christian counselors interested in using Scripture in counseling.

IMPLICATION 1: RESPECT

First, we must cultivate and maintain respect for the Bible. Scripture is our primary way of knowing God. It is God's authoritative revelation to humankind. We call it *special revelation.* Yes, we see God in nature, but nature worship without special revelation leads to animism and other heresies. Yes, we know God through prayer and meditation, but the New Age movement demonstrates the directionless confusion of spirituality unbounded by Scripture. We need Scripture to understand God. John Calvin writes that "Scripture, collecting in our minds the otherwise confused notions of deity, dispels the darkness and gives us a clear view of the true God."[18]

When we claim "all truth is God's truth," we are both correct and incorrect. All that is true, whether discovered through science, literature, philosophy, theology, counseling, or Scripture, comes from God. However, science, literature, philosophy, theology, counseling, and Scripture are not equally direct ways of knowing God, and every way of knowing God is limited by our hermeneutic methods for understanding truth. Scripture is the most direct way of knowing God; therefore it deserves our respect.

What does this mean for the Christian counselor? We must not hesitate to revere the God revealed in Scripture as the ultimate standard of truth. Postmodernism has pushed mental health disciplines toward accepting personal "truth" as equally valid to God's transcendent truth. Christian counselors should resist the trend. When we look for truth, we don't first look inside ourselves or inside our clients; we look to God. However, communicating our respect for Scripture without inducing shame or excessive submission in our clients can be challenging.

WHAT IF THIS HAPPENED?

Your client, Frank, has been reading books on relaxation and meditation techniques. The books were assigned by a previous counselor, and they seem to be helping him cope with his anxiety problems. In the middle of today's session, you are discussing the loneliness Frank felt as an only child raised by two busy professional people. He becomes tearful, puts his head between his hands, and sits silently for several minutes. Eventually he lifts his head, looks you in the eye, and says, "I've been thinking about this, about how lonely I feel. Sometimes I just feel stuck, as if there is nothing I can ever do to feel any better. But I know that's not true. There is a way out of this. I just need to keep looking inside myself. I'm learning a lot in these meditation exercises. If I keep looking inside myself, I know I will eventually find the truth."

How do you respond? Here are three possibilities:

Option 1: "Yes, it is important to keep searching inside yourself for your values and your ideas of what to do next. But I'm wondering why it is so important to find the answers inside yourself."

Option 2: "Good idea. It is really very important to keep searching for truth."

Option 3: "I don't think you'll have much luck looking inside yourself for truth. The Bible teaches we find truth through Jesus. Jesus said, 'I am the way, and the truth, and the life.'"

Though a good case might be made for any of these responses in some counseling situations, I prefer option 1. It gently challenges Frank's assumption that he will find truth inside himself without introducing harshness into the conversation. Option 1 is likely to lead into a meaningful discussion of the place and authority of

Scripture in Frank's life. Option 2 unintentionally reinforces Frank's idea that he will find truth inside himself. Option 3 may be so abrupt that it will stop Frank from exploring further. He might agree with the counselor only to avoid disapproval.

IMPLICATION 2: HUMILITY

Second, while we must respect the authority of Scripture, we should also assume an attitude of *humility* regarding our interpretations of Scripture. Although Scripture is special revelation, inspired by God, it is always interpreted by fallible humans (2 Tim. 3:16). Yes, knowing God helps us understand Scripture more clearly than before, but we still bump against the limits of humanity. Thus, our humanness and the hermeneutic strategies we use in interpreting Scripture limit our capacity to understand truth.[19]

WHAT IF THIS HAPPENED?

Nancy and Thom Baker come to see Roberta, a lay counselor, for marital help. One of the difficulties the Bakers face is conflict over their domestic roles. Nancy wants an egalitarian marriage, but Thom wants a more traditional, male-headship marriage. Roberta listens carefully to both Nancy and Thom, encourages them to express their desires and opinions to one another, and helps them look at the deeper psychological beliefs that are operating beneath the surface of awareness. Thom is operating from the assumption that only the strong survive and one has to be tough in this world to succeed. He tries to run his family the same way. Nancy is operating from the assumption that her worth depends on the approval she elicits from others. Most of her friends and extended family are in egalitarian marriages, and they frequently question and criticize her about her more traditional marital role. She wants to change her marriage to gain social approval from those she cares about.

Roberta considers her two possible responses. One option is to use Scripture to teach the "right way" to structure a marriage.

Roberta is committed to an egalitarian marriage and has been
persuaded by several recent books that her views are supported
in Scripture. She could try to persuade Thom. A second option is
to coach Thom and Nancy as they work to understand each
other better and to search Scripture themselves for the best way
to structure their marriage. Which option should Roberta
choose?

A hermeneutic of humility moves Roberta to select the second
option. Though she is convinced that Scripture teaches a certain
way to structure marriage, she also recognizes that others interpret
Scripture differently from the way she does and that her job as a
counselor is not to indoctrinate clients to her way of thinking.

I am not suggesting that Christian counselors should avoid taking
firm doctrinal positions on scriptural teaching. With careful hermeneutic strategies, we can minimize the intrusions of our faulty
human reasoning and boldly advocate scriptural truth in a
postmodern society that often overlooks transcendent truth. However, when we interpret controversial passages, we are wise to
remember the hermeneutic circle and humbly recognize that our
human biases and sin will influence and limit our understanding of
God and the Bible.

Spirituality

Two people see an apple. One responds analytically, investigates the
apple, and says, "This is red on the outside, crisp on the inside, and
tastes sweet and pleasant." The other reflects on past memories and
says, "My grandmother used to make the most delicious apple pie!
She sprinkled cinnamon sugar on the crust, baked it just right, and
served it piping hot." Both are responding to the apple; both are
correct; but they emphasize different aspects of reality.

So it is with Scripture. One person, a theologian, approaches
Scripture analytically, trying to understand how special revelation
can be accurately interpreted in order to understand God better.

Another person, or perhaps the same person at another time, approaches Scripture reflectively and experientially, contemplating God by meditating on Scripture. Though both approaches are important in both theology and Christian spirituality, the contemplative approach to Scripture is of central importance in spiritual formation. Richard Foster puts it well: "Whereas the study of Scripture centers on exegesis, the meditation of Scripture centers on internalizing and personalizing the passage. The written Word becomes a living word addressed to you."[20]

Dr. Jim Wilhoit, who teaches courses in spirituality at Wheaton College, loves to tell of the time when he and Carol brought their slightly jaundiced newborn daughter home from the hospital. They secured her in an infant seat and placed the seat next to a window so the natural light of the sun could heal her jaundiced body. What a beautiful picture of God's healing presence in our lives. But we have to place ourselves in the way of God's light. Meditating on Scripture is a way to place our frail, ailing selves in the presence of God's healing warmth. This is not an exercise in theology. In fact, Foster warns that meditating on Scripture is "not a time for technical studies, or analysis, or even the gathering of material to share with others."[21] Scripture meditation is deeply personal, providing healing light and spiritual sustenance for all who long for intimacy with God and who dare to admit their neediness.

There are at least two purposes for using Scripture during times of meditation. First, it provides substance for contemplation.[22] The psalmist writes of the godly, whose "delight is in the law of the Lord, and on his law they meditate day and night" (Ps. 1:2). Elsewhere in the Psalms we read, "Oh, how I love your law! It is my meditation all day long. Your commandment makes me wiser than my enemies, for it is always with me. I have more understanding than all my teachers, for your decrees are my meditation" (Ps. 119:97-99). Unlike meditation in Eastern religions, where the goal is to empty one's mind, the goal of Christian meditation is to fill one's mind with an awareness of God's presence. Scripture provides rich material to fill our thoughts and direct our paths.

WHAT IF THIS HAPPENED?

Pastor Neal is tired. He counsels fifteen people each week, prepares sermons, visits parishioners, and spends as much time as possible with his family. Lately, he has been feeling discouraged about the slow changes he sees in his counseling clients. Sometimes he feels angry that people resist change. Other times he feels bored and drowsy during counseling sessions.

Pastor Neal recognizes the signs of excessive stress and decides he needs a change. He blocks off a day on his calendar and arranges to go to a nearby retreat center for a day of solitude, prayer, and meditation. Pastor Neal takes only himself and a copy of the Bible. Scripture will be his food, his recreation, and his business for the day. Throughout the day he strolls the grounds, reads the Bible, naps, prays, meditates, and returns with renewed energy and a clearer image of God's nature.

Second, Scripture provides important theological boundaries for spiritual meditation. Richard Foster writes, "For all the devotional masters the *meditatio Scripturarum,* the meditation upon Scripture, is the central reference point by which all other forms of meditation are kept in proper perspective."[23] Without scriptural boundaries, the practice of spirituality slips into heresy and self-worship, as we see all around us in contemporary culture.[24] For example, one medical doctor, who describes herself as a practitioner of "soul work," reports that the "overriding bible" of her work is that "you attract what you dwell upon. You attract what your own vibratory rate is." She goes on to describe her interest in shamanic soul-retrieval work and past life therapy.[25] Although our imagination is a gift from God, we need Scripture to provide a theological and historical anchor for it. Otherwise, our imagination is guided by passing fads and self-interest disguised in various forms.

Scripture is an essential tool for spiritual formation. It provides both resources for spiritual contemplation and boundaries to keep us from slipping away from truth.

PSYCHOLOGICAL AND SPIRITUAL HEALTH

How and when should counselors use Scripture to move clients toward greater psychological and spiritual health? Let's look at this question in two important ways: one general and one more specific.

Generally, we are concerned about Scripture in choosing our counseling strategies and theories, even those that do not specifically involve using the Bible in counseling sessions. Dr. Stanton Jones, chairperson of the Wheaton College Psychology Department, has developed a useful system for considering how we might conceptualize Scripture in counseling, based on four types of counseling strategies.[26] First, some counseling strategies are directly derived from Scripture. For example, some cognitive therapists teach clients to use Scripture references to counter faulty dysfunctional thoughts, just as Paul taught Christians in Philippi to think about things that are honorable, pure, pleasing, and commendable.[27] Second, some counseling strategies are generally supported by implication in Scripture. For example, using religious imagery as a technique for depressed clients is consistent with Scripture, though not specifically taught or commanded in Scripture. Third, some counseling strategies are not discussed or implied in the Bible but are not inconsistent with Scripture. For example, using progressive muscle relaxation to control anxiety symptoms is neither advocated nor prohibited in Scripture. Fourth, some counseling techniques are inconsistent with Scripture. For example, the counselor who advocates adultery as a treatment for midlife depression is contradicting a principle of Scripture.

We can see several benefits to this classification system. First, it reminds us that using Scripture in counseling is not just a matter of quoting or memorizing Bible verses. Our views of Scripture can be considered in selecting every technique, even those that have no overt religious connections. Clearly, Christian counselors need to avoid interventions that fall into the fourth category—those that are incompatible with Scripture. Second, this classification allows us to recognize and confidently use counseling techniques that are compatible with Scripture, even if those techniques were developed by non-Christians. During some sessions, Christian counseling may be almost indistinguishable from other forms of counseling yet still be effective. Third, it reminds us to scrutinize our counseling strategies and perspectives carefully. In evaluating the messages of prophets, Paul instructed the believers at Thessalonica to "test everything; hold fast to what is good; abstain from every form of evil" (1 Thess. 5:21-22). We have a similar obligation as counselors. As we test new theories and techniques with Scripture, we can abstain from certain counseling strategies that contradict Scripture and hold fast to those that are compatible with Scripture.

In addition to making a general evaluation of scriptural support for counseling methods, it is also important to consider the specific effects of directly applying Scripture in counseling. When is it wise to quote Scripture to a client? Is Scripture memory appropriate in counseling? Is Bible meditation an appropriate homework assignment? To address these complex questions, it is helpful to consider the three questions derived from the model presented in chapter 2 as applied to two counseling scenarios.

WHAT IF THIS HAPPENED?

You arrive at the office, sit at your desk, sip on a cup of bitter coffee, and check the day's schedule. At 2:00 you are seeing Pete and Kate Balistic, and at 3:30 you are seeing Richard Yavis. Each session will pose different challenges. You start planning.

The Balistics have been coming to see you for two months, sometimes for individual sessions and sometimes for joint sessions. They started seeing you at Pete's insistence when he found out about Kate's affair. She dutifully stopped the affair, agreed to counseling, and has been working to move forward with her life. She is disappointed with her marriage and cannot yet promise Pete that she wants to stay married. Pete is trying to help you counsel Kate. He comes each week with a typewritten list of evidence that Kate has not truly repented and that she is refusing to submit to her marriage vows. Pete loves Scripture, and at the top of his list each week are one or two Bible verses that he uses to support his allegations that Kate is a vile sinner and an unworthy spouse. Interestingly, Kate never fights back. She recognizes that she is a vile sinner, expresses regret for her affair, but does not feel ready to commit to the marriage. From 2:00 to 3:30 ought to be interesting today.

At 3:30 Richard Yavis will be flipping through a *Sports Illustrated* in the waiting room. As you usher him into the office, he will make some comment about the NBA play-offs, but as soon as he sits down, he will be working. Insightful, motivated, articulate, Richard is the ideal counseling client. For the past three months he has been seeing you for help with depression and has been feeling much better recently. For the last several weeks, you and Richard have been exploring the profound sense of loneliness he experienced as a child and how he tries to be perfect in order to win approval and cope with his loneliness. Like Pete, Richard loves Scripture.

Will This Help Establish a Healthy Sense of Self?

Three people are involved in these two counseling sessions, and the proper use of Scripture in counseling may be different for each of the three. Pete does not have an accurate view of himself. Rather than acknowledge his anger and sadness about Kate's affair, he has shielded himself by using logic and by hurling accusations in Kate's direction. He has cloaked himself with self-sufficiency, not because of narcissism, but because it hurts too much to face his feelings of loss. How could Scripture be used to give Pete a healthier and more accurate awareness of himself?

Should a counselor use Scripture to confront Pete with his self-deception, perhaps reminding Pete of his obligation to love Kate as Christ loves the church or his obligation to forgive Kate as Christ has forgiven him? Probably not. Pete is already using Scripture to protect himself and remain self-sufficient. He can move forward and admit his need for comfort only by getting past his logical defense system.

With Pete, it makes more sense to focus on the therapeutic relationship, perhaps by meeting with him individually for several sessions and encouraging honest disclosure of his feelings of fear, sadness, and anger. Scripture might be used as a contemplative tool, either inside or outside of the counseling sessions. For example, Pete's counselor might teach him to contemplate passages from the book of Hosea or the passage in Matthew 11:28-30, paying close attention to his own emotional response to Kate's unfaithfulness. Once he acknowledges and begins to deal with his brokenness and pain, he will have less need to criticize and humiliate Kate.

Kate also has an inaccurate view of herself, but her self-sufficiency is rooted in a deep sense of inferiority. From as early as Kate can remember, she has considered herself worthwhile only if she has the approval of everyone around her. When she met Pete, she loved his rugged, decisive style. They married, and at first she loved to submit to his leadership. He appreciated her, and she was happy. But with time, the demands kept coming; he stopped showing as much appreciation; and Kate's happiness began slipping through her fingers. When another man showed her attention and appreciation, she was drawn off into another romance. Now she has no one's attention, no one's appreciation. She is sad, lonely, and confused, and she protects herself from further criticism by remaining aloof from Pete.

Should the counselor side with Pete and use Scripture to demonstrate Kate's apostasy? Probably not. Kate will see herself honestly only in the context of a nurturing counseling relationship. If the counselor takes Pete's side, it will make such a relationship impossible. Ultimately Kate needs to admit her sin, but she will not be able to if she is constantly feeling the need to defend herself. Once she feels safe with her counselor, she will begin exploring her sin. Scripture might be used effectively with Kate, but not in a harsh, confrontive way. Kate might find tremendous comfort in Scripture if it were not used to control her, as Pete has done for years. In the process, Kate might learn to view herself more accurately as a child of a loving Creator who provides us with moral boundaries that help us establish an abundant life that brings honor to God.

Richard's sense of self is changing. He has identified his self-sufficient efforts to earn approval through perfectionism and is learning about relationships based on love, respect, and honest expression of need. Explicitly using Scripture in counseling might be very helpful for Richard. For example, he might memorize Titus 3:4-7: "But when the goodness and loving kindness of God our Savior appeared, he saved us, not because of any works of righteousness that we had done, but according to his mercy, through the water of rebirth and renewal by the Holy Spirit. This Spirit he poured out on us richly through Jesus Christ our Savior, so that, having been justified by his grace, we might become heirs according to the hope of eternal life." Scripture might help Richard get his eyes off himself by experiencing God more richly, entering further into an awareness of God's gracious presence in his life.

Will This Help Establish a Healthy Sense of Need?

Pete has a clear sense of Kate's need, but he does not acknowledge his own brokenness. Thus, if Scripture is used in working with Pete, it should be related to his need and not Kate's. It is important to recognize that Pete already feels broken, but he has hidden his inner feelings beneath a facade of self-righteousness. His counselor will probably not need to confront Pete; just providing a safe relationship will be enough for Pete to begin exploring his feelings. Even if confronting Pete is necessary, it should be done only after a safe counseling relationship has been established.

Though Kate has not expressed much remorse about her affair, she is inwardly overwhelmed with brokenness and need. It is unnecessary, and probably damaging, to use Scripture to confront Kate with her sin. It is wise to follow the pattern Jesus used when confronted with a woman caught in adultery. First he said, "Neither do I condemn you" (John 8:11); then he said, "Go your way, and from now on do not sin again." Counseling with Kate should follow the same pattern, with a counselor first accepting and understanding her, then working with her to strengthen her commitment to marriage.

Richard has been insightful enough not only to recognize his unrealistic goals of earning approval through perfection but also to explore his long-standing feelings of loneliness. Although Scripture may be useful in other ways, it is probably not necessary to use Scripture to establish Richard's sense of need for God and others.

Will This Help Establish a Healing Relationship?

Pete, Kate, and Richard are different people, and each will have a distinctive response to the use of Scripture in counseling. Sometimes using Scripture in counseling helps establish a close working alliance, and at other times it distracts from a healthy therapeutic relationship. For example, Kate might have a negative response if her counselor uses Scripture and might become more resistant and cautious in exploring her thoughts and feelings. Even with good intentions, counselors can sometimes introduce relational problems by explicitly using Scripture in counseling.[28]

Problem 1: I thought you were a counselor. People often choose Christian counselors because their usual religious experiences have not helped them resolve their problems. They are looking for something different from what they find in church on Sunday morning. If counselors use Scripture unwisely, they may violate clients' expectations about counseling and slow down the rapport-building process.

Problem 2: May I say something? If counselors become too strident in providing Scripture for clients, they may end up talking when they should be listening. Many forms of counseling include didactic components, but when the sessions start feeling like lectures or lessons, clients will often distance themselves from the counseling process.

Problem 3: The safe zone. Some counselors may use Scripture in order to keep counseling sessions at an intellectual, logical level of communication. This may reflect the counselors' own sense of insecurity and desire to avoid emotions as much as an ideological commitment to using Scripture. Effective counseling usually reaches deep into a person's emotional state and requires more than an intellectual look at life. Of course, Scripture can be used in emotionally sensitive counseling as well, so this criticism does not apply to all uses of Scripture in counseling.

Problem 4: Overconfidence phenomenon. Many social-psychology studies demonstrate that humans are consistently more confident than they are correct. Even incorrect opinions are cherished and believed tenaciously. When we approach Scripture, we are vulnerable to the same phenomenon, so we may not readily recognize the limits to our hermeneutic strategies. Thus, counselors who use Scripture explicitly are vulnerable to appearing and being arrogant in the biblical interpretations. Arrogance hurts rapport!

Problem 5: Overreliance phenomenon. Finally, we may rely excessively on Scripture when we could be using other counseling strategies. Cognitive-therapy strategies can be quickly and effectively applied to treat panic disorders. Behavioral strategies reduce phobic reactions. If we rely too heavily on Scripture, we may miss other valid treatment options. Because the therapeutic relationship is built on the assumption that the counselor knows how best to treat the client's problem, overreliance on a less direct technique can hurt the therapy relationship.

One approach to this list of problems is to say, "I don't care. Scripture is truth, and I will continue to use it in counseling. I refuse to sugarcoat truth!" For those inclined to respond this way, it is important to remember that truth is almost always communicated in embodied form. Most of what we know about grace and salvation is accessible to us because Jesus was incarnated and demonstrated a living theology. To some extent, our understanding of God is affected by the ways our parents treated us. We remember movies and stories more than essays because we are quicker to observe and understand truth that is embodied. In the same way, truth is communicated more by who the counselor is than by what the counselor says. The vitality of Scripture in counseling is limited by the quality of the counseling relationship.

Though less important than a client's relationship with God, the counseling relationship is often the mechanism by which God's grace is introduced to a hurting person. By fostering a healthy Christian-counseling relationship, with or without the explicit use of Scripture, we provide clients with a glimpse of God's grace.

FACING THE CHALLENGES

Challenge 1: Moving from Two Areas of Competence to Three

Psychological competence in counseling is important. The best counselors use Scripture only after carefully considering the psychological implications and the effect on the therapeutic relationship. Unfortunately, as with other religious interventions, the use of Scripture is rarely discussed in graduate training programs, even programs with a religious orientation.[29] Not surprisingly, explicitly using Scripture in counseling is relatively rare for Christian counselors.[30] In reporting this, I am not suggesting a dismal state of affairs: it seems caution is appropriate in using Scripture in counseling. However, competence brings increased freedom, and Christian counselors who have carefully considered the implications of various religious interventions are better prepared to use Scripture confidently and appropriately in their clinical work.

Basic theological competence is also important. Counselors who understand the authority and position of Scripture in Christian living are better prepared to deal with the complex issues they uncover in the counseling office. Counselors without minimal theological competence are at risk of creating a theology based on the human problems seen in the counseling office, and they may distort Scripture to fit preconceived theological notions.

Understanding the role of Scripture in spiritual formation is also important for Christian counselors. We need to be concerned not only about theologically proper and correct use of Scripture but also about the power of Scripture. Scripture was given to help transform our lives. It is powerful, active, and useful for training ourselves to be righteous (Heb. 4:12; 2 Tim. 3:16). Competent Christian counseling calls us to know the power of God in transforming lives and the vital role Scripture plays in the transforming process. This type of training can rarely be accomplished in the classroom. But it calls us to lives of spiritual discipline and a personal love for Scripture.

Challenge 2: Blurred Personal-Professional Distinctions

In one sense, using Scripture in Christian counseling can be limited to a professional discussion. For example, certain Scripture passages can be used to dispute various forms of unhealthy self-talk.[31] These verses might be equally effective as counseling tools regardless of the counselor's personal religious values. In the same way, a counselor might learn to use facial expressions to communicate interest and active listening, and those expressions might be helpful even if the counselor is not actually listening.

But in another sense, the use of Scripture, like the use of active listening skills, is a reflection of the counselor's inner life. Appearing to listen is no substitute for listening. Appearing to love Scripture is no substitute for loving Scripture. Our inner life, shaped by God's transformation of our character through Scripture and other means, is our greatest resource in helping hurting people. A Christian psychiatrist writes, "The healer who would be spiritual, who would practice healing in a Christian context, must be constantly vigilant for the falsely spiritual in his/her practice. Genuine spirituality will be evidenced by the appearance of fruit of the Spirit (love, joy, peace, patience, etc.) *in the practitioner.*"[32]

When Scripture is used creatively, spontaneously, and confidently in counseling, it is only because the counselor is so close to God's Word that the ideas and principles in Scripture have become contagious. For counselors with this type of love for Scripture, the goal is not to carefully pick and choose verses that can be *integrated* into counseling practice but to be *saturated* by God's Word so that counseling practice (and every other part of life) is transformed and renewed by God's presence. Sometimes these counselors explicitly use Scripture in counseling, and sometimes they do not. But they routinely consider the themes of Scripture when evaluating, planning treatment interventions, and relating to clients.

Challenge 3: Expanded Definitions of Training

How do we train ourselves to use Scripture sensitively for the spiritual development of our clients? By first learning to use Scripture in our personal spiritual development. I offer two suggestions.

First, both Dallas Willard and Richard Foster describe study, including study of Scripture, as an important discipline for the spiritual life. Willard describes study as an important contribution that we make to our relationship with God.[33] This is not necessarily the cram-for-exam type of study that we learn in college and graduate school. It does not require us to have a desk filled with open commentaries, Bible dictionaries, lexicons, and so on. Rather it is a commitment to reading and to trying to understand God's will revealed in Scripture. Foster suggests selecting a book of the Bible and reading it straight through to identify the themes and flow of the book.[34]

Second, using Scripture for spiritual growth requires time for reflection. We get accustomed to reading quickly to survive the challenges of the academic and professional worlds, but reading quickly is not an effective goal when approaching Scripture. After reading a book of the Bible through in one sitting, it might be helpful to spend thirty minutes per day for the next year reading it very slowly and reflecting on the promises of Scripture. Willard instructs, "We not only read and hear and inquire, but we meditate on what comes before us; that is, we withdraw into silence where we prayerfully and steadily focus on it. In this way its meaning for us can emerge and form us as God works in the depths of our heart, mind, and soul."[35] Meditation is an essential part of the spiritual discipline of study.

Challenge 4: Confronting Dominant Views of Mental Health

Insofar as dominant models of mental health encourage clients to look inside themselves or to a counselor for standards of conduct and principles of morality, using Scripture takes counseling in a different direction by suggesting an external source of truth.

WHAT IF THIS HAPPENED?

Wendy cries softly as she describes her feelings of shame to her therapist, Dr. R. E. Teeguy. Unhappy in her marriage, Wendy agreed to go on a business trip with a coworker. While they were away together, she had sex with him. Since she returned, she has felt overwhelmed with guilt and shame.

Dr. Teeguy interrupts, "I'm wondering why you are upsetting yourself so much about your decision to sleep with Tom."

"Because what I did was terribly wrong. I cheated on Mike. I betrayed his trust, and now I don't even know how to act around Tom."

"I can see this is upsetting for you, but I don't agree that you have to be upset. Can you prove to me, logically, that what you did was terribly wrong? It sounds as if you're saying that you have broken the law or something and that you are now a worthless person because of having slept with Tom."

We can see where Dr. Teeguy is headed. He believes Wendy is upsetting herself unnecessarily with arbitrary standards of morality. By dismissing her "silly" ideas of right and wrong, Wendy might feel great relief after the session. Both Dr. Teeguy and Wendy think of it as a successful counseling session.

Though Dr. Teeguy might say that he holds no religious values, he actually has deified himself by assuming that his values of right and wrong are better and more carefully reasoned than Wendy's. He encourages Wendy to accept his values and feel greater peace about having slept with Tom.

This is an extreme example, chosen to illustrate the problem of removing external standards of right and wrong from the counseling office. Most counselors, regardless of their religious perspectives, are more sensitive to religious values than Dr. Teeguy. But even religiously sensitive counselors are sometimes guilty of undermining external standards of right and wrong and of encouraging clients to look inside themselves for truth. In his presidential address for the American Psychological Association's Division of Psychotherapy, Dr. Stanley Graham stated: "Quite early in the treatment process, the patient begins to use words like good and bad, and it is our tendency as therapists to diminish the intensity of these words since they relate to a value system within the individual that has led to the current state of stress. My own personal view of the last thirty years of psychotherapy is that we have collectively done an excellent job of diminishing the demonstration of good and bad and a very poor job of replacing these concepts with acceptable definitions that allow the individual self-acceptance and peace."[36]

Though Graham was not arguing for explicitly religious forms of psychotherapy, Christian counselors can resolve his concern by respecting Scripture as an external authority for values and morality. Christian counseling, rooted in a commitment to Scripture, retains words such as *right* and *wrong*. Clients can still look inside themselves for feelings, experiences, thoughts, and assumptions, but they do not have to find truth inside themselves. Christian counseling leaves room for external authority: God can still be God.

Of course, we must be careful not to be too strident in our assertions about Scripture in counseling because our interpretations of Scripture are limited by human fallenness and our imperfect hermeneutic strategies. Some clients have unhealthy beliefs that they support with a distorted understanding of Scripture. So do some counselors. We must be humble, submit ourselves to God's guidance, and learn from one another.

Challenge 5: Establishing a Scientific Base

Unfortunately, the use of Scripture in counseling has received very little scientific attention. The hypothesis, which awaits scientific verification, was stated well by Dr. Siang-Yang Tan: "It is proposed that a biblical approach to counseling . . . that explicitly utilizes Christian religious values or perspectives and interventions (e.g., prayer and the use of Scriptures) and relies on appropriate spiritual gifts and the power and ministry of the Holy Spirit, makes unique contributions to counseling effectiveness, especially with religious, Christian clients. Further research is needed to determine the empirical validity of this proposal."[37]

In 1993, when Dr. Brad Johnson reviewed the outcome literature on religious forms of psychotherapy, he found only five studies reporting the effectiveness of Christian forms of therapy.[38] Of these, only three used Scripture as a direct intervention. In the best designed of these studies, Johnson and his colleagues used two different forms of Rational-Emotive Therapy (RET) and tested their effectiveness. One form, Christian RET, used Scripture rather than the human reason of the therapist as the source of truth. Clients learned to challenge irrational beliefs with Bible passages.

Although the treatment effectively reduced depression, the researchers found no differences between the overall effectiveness of RET and Christian RET among their depressed Christian participants.[39] Two other published studies, both using Scripture as a tool to combat irrational beliefs, produced similar results.[40] Interestingly, two studies in Johnson's review showed religious interventions to be more effective than nonreligious interventions, but both of these studies relied on Christian imagery more than Scripture for the religious interventions.[41]

At this time, the research is so limited that it is premature to draw any conclusions about the effective use of Scripture in counseling. As academicians and clinicians work together to collect additional information and report results, we will be better prepared to use Scripture in effective and sensitive ways in counseling.

Challenge 6: Defining Relevant Ethical Standards

Many of the same ethical issues considered at the end of chapter 3 are relevant here. The principle of competence suggests that counselors should use Scripture only in ways that are consistent with their training. For example, the psychologist who has no training in theology needs to exercise special caution when using Scripture in counseling. The principle of informed consent requires counselors who use Scripture extensively in counseling to tell their clients so near the beginning of the counseling relationship. The counselor should also disclose the client's alternatives by discussing other models of treatment available elsewhere. Charging fees and filing insurance claims for scripturally based interventions creates the tensions already discussed in chapter 3.

Using Scripture in counseling introduces another risk not discussed previously: the risk of significantly reducing client freedom by imposing the therapist's values on the client. Religious psychotherapy, in general, introduces the risk of imposing unwanted values or beliefs on a client, and explicitly using Scripture in counseling quickly magnifies this risk.[42]

WHAT IF THIS HAPPENED?

Ms. Young is seeing a counselor at the Ridge Id Counseling Center. She is facing a difficult decision about her future education and is looking for Christian guidance. Ms. Young has always dreamed of being a pediatrician, but her parents and her fiancé want her to matriculate in a two-year nurses-training program. With nurses training, they tell her, she can more quickly enter the workforce and will have an easier time giving up her career when her children are born. The counselor at Ridge Id joins forces with Ms. Young's many advisers and, based on a questionable interpretation of Titus 2:5, tells her that Scripture instructs women to stay at home once they have children. Her counselor makes it very clear: Nursing school is the option best supported with Scripture.

Ms. Young leaves counseling feeling confused and frustrated, intent on giving up her long-standing goal in order to do what God wants her to do.

This counselor not only communicated a personal preference for Ms. Young to choose nursing school but also suggested, by referring to Scripture, that God wants her to choose nursing school. Under such circumstances, Ms. Young has lost freedom. In her mind, she can choose only to give up her goal to be a pediatrician or to rebel against God. Using Scripture in counseling magnifies the risk of unethical coercion or inappropriate value imposition. This is not to say that we should always avoid using Scripture in counseling but that we are wise to consider the risks and exercise appropriate caution.

Although the greatest attention has been given to whether or not it is ethical to use explicitly Christian techniques in counseling, one author has turned the question around: Is it ethical for a Christian counselor *not* to use explicitly religious interventions in therapy? David Holling argues that a pastoral psychotherapist has an obligation to treat patients differently from the way a traditional therapist might, by using Scripture, prayer, rituals, doctrines, and sacraments.[43] His point is worth considering. If we claim to be specialists in Christian counseling, then our work with religious clients ought to look different from the work of those who specialize in different forms of counseling.

SUMMARY

Scripture is powerful and can keep us focused on timeless truth in the midst of professions vulnerable to fads and shifting standards of right and wrong. Some Christian counselors have used Scripture to support counseling models or as a specific intervention tool in counseling, but survey research suggests that the explicit use of Scripture is quite rare among Christian counselors.

When counselors choose to use Scripture in counseling, it is important to consider the specific effects it might have on a client, based on a careful assessment of the client's needs, the therapeutic relationship, and ethical standards. Also, it is important to balance a healthy respect for Scripture as God's special revelation with personal humility, recognizing that all interpretations of Scripture are limited by our imperfect hermeneutic methods. Our knowledge of God, self, and Scripture are all interrelated, and our capacity to understand any one of these elements will add to our ability to understand the others.

In order for Scripture to effect significant change in the lives of counselors and clients, it must be internalized and personalized outside of counseling sessions. Meditating, contemplating, and praying from Scripture are often helpful in spiritual growth, especially when we discard the notion that more is better. Sometimes thirty minutes are better spent contemplating one or two verses than reading several chapters.

5/ SIN

It is striking to observe the difference one word can make in the meaning of a sentence. Richard Lederer, a New Hampshire English teacher, has written a delightful little book titled *Anguished English,* which illustrates the significance of the ways we place and use words in writing and speech. In one chapter he lists humorous excuse notes he has received from parents over the years. For example, "My son is under the doctor's care and should not take P. E. today. Please execute him."[1] One strategically placed or misused word makes a big difference!

Similarly, one word makes a big difference in the way two counselors describe the relationship between sin and psychological disturbance. Albert Ellis has argued that the *concept* of sin is the cause of virtually all psychopathology.[2] Jay Adams has argued that sin is the cause of virtually all psychopathology (except that which is caused by organic factors).[3] At first glance these two positions might appear almost identical. Actually they are diametrically opposed. When Ellis refers to the *concept* of sin as the problem, he means that all we need to do to be healthy is to dismiss our silly ideas about right and wrong and live a life of responsible pleasure seeking. Adams leaves out the word *concept,* suggesting that sin itself is the problem. People are emotionally disturbed because they are sinners who have been damaged by other sinners and who need to repent and live more obediently. Ellis calls us to eliminate our sensitivity to sin; Adams calls us to heighten our sensitivity.

Though both Ellis and Adams have been misunderstood and misrepresented by many Christian counselors, they nonetheless represent extremes on an ideological continuum regarding the relationship of sin and psychopathology. Where should Christian counselors position themselves on this continuum? And once we position ourselves, how forthright should we be about confronting our clients regarding the sin in their lives?

FOUNDATIONS

Psychology

The most striking thing about the psychological literature on sin is its relative absence. Though a few authors have written about the role of sin in mental illness, their articles are scattered sparingly through volumes of journals and books that line the shelves of university libraries. From among the few published works, two themes—similar to the perspectives of Ellis and Adams—can be distilled.

SIN AS A CAUSE OF PSYCHOPATHOLOGY

First, a few writers have argued that sin ought to be seen as an important cause of emotional disturbance. Biblical counselors have been saying this for several decades, but their writing is usually not visible among the general psychological literature. A few psychologists have agreed with biblical counselors in seeing sin as a cause of psychopathology.

Thirty years ago, O. Hobart Mowrer developed a group therapy approach called integrity therapy, which emphasized honesty, responsibility, and mutual concern in counteracting the psychopathological effects of sin.[4] Mowrer writes:

> For several decades we psychologists looked upon the whole matter of sin and moral accountability as a great incubus and

acclaimed our liberation from it as epoch-making. But at length we have discovered that to be "free" in this sense, i.e., to have the excuse of being "sick" rather than sinful, is to court the danger of also becoming lost. This danger is, I believe, betokened by the widespread interest in Existentialism which we are presently witnessing. In becoming amoral, ethically neutral, and "free," we have cut the very roots of our being; lost our deepest sense of self-hood and identity; and, with neurotics themselves, find ourselves asking: Who am I? What is my destiny? What does living (existence) mean?[5]

Mowrer reported both empirical and anecdotal evidence to support the connection between moral accountability and mental health—evidence that he claims was selectively ignored by psychologists.[6]

In 1973 Karl Menninger, of the Menninger Clinic, published what has become a widely cited book, *Whatever Became of Sin?*[7] Menninger argued that both good psychotherapy and good religion help people confront their self-centeredness and move beyond their arrogance to a healthier understanding of self and others. More recently, several pastoral counselors have argued for the importance of considering sin in counseling.[8]

Mowrer, Menninger, and those writing in the pastoral counseling field do not represent mainstream psychology in their understanding of and emphasis on sin. Most psychologists who write about sin are interested in the cognitive processes used in understanding sin and the effects of those processes. They are more interested in the human *concept* of sin than in sin itself.

THE CONCEPT OF SIN AND PSYCHOPATHOLOGY

Are we sinners, or are we sick? Do we have moral problems or psychological problems? Our answers to these questions reflect our *attributional style,* and they shape the way we do counseling. By attributional style, psychologists mean the way people explain good and bad events in their lives and the lives of others.

WHAT IF THIS HAPPENED?

Jeff is HIV positive and anticipates dying of AIDS eventually. He seeks counseling to deal with his emotional turmoil. Alison is married to Jeff and is dealing with her own emotional reaction to Jeff's illness. She is seeing a different counselor. Notice that Jeff and Alison's attributional styles will affect the emotions they are confronting in counseling. Here are two possible attributional styles:

Attributional style 1: Jeff as a sinner. Jeff believes he is HIV positive because he is a sinner. He says to himself, "If I had managed my homosexual desires better, I would not have had sex with other men and would not be HIV positive now." Alison has a similar attribution. She says to herself, "Jeff behaved like a fool, and now he has ended up hurting his entire family." Because of these attributions, Jeff is dealing with feelings of shame and guilt in counseling. Alison is working on her anger.

Attributional style 2: Jeff as sick. Jeff sees AIDS as a terrible sickness. He says to himself, "I am likely to become a victim of a terrible disease, a tragic illness." Alison sees Jeff's illness similarly and says to herself, "This is a tragic example of how unfair life can be. A young man will be struck down in the prime of his life, leaving a family that needs him." Jeff and Alison both deal with their fears and sadness in counseling.

These examples illustrate how attributions lead to different emotional consequences.[9] When we view people as sinners, we assume that they had a choice and that they are therefore responsible for the consequences of their choices: "Jeff is HIV positive because he chose to have sex with another man." This is an example of an *internal* attribution. A frequent response to internal attributions is to become angry at, and often to punish, the sinner. When we view people as sick, we assume that they had little or no control over their current state: "AIDS is a random killer, striking people down in the prime of their lives." This is called an *external* attribution. A frequent response to external attributions is to feel sympathy for the victim.

A number of psychologists have provided evidence that our attributional style affects mental health. Depressed people, for example, are more likely than others to attribute bad events to their own internal flaws and good events to external causes, such as luck or random chance. Those who resist depression most effectively see bad events as resulting from external or unstable factors, such as a lack of effort or bad luck, and good events as resulting from internal, stable qualities such as good ability and dedicated effort.[10]

Thus, based on attributional theory, it is reasonable to assume that those who attribute bad events to personal sin are more likely to be depressed and angry than those who see themselves as sick or as victims of unfortunate circumstances. Not surprisingly then, the prevailing model of mental health found in psychology is to view people as sick, an external attribution, rather than as sinners, an internal attribution. In order to break through dysfunctional cycles of shame and overwhelming feelings of guilt, counselors often help their clients externalize their attributions for failures in life. For example, a number of articles in the substance-abuse literature argue that attributing addictions to sin rather than disease is harmful and destructive. Producing guilt and shame appears to drive people further into a state of addiction.

Christian counselors find themselves caught in the middle of these two worlds, each of which prefers a different attributional style. In our Christian domain, we believe that sin is a willful rebellion against God and that it often carries painful consequences for oneself or others. People are sinners, and sin has bad consequences. In our counseling domain, we are sometimes told that emotional problems result from things beyond a person's control: addictions, diseases, bad parenting, unfortunate circumstances, chemical imbalances. One system tells us that people are sinners; the other tells us that people are sick. How can we reconcile these two attributional systems without giving up either our commitment to Christianity or our commitment to counseling and mental health? To reconcile these two seemingly distinct perspectives, we need to consider the contributions of Christian theology and spirituality.

Christian Theology

In the psychological world, the distinction between sin and sickness is presented as a rather simplistic dichotomy. In the world of Christian theology, where sin and sickness are inextricably connected, the dichotomy disappears. Consider Millard Erickson's definition of sin: "Sin is any lack of conformity, active or passive, to the moral will of God. This may be a matter of act, of thought, or of inner disposition or state."[11] Here we see that sin and sickness are intertwined and inseparable. Sin can be a matter of act or thought, as is generally assumed, but sin is also an inner disposition, a part of our character that resembles a chronic sickness. Theologian Edwin Zackrison explains: "Biblically, the sin problem involves more than simply our bad actions, whether personal or social in their implications and complications. In Scripture and theology sin is a condition that goes to the root of our being for it has to do with our relationship to our origin and to God."[12] Christian theology includes both a personal and an original concept of sin.[13] Too often counselors who are not Christians understand only the personal concept of sin and thereby misrepresent Christianity.

WHAT IF THIS HAPPENED?

Dr. Best is a psychologist who works with depressed patients, many of whom have religious beliefs. She notices that her patients come to therapy feeling guilty, often because their behaviors are not consistent with their religious belief systems. Dr. Best assumes the problem is religion and writes angry articles and books about the pathological effects of religion. Her books are quite popular, and many other psychologists begin noticing similar patterns in their clients.

In this example, Dr. Best is using a partial understanding of sin, recognizing only its personal nature and overlooking its original, universal nature. Like Dr. Best, psychologists writing about sin have generally assumed that the most devout Christians are the ones most preoccupied with managing sinful thoughts and behaviors, and they conclude that religion promotes psychopathology. Eric Fromm suggested that the goals of Christianity are powerlessness and obedience, resulting in a prevailing mood of sorrow and guilt.[14] This is the same guilt that Albert Ellis observed in his religious clients, leading him to conclude that the concept of sin causes psychopathology.

Unfortunately, Fromm and Ellis are not completely wrong. Some Christians assume the same—that sin is only personal and that Christian piety is best defined by controlling specific behaviors. This is known as the heresy of Pelagianism: sin is just a set of bad habits that we need to eliminate. When we view sin as limited to personal behaviors or thoughts, we fall prey to a sin-management mentality and become vulnerable to legalism and asceticism and to excessive guilt reactions. The apostle Paul had strong words for those who tried to control their sin nature using sin-management techniques: "If with Christ you died to the elemental spirits of the universe, why do you live as if you still belonged to the world? Why do you submit to regulations, 'Do not handle, Do not taste, Do not touch'? All these regulations refer to things that perish with use; they are simply human commands and teachings. These have indeed an appearance of wisdom in promoting self-imposed piety, humility, and severe treatment of the body, but they are of no value in checking self-indulgence" (Col. 2:20-23).

Sin is more than a set of personal behaviors, and managing sin requires more than keeping a checklist of dos and don'ts. Sin is an original part of our character, a pervasive element of the human condition. Sin is our sickness. It is a sickness dating back to the Fall, when Adam and Eve chose to sin in the Garden of Eden. Ever since the original sin, every human being has struggled with sin. "Therefore, just as sin came into the world through one man, and death came through sin, and so death spread to all because all have sinned" (Rom. 5:12).

The ubiquity of sin is both bad news and good news. It is bad because we are indeed sick, burdened by sin that affects every attitude, behavior, relationship, and thought in our lives. We are bundles of mixed motives, constantly fighting to yield more control to God and less to our sin nature. It is good because this view of sin disqualifies the objections of psychologists who claim Christians are destined to be emotionally sick.[15] Christians who understand sin properly view themselves as part of a universal community of sinners. If sin is a sickness, something that affects all people and interferes constantly with our capacity to make good choices, then our attributions no longer need to be internal and shame producing. We are all pilgrims together, struggling with common temptations and burdens. Those who understand sin most accurately are able to make both internal (personal) and external (universal) attributions for the causes of their problems.

WHAT IF THIS HAPPENED?

Jeff is HIV positive, and both he and Alison are working to make sense of their future. Earlier in the chapter, two possible attributional styles were suggested. Either Jeff could be viewed as a sinner (an internal attribution), getting what he deserves for rebellious behavior, or he could be viewed as a victim of a terrible sickness (an external attribution). Now we have a third alternative that combines these two attributional styles. Yes, Jeff is a sinner, and so is everyone else. Sin is a pervasive force that affects us all in various ways. Jeff's sin carries particularly harsh consequences because sickness abounds in our fallen world, including the sickness of AIDS. Jeff's situation is an illustration of the sometimes harsh consequences of sin, but it is not an illustration of judgment; most of us sin without the consequences Jeff faces. This attribution is both internal and external, both personal and original, leaving room for sympathy and compassion as well as disappointment, sadness, and anger.

Those who understand both the personal and original nature of sin are able to adjust to the nagging ache of fallen existence without succumbing to the excessive self-condemnation and guilt that psychologists have often associated with religion. The best response to sin is not to sink further into self-absorption and self-abasement but to recognize our need and look for healing in relationship with God.

Spirituality

Entering deeply into the spiritual life requires us to abandon sin-management and to seek inner transformation through the work of the Holy Spirit. Richard Foster puts it well: "Our ordinary method of dealing with ingrained sin is to launch a frontal attack. We rely on our willpower and determination. . . . We determine never to do it again; we pray against it, fight against it, set our will against it. But the struggle is all in vain, and we find ourselves once again morally bankrupt or, worse yet, so proud of our external righteousness that 'whitened sepulchers' is a mild description of our condition."[16]

WHAT IF THIS HAPPENED?

John sees a lay counselor at his church because he has been feeling sad and lonely lately. His counselor helps him discover some sinful attitudes and hidden resentments about his past, repent of his unforgiving attitude, and write a letter of forgiveness to his parents. John feels better after writing the letter, and he and his counselor decide their work together is finished.

This straightforward approach to counseling may have some benefits, but it is doubtful that John will experience lasting spiritual and personal growth with this approach. Though he has identified sin and vowed to stop feeling resentful, he has learned little about a more intimate relationship with a loving, gracious God, and he may find that releasing resentment is more difficult than he and his counselor anticipate. John is trying to forgive by using willpower, and willpower may not be the most effective approach. For most people in John's situation, repenting of resentment and coming to true forgiveness requires a daily "letting go" that is found most perfectly in profound communion with Christ.

Because sin is original as well as personal, even our willpower is tainted with evil. We deceive ourselves, justify our actions, value reputation above virtue, compare ourselves with those who sin more (or at least more blatantly), smugly reassure ourselves that things could be worse, and substitute one sin for another. Human willpower alone can never conquer sin because the human will is saturated with it. To cope with sin, we need a power greater than human nature. We need God. Thomas à Kempis wrote about this in the fifteenth century: "We must not despair when we are tempted but instead, seek God more fervently, asking for his help in this time of tribulation."[17] And Thomas Merton suggests something similar in the twentieth century: "Perfection is not a moral embellishment that we acquire outside of Christ, in order to qualify for union with him. Perfection is the work of Christ himself living in us by faith."[18] And even this faith, the apostle Paul reminds us in Ephesians 2:8-9, is a gift from God, not an act of human will.

Coping with temptation and managing sin cannot be done with willpower alone because even the human will is sinful. How do we cleanse our hands from sin and purify our hearts from duplicity? By drawing near to God and allowing God to draw near to us.[19] There are no rugged individualists living a victorious Christian life, only those who lean on God. Augustine wrote: "From Thee, O God, are all good things, and *from my God is all my health.*" [20]

Because properly managing sin requires us to transcend will-power and seek God, the spiritual disciplines become essential tools for holiness. The disciplines themselves do not make us holy, but they open a door to our soul, allowing God's grace and truth to fill us. "The demand is for an inside job, and only God can work from the inside."[21]

PSYCHOLOGICAL AND SPIRITUAL HEALTH

This discussion of sin leads to some important questions for Christian counselors: Should I confront sin in my clients' lives? Will confronting them help them experience greater psychological and spiritual health? Depending on personality style and theoretical orientation, some counselors routinely answer no to these questions and avoid confronting their clients. Though I recognize that some theoretical orientations require this nonconfrontive environment to be effective, I believe confrontation should be a valid option for most Christian counselors under many circumstances.[22] But the question Should we confront sin in counseling? like many others posed in this book, is too general. A more appropriate question is, *"Which* clients should I confront with their sin, and *how* should I go about confronting them?"

In counseling, four approaches to confronting sin are appropriate in various situations: silence, pondering, questioning, and direct censure. In addition, there is the option of not confronting sin. Each approach must be carefully selected with regard to the particular client, the situation, and the nature of the therapeutic relationship. The following examples illustrate each of these approaches.

SILENCE

Sometimes the best way to confront sin is to remain silent and let clients work out their feelings of guilt and questions of blame on their own. This approach may be especially helpful for those who seem overly dependent on the counselor's opinion.

Client: She thinks she owns me. I am thirty-five now, and I need her to be my friend more than my mother. It's really not her business whom I date and whether I choose to sleep with him. It's my business. I will sleep with Tom whenever and wherever I feel like it.

Counselor: (Silence)

Client: I'm not a bad person. I think that's what she wants. She wants me to feel bad, as I did when I was a teenager.

Counselor: (Silence)

Client: Do you know what I mean? I just am tired of feeling like a bad person.

Notice here how the client is looking for approval from the counselor. Sometimes even an affirming head nod or verbal acknowledgment ("I see, Uh-huh") is enough to feel approval from a counselor. If the counselor had acknowledged the client's first statement, the client might leave the session feeling that her counselor agrees that she has the right to sleep with Tom anytime and anyplace she chooses. Silence is a relatively gentle form of confrontation that prevents counselors from inadvertently permitting or encouraging sinful behaviors.

PONDERING

Pondering aloud is sometimes a helpful way to confront clients indirectly and cause them to think more intently about their choices. This has sometimes been called the "Columbo technique," named after the television detective who mastered this strategy.

> *Client:* She thinks she owns me. I am thirty-five now, and I need her to be my friend more than my mother. It's really not her business whom I date and whether I choose to sleep with him. It's my business. I will sleep with Tom whenever and wherever I feel like it.

> *Counselor:* Help me out here a minute. You are saying that you don't really think you need to behave according to your mom's wishes. But there is tension on your face and in your voice, as if you don't really believe what you are saying.

> *Client:* I do believe it. It's just that she seems so powerful. I've been living on my own for eighteen years, but it's as if she's still here, still controlling me.

> *Counselor:* So it's almost as if her voice is inside you.

> *Client:* Yeah, that's exactly what it's like.

Here the counselor is easing the client toward a more complete understanding of conscience. The client wants to blame her mom but actually has internalized many of her mother's values. Perhaps she feels bad about sleeping with Tom, and the counselor is helping her uncover and explore her feelings. As with silence, this is a relatively gentle form of confrontation.

QUESTIONING

By asking specific questions, counselors are sometimes able to access clients' values of right and wrong. This approach can help give clients a feeling of ownership over their decisions rather than simply conforming to meet the expectations of a confrontive counselor.

Client: She thinks she owns me. I am thirty-five now, and I need her to be my friend more than my mother. It's really not her business whom I date and whether I choose to sleep with him. It's my business. I will sleep with Tom whenever and wherever I feel like it.

Counselor: What are your values about sleeping with Tom?

Client: Well, I don't think it's the best thing to do, but it's not like the worst crime I could do either. My mom seems to think I'll go to hell if I sleep with someone.

Counselor: It sounds as if her religious views are important to her. And it sounds as if yours are different from hers. What about your religious values? How do they affect your choices with Tom?

Though this is more confrontive than either of the first two examples, it respects the client's right to articulate her own values of right and wrong.

DIRECT CENSURE

This technique should be considered only when there is a high level of trust established in the therapeutic relationship. Under ideal circumstances, it can lead to quick changes. Unfortunately, if it is misused it can also cause severe damage to a therapeutic relationship and reduce the authenticity of future sessions.

Client: She thinks she owns me. I am thirty-five now, and I need her to be my friend more than my mother. It's really not her business whom I date and whether I choose to sleep with him. It's my business. I will sleep with Tom whenever and wherever I feel like it.

Counselor: Your mother may not express herself well in many situations, but it's interesting that the Bible presents values that are very similar to hers.

Client: What do you mean?

Counselor: God's Word instructs us that sex is only for marriage, and you and Tom aren't married. Hebrews 13:4 reads: "Let marriage be held in honor by all, and let the marriage bed be kept undefiled; for God will judge fornicators and adulterers." Perhaps that is what your mom is concerned about, too.

Clearly, this is the most extreme form of confrontation, elevating the counselor's values to a position above the client's values. There are times when direct confrontation is appropriate, but in my opinion it should be used very sparingly. In my years of clinical work, I have used direct censure very rarely.

NOT CONFRONTING

Sometimes confronting sin is not the best therapeutic strategy. In this example, the counselor chooses to move the session in a different direction.

Client: She thinks she owns me. I am thirty-five now, and I need her to be my friend more than my mother. It's really not her business whom I date and whether I choose to sleep with him. It's my business. I will sleep with Tom whenever and wherever I feel like it.

Counselor: You're feeling angry. I'd like to hear more about it.

Client: She's always calling, always wanting to know everything about my life. And I feel I'm a grown-up now. I can make my own choices.

Counselor: It sounds as if you are feeling a need for a better boundary between you and your mom.

Client: I guess so. I'm just not sure how to tell her that.

In this example, the counselor may have determined that other important therapeutic work must be done before considering the sinfulness of the client's behavior, such as discussing ways of asserting better communication boundaries between the client and her mother.

These examples illustrate five legitimate alternatives when discussing sinful behavior in counseling. Choosing which approach to use in a specific counseling situation requires discernment, wisdom, an understanding of the counseling relationship, and self-awareness. As in previous chapters, the following three questions should be used in coming to careful decisions about confronting sin.

Will This Help Establish a Healthy Sense of Self?

The Christian life is not a matter of fine-tuning our previous self to reduce our propensity to sin. Rather, Christ calls us to exchange our old self for a new self. We are to be transformed, radically changed, born again. The apostle Paul put it this way: "Therefore we have been buried with him by baptism into death, so that, just as Christ was raised from the dead by the glory of the Father, so we too might walk in newness of life. For if we have been united with him in a death like his, we will certainly be united with him in a resurrection like his. We know that our old self was crucified with him so that the body of sin might be destroyed, and we might no longer be enslaved to sin" (Rom. 6:4-6).

A Christian view of self calls us to give up one life for another.[23] In *Mere Christianity,* C. S. Lewis describes our normal tendency to try adding the Christian life on top of our natural self. We only hope that our natural self will still have time to be expressed and nurtured. So we struggle, trying to figure out how to give more time or money or resist certain temptations and sins, and we end up feeling deprived, hampered, and angry. Lewis writes: "The Christian way is different: harder, and easier. Christ says, 'Give me All. I don't want so much of your time and so much of your money and so much of your work: I want You. I have not come to torment your natural self, but to kill it.'"[24]

Christian counselors have discussed confronting sin in counseling for many years, but too often we limit our discussion to confronting personal sin and end up teaching our clients the type of dysfunctional religion that C. S. Lewis is discussing. Consider the client, previously discussed, who wants permission to sleep with her boyfriend, Tom, anytime and anyplace. By directly confronting her sin we might, under the best circumstances, be able to change her behavior. She might become chaste and wait until marriage for sex, though this seems an idealistic outcome. But even if she succeeds in behavioral change, have we helped her accomplish real inner transformation? Has she replaced an old self with a new self, or has she merely added a behavioral proscription to the old self? Has she confronted the reality of original sin, or has she just mastered some sin-management strategies to control personal sin? Has she given Christ all of herself, or has she given just one small part of herself?

All these questions can be summarized into one global question for Christian counseling: Do we push people or attract people toward spiritual transformation? I suspect the only effective way is to attract people to the spiritual life. Christian counselors who confront sin but do not live out the fruit of a Spirit-transformed life (love, joy, peace, patience, kindness, generosity, faithfulness, gentleness, self-control) inadvertently teach their clients a faulty approach to spiritual formation by trying to push them toward spiritual maturity.

In the midst of life's hurried and frantic pace, we easily resort to behavioral-management strategies, assuming we can change from the outside in. But in times of quiet, moments of calm, as we set aside life's hurried pace and renew ourselves in God's presence, we recognize that God wants to change us, and our clients, from the inside out. God wants surrender, not sin-management tactics.[25]

Here are two more examples. Consider which has the greatest likelihood of eventually leading to inner transformation and surrender.

OUTSIDE-IN APPROACH

Client: She thinks she owns me. I am thirty-five now, and I need her to be my friend more than my mother. It's really not her business whom I date and whether I choose to sleep with him. It's my business. I will sleep with Tom whenever and wherever I feel like it.

Counselor: Your mother may not express herself well in many situations, but it's interesting that the Bible presents values that are very similar to hers.

Client: What do you mean?

Counselor: God's Word instructs us that sex is only for marriage, and you and Tom aren't married. Hebrews 13:4 reads: "Let marriage be held in honor by all, and let the marriage bed be kept undefiled; for God will judge fornicators and adulterers." Perhaps that is what your mom is concerned about, too.

Client: So you think she's right. I guess I do too, but it's just so hard not to feel like a kid again when she is constantly telling me that I'm doing the wrong thing.

Counselor: Is it any easier to think about God telling you what is right and wrong?

Client: I guess so. I mean, that has always been important to me. But when Mom tells me not to do something, it makes me want to do it all the more.

Counselor: How about when God tells you?

Client: It's easier. I know God wants the best for me. And sometimes I think Mom just wants me to look good so she looks good. Yeah, I think I need to make some changes.

Counselor: Let's spend some time talking about how you might make those changes. . . .

At times, direct censure is an appropriate approach to sin. But most of the time, in my opinion, it is more appropriate simply to model the fruit of a transformed life with the ultimate goal of helping people find their deep inner cry for intimacy with God and others.

INSIDE-OUT APPROACH

Client: She thinks she owns me. I am thirty-five now, and I need her to be my friend more than my mother. It's really not her business whom I date and whether I choose to sleep with him. It's my business. I will sleep with Tom whenever and wherever I feel like it.

Counselor: (Silence)

Client: I'm not a bad person. I think that's what she wants. She wants me to feel bad, as I did when I was a teenager.

Counselor: (Silence)

Client: Do you know what I mean? I just am tired of feeling as if I'm a bad person.

Counselor: I'm wondering if that is a familiar feeling for you.

Client: I've always felt bad. Nothing I do is good enough. Even now, I feel as if you aren't saying anything. As if you think I'm a bad person.

Counselor: That's an important feeling for us to explore.

Client: Well, do you? Do you think I'm bad?

Counselor: Tell me what you think.

Client: (pause, followed by tears) I feel bad. I feel bad all the time.

In this example, the counselor is kind and direct without condoning sin yet focuses the discussion toward the inner life of the client. From here, the client can begin to explore how she has always felt unworthy and bad. Whereas the non-Christian counselor might then dissuade her and convince her she is a good person, the Christian counselor will help her see the universality of her concerns. The client is like every human, plagued with self-serving desires, an unhealthy need for approval, and the grief and loneliness that come from living in proximity with other fallen humans. Fortunately, a gracious God loves her despite her humanness and is willing to transform her character into something beautiful.

Will This Help Establish a Healthy Sense of Need?

We often assume that confronting sin will help people recognize their errors and admit a need for God. Fortunately, this is sometimes true. In the context of a trusting therapy relationship, direct confrontation is sometimes helpful. Unfortunately, this assumption is only *sometimes* true. At other times, confrontation pushes people away, driving them further into patterns of denial and defense. In these cases, a less direct confrontation of sin is almost always a better approach. How can we tell the difference? Which clients can handle direct confrontation, and which should we treat more gently? Four factors should be considered.

PERSONALITY DISORDER

The majority of the people who seek help from counselors have the flexibility and adaptive capacity to adjust to new situations, learn new ways of thinking, explore their feelings openly, and make substantive behavioral changes. However, a portion of counseling clients come with personality disorders, a term used in the American Psychiatric Association's *Diagnostic and Statistical Manuals of Mental Disorders* to indicate marked inflexibility and maladaptive relational skills.[26]

Clients with personality disorders are likely to respond poorly to confrontation. Some may become excessively compliant in order to please the counselor but not make significant internal changes. Others may become defensive and angry and may withdraw from the therapeutic relationship. Still others may work to make the recommended changes but may do so in an obsessive-compulsive manner that worsens their psychopathology. Whenever possible, it is important to have an accurate diagnosis, including the presence or absence of a personality disorder, before making decisions about directly confronting clients.

I recently surveyed Christian counselors to find out how frequently they used controversial diagnoses, such as multiple personality disorder (now called dissociative identity disorder), ritual abuse, and childhood sexual abuse. To disguise the purpose of the study, I also listed several other diagnoses that I was less interested in, including personality disorders. I sent the same survey to a control group of psychologists selected randomly from one division of the American Psychological Association. The surprise finding of the survey was that Christian psychologists and lay counselors report seeing more people with personality disorders than psychologists selected without regard to their religious identity![27]

As I thought about this surprising finding, it made sense. Within our Christian circles, we have an extensive counseling network for people with relatively minor problems. Christians generally see a pastor or a church-based counselor first. If they do not improve, they may be referred to a Christian psychologist for help. When they need long-term care that their insurance benefits will not cover, they may be sent to see a lay counselor who works without charge. In the non-Christian world, people will often see a psychologist first, without working through the layers of help available to Christians. Thus, Christian psychologists and lay counselors may see the most difficult and chronic counseling cases, including clients with personality disorders.

Whatever the reason for these findings, it is important to recognize that some Christian counselors work with many clients who have personality disorders. Directly confronting sin is usually not wise with these clients, especially in the early stages of treatment.

START SMALL

It is wise to start with smaller, less intimidating types of confrontation before trying to confront a cherished belief or behavior. This gives a counselor the opportunity to see how a client handles confrontation. Consider the following example.

WHAT IF THIS HAPPENED?

Counselor: As we begin today, I would like to discuss the starting times of our sessions with you. I've noticed that you have been ten minutes late to each of the last two sessions. It's your time, but I've been concerned that the shorter sessions might interfere with what we're trying to do in counseling.

A client's response to this confrontation can be used to predict how he or she will respond to more significant confrontation later. Here are three possible responses:

Response A: "Yes, I've been caught in traffic both weeks. I'm sorry, and I realize it is to my benefit to be here on time."

Response B: "Oh, I know, I am so sorry. I really don't have any excuse. I feel so bad. Are you mad?"

Response C: "Hey, I figure I'm paying the bill. It's my time, and I can use it however I want. Right?"

If the client responds to a minor confrontation by affirming appropriate responsibility for the problem, as in response A, this client probably has the emotional resources to handle other confrontation well also. If the client responds by acquiescing or wallowing in shame, as in response B, it is important to help the person gain more self-confidence and a clearer sense of identity before directly confronting sin. Those who respond in anger or by becoming highly defensive, as in response C, will probably respond in a similar way to other forms of confrontation. It will be important to let the therapeutic relationship have a softening effect on these clients before actively confronting sin.

THERAPEUTIC ALLIANCE

I remember making a driving error once and having an angry cowboy in a Ford pickup lean out his window, shake his fist at me, and yell, "Hey, buddy. Learn to drive!" For some reason I didn't take him very seriously. I didn't go home and pull out my driver's manual. I didn't enroll in a driver's education course. I didn't even reread the owner's manual to my car.

My response would be different if Lisa, who has known me for twenty-four years and has been my spouse for seventeen years, sat me down on a quiet evening and said, "Mark, I've been concerned about your driving. You seem to put yourself and the family at risk, and I would really like you to consider taking a refresher course in driving." I wouldn't be much happier with Lisa than I was with the cowboy in the Ford, but I would be more likely to comply. If Lisa, whom I know and trust, believes I need to improve my driving, then I need to take her seriously. The same is true in the counseling relationship. It is easy to discount the words of strangers. But as a counseling relationship deepens and as trust is established, words of confrontation are taken more seriously. This suggests that we should not hurry to confront sin. Confrontation will be only as successful as the trust we have built through hours of intent listening and understanding. Counselors must earn the right to confront, not just assume the right.

PERSONAL INTEGRITY

Part of earning the right to confront involves the therapeutic relationship; another part involves the counselor's personal life. It is important to remember a warning Jesus gave: "Do not judge, so that you may not be judged. For with the judgment you make you will be judged, and the measure you give will be the measure you get. Why do you see the speck in your neighbor's eye, but do not notice the log in your own eye? Or how can you say to your neighbor, 'Let me take the speck out of your eye,' while the log is in your own eye? You hypocrite, first take the log out of your own eye, and then you will see clearly to take the speck out of your neighbor's eye" (Matt. 7:1-5).

Thus, our first concern should always be to consider the grip of sin in our own lives as counselors and to seek to move closer to God in response to our sin. Before confronting others, we ought to confront ourselves. Before helping others confront their state of brokenness and need, we must confront our own.

Will This Help Establish a Healing Relationship?

Confronting sin can sometimes help establish a deeper, more complete healing relationship. A biblical proverb reminds us: "Well meant are the wounds a friend inflicts, but profuse are the kisses of an enemy" (Prov. 27:6). Counselors who refuse to confront may limit the effectiveness of the counseling relationship.

Of course, every road has two ditches, and counselors can easily become too confrontive or too direct in their confrontation, as illustrated in some of the examples given earlier in this chapter. When counselors confront too often, too directly, or without establishing adequate trust, clients will usually distance themselves from the counseling process and progress will be inhibited.

I believe *empathic confrontation* is the best tool in striking this balance. Too often we separate empathy and confrontation, assuming they are mutually exclusive. But many forms of confrontation allow empathy and confrontation to coexist.

EMPATHIC CONFRONTATION

Client: I just get so tired of my husband's behavior. He thinks he can do whatever he wants and I will be the good wife, staying at home, taking care of the kids, and abiding by his every desire. So I just refused. I left the kids a few hours and went shopping for myself. They may be a little young to be left on their own, but he didn't have to get so angry about it. He has no right to treat me like property.

Counselor: It all feels pretty overwhelming right now.

Client: Yeah. What gives him the right?

Counselor: Uh-huh. And inside it creates this desire to rebel.

Client: Yeah. I don't like it, but I feel it so strongly.

In this example, the counselor is able to be confrontive just by reflecting the content of the client's speech. She is confronting herself, but the counselor is directing the flow of the conversation so she can recognize her thoughts and feelings. Empathic confrontation can also be used in the context of three techniques described earlier—silence, pondering, and questioning. With silence, the empathy must come through facial expressions. With pondering, the counselor adopts an attitude of trying to understand what the client is saying, though actually the counselor is more concerned about the client's understanding what he or she is thinking and feeling. With questioning, the counselor is supportively helping the client find resources for determining what is right and wrong. In all these forms, empathic confrontation requires a collaborative stance. The counselor is not exercising power over the client but standing alongside as a joint pilgrim in the spiritual life.

The perfect example of empathic confrontation is found in Jesus, when he instructed his followers: "Come to me, all you that are weary and are carrying heavy burdens, and I will give you rest. Take my yoke upon you, and learn from me; for I am gentle and humble in heart, and you will find rest for your souls. For my yoke is easy, and my burden is light" (Matt. 11:28-30). Jesus did not deny the burden of original sin; he had watched the effects of sin throughout human history and had even experienced the same temptations we experience (Heb. 4:15). Jesus empathically acknowledged that the burden of sin is heavy and creates weariness. This burden of sin is what A. W. Tozer calls "a crushing thing."[28] When our clients want to deny or excuse sin, we can empathize with them as we recall that we are all caught underneath this crushing load of original sin that affects personal behavior.

And Jesus is gentle and humble in heart. Jesus was not worried about positioning himself for greatness. He came to humble himself, to pour out his life, to be "obedient to the point of death" (Phil. 2:8). Counselors are called to the same gentleness and humility. Even when we must confront, we are to do it gently with a spirit of empathy and compassion. "My friends, if anyone is detected in a transgression, you who have received the Spirit should restore such a one in a spirit of gentleness. Take care that you yourselves are not tempted. Bear one another's burdens, and in this way you will fulfill the law of Christ. For if those who are nothing think they are something, they deceive themselves" (Gal. 6:1-3).

FACING THE CHALLENGES

The beginning of this chapter suggested a continuum with Albert Ellis and Jay Adams anchoring the scale at each end. Ellis believes that counselors need to help clients dismiss their ideas about sin and live as responsible hedonists. Adams believes that sin itself causes many (or most) emotional problems and that counselors will not be completely effective until they help their clients change patterns of sinful living. Both Ellis and Adams have made important contributions: Ellis has pointed out the self-destructive cycle of excessive guilt and shame; and Adams has stood against the social tide, boldly reminding us that sin matters. The position I am advocating is between these two extremes.

In this middle position, Christian counselors take sin seriously while emphasizing the original nature of sin. Sin is the poison that burst into a perfect creation through Adam and Eve's transgression. It affects every human every day. To minimize or deny the power of sin is to close our eyes to the spiritual world that surrounds us. Because sin is original as well as personal, it does no good for our clients to wallow in guilt or shame. In fact, shame seems only to strengthen sin's grip on our lives.

When a counselor confronts personal sin with direct censure, it often heightens the power differential already present in the counselor-client relationship; it sometimes adds to a client's sense of shame; and it minimizes the generational and social effects of sin. Instead, we ought to emphasize the original nature and effects of sin as we position ourselves alongside clients who struggle with the same sins and temptations that we ourselves face. Even if we cannot empathize with the exact temptations our clients face, we should be able to recognize the sparkle and lure of sin as well as the emptiness and death that it produces. Empathic confrontation is an attempt not to minimize the significance of personal sin but to provide a safe, collaborative atmosphere that fosters genuine, honest self-exploration and discovery. When used properly, empathic confrontation through silence, pondering, or questioning helps a client honestly explore thoughts and feelings, and the change that results tends to be lasting change stemming from insight and growth.

This approach to confronting sin does not require self-disclosure during counseling sessions, but it does require personal honesty. Excessive self-disclosure confuses therapeutic boundaries and is unfair to clients; our clients do not need to know our personal struggles and temptations. However, as counselors we need to recognize and honestly confront our humanity, including our temptations and struggles. This requires a counselor to be genuine, devoted to spiritual growth and wisdom. So again we consider the six challenges described in chapter 1.

Challenge 1: Moving from Two Areas of Competence to Three

Psychologists who write about sin often have only one area of competence—psychology. They approach sin from a distinctly theoretical perspective and end up oversimplifying and misunderstanding the Christian notion of sin. For example, Weiner's dichotomy between sin and sickness has broad appeal within the psychological community, but it is a simplistic dichotomy based on a partial understanding of the Christian notion of sin.[29] Personal sin and sickness, from a Christian perspective, have the same point of origin in the Fall and cannot be separated as two extremes in a dichotomy. Dr. Weiner is a brilliant researcher, and his work on attribution theory has made a strong contribution to psychology. Unfortunately, by choosing the word *sin* to describe an attributional style, he perpetuates a wide-scale misunderstanding of sin within the psychological community.

Similarly, Mowrer's integrity therapy is a worthy notion that oversimplifies sin. He is probably correct in noting that psychology has drifted away from an understanding of personal responsibility and accountability, and his plea for more emphasis on personal sin is admirable. But he tends to overlook the significance of original sin by focusing intently on personal sin.

To understand sin properly, psychologists and Christian counselors need the contributions of theologians and devotional writers. Christian spiritual writers throughout the past two millennia have emphasized the universality of human sin. If we take these writers seriously, we must confront some problems in a modern-day psychology that considers self-esteem a goal we can attain on our own with various self-help strategies. Until we honestly confront the problem of sin, we cannot know the miracle of grace and true self-acceptance. Blaise Pascal, a seventeenth-century philosopher, reminds us that "it is in vain that you seek within yourselves for the cure for your miseries. All your intelligence can only bring you to realize that it is not within yourselves that you will find either truth or good."[30] Using words that were strong even in the sixth century, Benedict's (of Nursia) seventh step of humility is this: "The seventh step of humility is when we declare with our tongue and believe in our inmost soul that we are the lowliest and vilest of all, humbling ourselves and saying with the Psalmist, 'But I am a worm, and I am the reproach of all, the outcast of the people.' The Scriptures teach us that it is good to be humbled so that we may learn God's commandments." [31]

For many mental health professionals, Benedict's prescription for humility may seem almost intolerable, but it is important to notice that Pascal and Benedict direct their words to all humans. We are all vile, broken, sick with the infection of sin. No, it's not just personal sin; it is also the sin of our parents, our children, our coworkers, our employers, and our friends. When we break through the glossy look-good exterior, we see a common human core of loneliness and grief that we all know too well. We are sinners in a world broken apart by sin, living in relationships with other sinners. None of the science-fiction movies portraying life after nuclear disaster comes close to capturing the contrast of a perfect creation falling to become a world devastated by sin. Once we recognize the universality of sin, we stop trying to convince ourselves that we are good people; we stop trying to compute who is better than whom; and we fall helplessly at the feet of a loving Savior who graciously gives hope, meaning, purpose, and peace.

Challenge 2: Blurred Personal-Professional Distinctions

If Christian counselors are to take sin seriously in their professional work, we must also be devoted to understanding the impact of sin in our personal lives. The haunting words of Jesus remind us to take the log out of our own eye before considering the speck in our neighbor's eye. How dare we confront sin in others' lives without looking honestly at our own?

Though not all counselors agree about the role of personal therapy for counselors in training, I believe it is almost always a wise choice. Having been trained in a research-based university setting, I did not consider personal therapy during my training years. Sometime later, as I became aware of the ache of life, I engaged in a one-year journey in personal therapy. My therapist, psychodynamic in orientation, helped me understand many things. She was not directly confrontive, but she supported me as

I explored my values and priorities, my feelings about past events and present relationships. Sometimes she pushed a bit harder than I would have liked: I remember hoping for an empathic Rogerian response once, and instead hearing, "That sounds like a narcissistic fantasy to me." What did I learn through personal therapy? I learned about sin, not because my therapist ever talked about sin,—I don't recall her ever using the word—but because I was given a safe Christian environment in which to explore. First, I explored the sins of others: my parents, spouse, friends. As I submerged myself into the depths of self-pity, I found the loneliness that I had tried to mask with frantic activity and professional success. Discussing others' sin was relatively easy, but my therapist seemed to think there was more to explore. Eventually, I was able to understand and acknowledge personal sin: my self-protective mechanisms, my self-centeredness, my arrogance.

Personal therapy was one of two experiences that radically transformed my clinical work. The second experience was auditing a course in spirituality during my first year as a faculty member at Wheaton College. For years I had been immersed in a psychological worldview that emphasized the goodness of humankind. I found it liberating to romp around in a different worldview, one that acknowledges human fallenness and need and then looks to God for help.

As these two experiences helped me see myself as a sinner in a fallen world, I became more empathetic, more collaborative, and less directive in my professional work. I became less interested in fixing symptoms than in exploring the deep aches that reside under layers of defense and self-protection in my clients. Though I still call myself a cognitive therapist, my colleagues tell me I am becoming more psychodynamic. Perhaps.

The point of these stories is to illustrate the fact that personal experiences in understanding sin affect the professional work of counselors. We bring our whole person into the counseling office.

Challenge 3: Expanded Definitions of Training

How then shall we train ourselves to understand the role of sin in human problems? Perhaps the greatest resource is not found in the fields of counseling and psychology but within the spiritual disciplines.

Too often we think of the disciplines as ends in themselves. Actually, they are only means to a spiritual end, a mechanism by which we receive God's grace. Fasting, for example, should not produce the pride of accomplishment but the humility of greater insight. Fasting brings us face-to-face with our neediness. Richard Foster writes, "More than any other Discipline, fasting reveals the things that control us."[32] Fasting provides an opportunity for us to understand the nature and consequences of sin, and it "confirms our utter dependence upon God."[33] It can also be a useful mechanism of insight for many clients, but counselors should have first-hand experience with fasting before suggesting it to clients.

Meditating on Scripture can also help us understand the nature of sin. In Luke 18:13 we read of a penitent tax collector who beat on his chest and cried out, "God, be merciful to me, a sinner!" Counselors interested in personal spiritual training will find it helpful to meditate on this verse for a week or more.[34]

Here is one more suggestion. For every page we read in contemporary counseling books, including self-help books, perhaps we ought to read at least one page in the spiritual classics and one chapter of Scripture. There is a worldview implicitly assumed in modern culture, and we are wise to balance our exposure to it with the spiritual worldviews prevalent in centuries past. Our diet affects our health.

Challenge 4: Confronting Dominant Views of Mental Health

The contributions of psychology to contemporary culture have, in my opinion, been overwhelmingly positive. The research advances and innovative clinical theories and methods of psychology have revolutionized our understanding of behavior and mental processes.

Given a chance to decide again, I would happily choose psychology as my profession.

However, my biggest criticism of psychology has undoubtedly been evident throughout this chapter. Specifically, I believe the worldview assumptions promoted by many well-meaning psychologists have done enormous damage to contemporary culture. Lining shelves in every bookstore throughout America we find books on self-esteem, self-affirmation, autonomy, and independence. At some point, we must stop and ask ourselves, Why do we care so much? Why are we so preoccupied with human worth?

A recent *Newsweek* article described the problem succinctly: "Ninety percent of Americans say they believe in God. Yet the urgent sense of personal sin has all but disappeared in the current upbeat style of American religion. . . . In earlier eras, ministers regularly exhorted congregations to humbly 'confess our sins.' But the aging baby boomers who are rushing back to church do not want to hear sermons that might rattle their self-esteem."[35]

Perhaps our obsession with self-esteem is nothing more than a massive worldwide defense mechanism used to protect us from what we all instinctively know—that we are sinners living in a world of sin. We have become so familiar with the defense mechanism that the alternative of admitting sin seems dismal and depressing. But could it be that we have it all backward? Could it be that true freedom comes only after we have acknowledged our problem?

Christian counselors have an opportunity to confront dominant views of sin and provide an alternative view. In Scripture, admitting sin is not merely a dismal, depressing thing. Rather, it is a step toward understanding grace and finding opportunity for true celebration.

Challenge 5: Establishing a Scientific Base

With regard to this challenge, there is both good news and bad news. The good news is that there appears to be little or no relationship between religion and mental health. This is also the bad news.

It is good news because prominent psychologists have argued that religion makes people sick.[36] Major literature reviews and meta-analyses provide no evidence for this conclusion.[37] Religious people, including Christians, appear to be just as healthy as others despite their belief in sin. In fact, some researchers conclude there is a small positive correlation between religious beliefs and mental health.[38]

It is bad news because we might expect Christian beliefs, including beliefs in sin, repentance, and grace, to produce better adjustment and mental health than the beliefs of non-Christians. One possible explanation is that religious people have been grouped together in most studies, and not all religious experience is the same. For example, those with deeply committed, internalized religious views appear to be healthier than those who see religion as a means to an end.[39] By combining these two groups in research studies, the beneficial effects of devout faith may be masked. Thus, we need more scientific studies with more careful distinctions between various religious views and perspectives.

As described in chapter 1, several outcome studies using religious forms of therapy have been reported, but none of the religious forms of therapy have challenged the underlying worldview implicit in traditional cognitive therapy.[40] If our views of sin make a difference in the way we counsel, then we must do more than add Scripture verses or Christian images to a standard form of therapy before calling it Christian counseling.

Though an ambitious goal, we ultimately need Christian counseling that is based on a Christian view of sin and redemption.[41] This model needs to be empirically validated by putting it head-to-head with traditional counseling models and testing its effectiveness.

It is daunting to see the thousands of books and journal articles published each year in psychology and counseling. Surely every topic must have been thoroughly covered in those many pages of scholarship! Actually not. Surprisingly little has been written about counseling and sin, and virtually nothing of a scientific nature has been reported.

Challenge 6: Defining Relevant Ethical Standards

Many of the same ethical challenges discussed in previous chapters apply to our understanding and confrontation of sin. In addition, there is a global ethical guideline that deserves special consideration here: *do no harm.* This is an ancient obligation for health-care providers, dating back to the Hippocratic oath. Whatever we do, it should be for the good of the client. In their zeal to confront sin, some Christian counselors forget that the good of their client is their first priority.

WHAT IF THIS HAPPENED?

Mr. Stu K. Fingers is referred for counseling with Dr. S. Trey Tenarrow. The referral comes from Mr. Fingers' employer, who says she is concerned that Stu may be drinking alcohol excessively. During the initial interview, Mr. Fingers denies using alcohol but admits to vague concerns involving anxiety and fear about the future. Dr. Tenarrow agrees to meet with Mr. Fingers for ten sessions with the understanding that the sessions will be confidential.

During the fifth session, Mr. Fingers admits that he is stealing money from the company, and he fears that his employer suspects him. Though his employer cannot prove that he has stolen money, she seems to be trying to find other reasons to dismiss him, including the false charges of alcoholism. Mr. Fingers appears angry toward his employer and fearful for the future, but he shows no evidence of remorse for stealing.

Dr. Tenarrow, feeling indignant and concerned about Stu's lack of remorse, confronts Mr. Fingers immediately: "I believe you have reason to be afraid because what you are doing is wrong. You need to take responsibility for your actions here. You need to be honest with your employer. Your employer needs to know about this." Mr. Fingers becomes defensive and leaves the session. He misses the remaining sessions and becomes increasingly anxious, wondering if Dr. Tenarrow plans to report him to his employer.

This is a difficult situation for a number of reasons, including ethical concerns about confidentiality, privacy, competence, and a counselor's duty to protect others. Dr. Tenarrow went wrong when he forgot his first obligation to his client. When he learned about Mr. Fingers' stealing, he became overwhelmed with his own emotions and responded out of his anger rather than considering the welfare of Mr. Fingers. A more reasoned response still might have involved confrontation but in a less threatening way. By threatening an already anxious man, Dr. Tenarrow introduced potential for harm. Reporting Mr. Fingers to his employer would have violated ethical standards and state law (in virtually all states) regarding confidentiality. To even hint at such a report is irresponsible and damaging.

Confronting sin, especially when done as direct censure, introduces power into the counseling relationship. At times this may be appropriate, but as the power differential increases, so must our sensitivity to the ethical implications of our words and actions.

A related ethical concern is that an awareness of sin can lead clients in one of two directions. For some, their natural response to understanding sin will be shame. For others, an awareness of sin leads them to an awareness of God's grace, as Paul describes in his epistle to the Romans. If Christian counselors help their clients confront sin, they have an ethical obligation to also point them toward grace as a resolution to sin.[42] Those who are left to wallow in shame will be worse because of their awareness of sin. Those who experience grace will be enriched by their awareness of sin. This will be discussed in greater detail later.

SUMMARY

Psychologists have generally been uninterested in sin, preferring to ignore it or to discuss the effects of the *concept* of sin. Because internal attributions heighten feelings of guilt and depression in many situations, mental health professionals have tended to avoid sin as an explanation for emotional problems, a practice based on a misunderstanding of the Christian notion of sin. To practice competent Christian counseling, we must understand sin from theological and spiritual perspectives. Properly understood, the original nature of sin allows Christians to give up unproductive and shame-producing efforts to manage personal sin by willpower alone. Instead, we need transforming encounters with Christ.

In Christian counseling, sin can be confronted in humble and empathic ways that encourage spiritual growth more than guilt and shame. These methods include silence at strategic moments, pondering aloud inconsistencies in clients' narratives, and questioning clients in order to understand their values of right and wrong. Understanding and changing the inner life of a client is more important than merely changing behavior. This calls Christian counselors to personal and spiritual disciplines that promote personal honesty, humility, and discernment.

6/ CONFESSION

After several effective counseling sessions, Chris is finished counseling for the day. As she leaves the office and heads for her car, she reflects with satisfaction on her day. Mr. Gregory is feeling some relief from his headaches. Ms. Martinez is less depressed than she has been in months. And Jeremy is back at school after several days of a severe school phobia. It has been a good day.

As she pulls out of the parking lot, Chris entertains the question that visits every counselor from time to time. Why? Why are these people getting better? Is it because Chris is a good counselor? Is it because her cognitive-behavioral techniques are effective? Or is there some other reason?

I suspect the correct answer to Chris's question is that all of the above are true. Her counseling skills, her theoretical model, and a plethora of other factors all contribute to the successes that Mr. Gregory, Ms. Martinez, and Jeremy are feeling. As discussed earlier, one of the tasks facing researchers and counselors is to figure out the nature of these other factors, often called nonspecific factors.

Perhaps one of the nonspecific factors that helps make counseling effective is its confessional nature. In counseling offices clients unload burdens of pain and well-kept secrets, often secrets that they have never verbalized to anyone before. When counselors respond in a caring, nonjudgmental way, clients feel relief. They leave with a lighter step than when they came.

The idea of confession has not enjoyed popularity in contemporary American society. Even among Roman Catholics, where the sacrament of penance has been valued for centuries, the practice of confession is waning. "According to the latest survey, in 1989, only 40 percent of Catholics confess their sins at least twice a year."[1] As the practice of confession has declined, the prominence of psychotherapy and counseling has increased. Americans have exchanged one form of confession for another, preferring to see a counselor for an emotional problem rather than a pastor or priest for a spiritual problem. Sharon Hymer, a psychotherapist, writes: "The decline in religious belief and church attendance in our culture has forced individuals to look elsewhere for confession. . . . With the disappearance of traditional avenues of confession, psychotherapy has arisen to provide an outlet for the confessional impulse."[2]

Though not all counseling is confessional in nature, much is. Thus, Christian counselors need to think carefully about the confessional aspects and implications of counseling. As counselors have been asked to listen to their clients' confessions, some have exaggerated their role as priest and reduced complex emotional problems to simple formulas of personal sin. They emphasize repentance and behavioral change without properly understanding the relational nature of counseling and their spiritual need for humility. Other counselors have rebelled against the confessional nature of counseling altogether and have tried to teach their clients that there is nothing to confess: "I'm okay, and you're okay." Between these two extremes is a place for competent Christian counseling, where confession is humbly accepted as a valid part of the counseling process and where the counseling relationship models the grace and kindness of Christ.

FOUNDATIONS

Psychology

The few published articles about psychology and confession are written from a variety of perspectives, sampled briefly here.

PSYCHOLOGICAL EFFECTS OF CONFESSION

Some authors have attempted to understand the effects of confession by using the tools of psychological science. Two examples of these studies include testing the impression-management effects of public confession and testing the physiological effects of private confession.

Bernard Weiner and his colleagues reported five role-playing studies to test the effects of public confession (not in a church setting).[3] They found that public confession, especially confession that is not prompted by an accusation, makes observers less angry and causes them to judge the offender as less culpable than offenders who do not confess. It is difficult to generalize the results of these studies to counseling practice because the private confession of counseling differs in significant ways from the public confession studied by the researchers. Much more research is needed before counselors understand how their views of their clients are affected by the types of confession used by the client.

James Pennebaker and colleagues have investigated the physiological effects of disclosing personal and traumatic experiences.[4] Among other measures, they used skin conductance as a measure of anxiety. Those who disclosed high levels of personal information showed lower levels of skin conductance (less anxiety) after disclosing personal information than they did after talking about innocuous topics. Thus, confession appears to have physiological benefits. However, it is important to remember that the same findings were not observed among those more cautious in their disclosing style. Thus, it is difficult to translate these findings into clear principles for counseling. One possible implication is that people who naturally disclose more in counseling will be less prone to psychosomatic ailments than those who are naturally more cautious. This is supported by another of Pennebaker's studies showing that those who expressed grief after the loss of a spouse had fewer physical ailments than those who tried to deal with their grief privately.[5]

CONFESSIONAL NATURE OF PSYCHOTHERAPY

If confession has psychological benefits, as it appears to, then how can confession be introduced into counseling? This probably requires little effort on the part of the counselor because confession is a natural, automatic part of counseling. Counselors, just by being available to clients, hear confessions much as Roman Catholic priests have for centuries. Both counselors and priests help hurting people seek restoration and the resolution of problems such as anger, guilt, and shame.[6] Counseling and religious confession both reflect the rhythm described in chapter 2: a person recognizes and admits need and is then drawn into a healing relationship through the understanding or absolving words of a priest or counselor. Swiss psychiatrist Carl Jung observed that confession to a therapist naturally produces relief because after people confess they feel reunited with the human community.[7]

Despite the confessional nature of counseling, there are distinctions between religious confession and counseling. Religious confession assumes moral error on the part of the confessor, whereas counseling usually assumes "a larger problem that is unconsciously motivated."[8] For example, if a client admits hitting his wife, a priest will focus on confession of moral error, penance, and forgiveness. A counselor, in contrast, might focus more on helping the client explore his anger about being abused himself as a child, his misconceptions about gender roles, and his current struggles for control in his marriage. The priest focuses on the immediate moral problem, whereas the counselor looks for a psychological context to help explain why the man hit his wife. Both are concerned with changing the behavior, but the methods are different. Confession assumes moral violation, and counseling assumes moral neutrality.

Although this distinction between the methods of confession and counseling is often valid, we must be careful to recognize that it is not an entirely adequate distinction because it returns us to the sin–versus–sickness dichotomy criticized in chapter 5: priests attribute problems to sin, and counselors attribute problems to sickness.

Yet Christian counselors often find themselves somewhere in the middle, believing that both sin and sickness contribute to dysfunctional human behavior. Because of this, Christian counseling should not always be morally neutral; moral discourse ought to be included in some counseling situations.[9]

Several religious psychotherapists have recently made similar recommendations, suggesting that counseling can and should, at times, have a moral dimension. Rather than perpetuating acceptance, which Richard Erickson describes as an attitude that communicates that all things are acceptable, Erickson believes psychotherapists should introduce a moral dimension in counseling by assisting clients in their desire for restoration: a process of confessing wrong, making amends, and taking responsibility for future actions. Psychologist Allen Bergin seems to agree with Erickson. In 1980, Bergin published a landmark article entitled, "Psychotherapy and Religious Values."[10] In the article he described two broad classes of values that are prominent in the mental-health fields. *Theistic* values are based on the presupposition that human morality is best understood in light of God's existence and revelation. *Clinical-Humanistic* values are based on the presupposition that humans are supreme and in charge of their own destiny. One of the differences between theistic and clinical-humanistic values involves the way confession is handled. Bergin writes of theistic values in mental health: "Personal responsibility for own harmful actions and changes in them. Acceptance of guilt, suffering, and contrition as keys to change. Restitution for harmful effects."[11] This value statement suggests that sin is sometimes an accurate and helpful attribution for many human problems. In contrast, he describes clinical-humanistic values this way: "Others are responsible for our problems and changes. Minimizing guilt and relieving suffering before experiencing its meaning. Apology for harmful effects."[12] This value statement suggests that psychological sickness, not sin, causes human problems. Thus, one of the primary distinctions between theistic and clinical-humanistic values seems to hinge on the way theistic counselors deal with clients' desires to confess wrongdoing.[13]

Should Christian counselors view clients' confessions as sin and emphasize the need for repentance and restitution, or should they view clients' confessions as resulting from sickness and emphasize the need for psychological insight and self-understanding? As discussed in the previous chapter, this dichotomy is too stark. The best counseling approach is found somewhere between these two extremes. The challenge for Christian counselors is to look at a broad psychological context for moral errors, which has traditionally distinguished counselors from clerics, and yet not slip into a moral relativism that discounts the significance of sin and the healing power of remorse and confession. This challenge is illustrated in the following case.

WHAT IF THIS HAPPENED?

R. E. Morse comes for counseling to deal with her depression. But in the midst of the third session, she unloads her deepest secret. Shortly after she had married her husband, she had a brief affair with a former boyfriend. She has never told anyone until now.

Her counselor has a choice. Which attitude should she use in talking with Ms. Morse?

> *Attitude A:* "This is a tragic event, and I can understand why it has been difficult to talk about. I want to help you think through the implications of the affair, including ways it has hurt you and others, how it can help you learn about yourself, and your need for restitution and reconciliation. The ultimate goals should be growth—that you understand yourself and others better—and forgiveness—that you experience God's forgiveness, forgive yourself, and be reconciled to those affected by your past attitudes and actions."

> *Attitude B:* "This is a bad event, and we need to understand what deep emotional needs you were trying to fill with this

affair. But there is little use in yelling at yourself or condemning yourself. Perhaps you were experiencing ambivalent feelings after your marriage, longing for intimacy that you missed as a child, and your affair was a way to cope with the loneliness and confusion you felt inside. Several years have passed, and no one appears to have been hurt by your actions, except that you are depressing yourself with self-condemning thoughts. It is time to be nice to yourself, understand the motives that compelled you toward this affair, and move ahead with your life.

Whereas attitude B reflects the belief that Ms. Morse acted out sexually and has been depressed because of psychological sickness, attitude A also emphasizes the healing nature of guilt, remorse, and restitution.

GUILT: A CONCEPT RELATED TO CONFESSION

The case of Ms. Morse raises another question that is related to confession: should guilt be encouraged or discouraged?[14] Though guilt has been theoretically linked to psychological disturbance, the relationships among religion, guilt, and disturbance have been debated vigorously. Guilt has sometimes been perceived as a harmful and self-defeating emotion accompanying religious faith.[15] At other times, guilt is perceived as an emotion that reflects empathy for others and leads to useful reparative actions.[16] Recent research suggests there may be a place for healthy guilt.

In a 1991 study, intrinsically religious participants (those whose faith is central to their lives) scored higher on a guilt-proneness scale than extrinsically religious participants (those who evaluate their religious faith in light of their other needs). Despite their proneness to guilt feelings, intrinsic participants did not report more depression or less existential well-being than extrinsic participants.[17] Similarly, June Price Tangney and her colleagues have reported several studies suggesting that proneness to guilt, unlike proneness to shame, is unrelated to psychological maladjustment.[18] In fact, recent evidence suggests that those most prone to shame-free guilt are less likely than others to experience anger, hostility, and resentment.[19]

In an analog study involving eighty-three college students, two colleagues and I presented participants with a continuous narrative containing three scenarios in which they first committed a dishonest act and then felt compelled to confess what they had done.[20] The final scenario contained a manipulation of grace or no-grace, in which half of the participants were forgiven for their act and half were not. Following each scenario, participants were tested for feelings of guilt and related behavioral and emotional responses. Those students who were highly committed to their religious faith were more prone to guilt and more inclined to confess their misdeeds than other participants; at the same time, the highly committed students were less prone to other negative emotions, such as depression, anxiety, and hostility. We concluded that some forms of guilt may be beneficial.

Several religious psychologists have noted a positive role for certain forms of guilt. S. Bruce Narramore distinguishes between constructive sorrow—a remorseful response leading to confession and reconciliation—and self-focused guilt (similar to what Tangney calls shame)—a response that damages one's self-image.[21] P. Scott Richards exhorts counselors to make a similar distinction in their work with religiously devout students: "Thus, although religiously devout students may be more prone to guilt, counselors should not assume that this is dysfunctional for them. In their desire to help clients feel better, practitioners have at times indiscriminately attempted to neutralize clients' guilt without giving sufficient consideration to whether the guilt was an appropriate emotional response to actual wrongdoings."[22]

Thus, guilt is not always a negative phenomenon. Guilt helps us understand and adhere to moral standards, supports our sense of order in the universe, and motivates us to reconcile with one another.[23] Guilt not only sometimes prevents blaming, resentment, and anger, but it can also lead to a greater understanding of God's grace. When Israel's King David committed adultery and murder, he felt deep remorse. He wrote: "Wash me thoroughly from my iniquity, and cleanse me from my sin.

For I know my transgressions, and my sin is ever before me. Against you, you alone, have I sinned, and done what is evil in your sight, so that you are justified in your sentence and blameless when you pass judgment" (Ps. 51:2-4). David's sorrowful remorse led him to marvel at God's grace rather than fall into a state of excessive self-deprecation. He later concluded: "Purge me with hyssop, and I shall be clean; wash me, and I shall be whiter than snow" (Ps. 51:7).

King David knew a simple truth that we have often overlooked in contemporary society. He knew that proper guilt and confession is the only path to forgiveness and restoration. Today we prefer to blame or excuse or even to wallow in shame. David Belgum, a theologian and counselor, observes: "Our generation may well be characterized as an age of *irresponsibility*. Rather than accepting our guilt for misdeeds, we rationalize our way out, blaming 'conditioned' causes; we attribute our behavior to our environment or heredity, or to our faulty training or lack of need-gratification."[24]

King David took a different route. He confessed his guilt and embarked on the path to reconciliation with God. When we deny or disqualify guilt from counseling, we rob our clients of opportunities for godly sorrow, repentance, and restoration.

Christian Theology

CONFESSION AND THE SACRAMENT OF PENANCE

The Christian church has always been interested in confession, but the means of confession has changed throughout the past two millennia. We know from Scripture (see Acts 19) that a form of public confession was practiced by the early church. Confession continued as an important part of early Christianity, as evidenced by written confessions of spiritual leaders. Several centuries after Christ, Saint Augustine and Saint Patrick each wrote their confessions, Augustine around A.D. 397 and Patrick around A.D. 460. Their confessions are illuminating combinations of autobiography, confessions of faith, and confessions of sin.[25]

Augustine's *Confessions* and his other writings served as a partial
foundation for scholasticism, a movement that attempted to analyze
faith intellectually. Scholasticism grew throughout the twelfth century,
and with it came the doctrine and sacrament of penance. Scholastics
believed three things were necessary for repentance: feelings of remorse,
verbal confession, and restitution. These three tenets of the doctrine of
penance seem reasonable, but the practice of repentance soon became
externalized—a matter of fulfilling the church's rules rather than a
matter of the heart. When John Calvin wrote his *Institutes of the Christian
Religion* in the mid-1500s, he sharply criticized the scholastics' doctrine
of penance and the related practice of buying indulgences from the
Catholic Church. Long before the days of Prozac, Calvin recommended medication for the scholastics: "These men are fit to be treated
by drugs for insanity rather than to be argued with."[26] In contrast to
the doctrine of penance, Calvin argued that confession should be
offered secretly to God, and when public confession was necessary, it
should be a voluntary act of contrition before other humans.

Calvin and the other Reformers called Christians to a personal
encounter with God. Before the Reformation, church members
approached the Catholic priest as a mediator to God. Thus, the
natural place to go for confession was to the priest. As a direct result
of the Reformation, Protestants now believe God can be approached directly, without an intervening cleric. Thus, confession is
personal, secret, and directly addressed to God.

This Protestant view of confession closely parallels the view of sin
presented in chapter 5. If our human problem were limited to
personal sin, then salvation could be found by confessing our personal
sins to God or one of God's representatives, such as a priest. But
because our human problem also involves original sin, our confession
must be more general than acknowledging personal acts of rebellion.
We must confess our chronic human need for God. Even on days
when we think we violate no scriptural commands, we are still
plagued by human frailties. The spirit of confession cannot be captured by the doctrine of penance; confession is a humble and contrite

posture that we should assume continually in the presence of God. Martin Luther put it this way: "When I admonish men to come to confession, I am simply urging them to be Christians."[27]

Having argued for the Protestant view of confession, it is also important to remember that the Roman Catholic views of confession and penance also have merit.[28] First, regular confession forces us to confront our sin. In the midst of everyday life, it is easy to overlook or minimize our misdeeds. Those who regularly confess wrongdoing may take sin more seriously than those who don't. Second, the act of penance—paying a price for sin—produces an awareness of the seriousness of sin. A sloppy understanding of Reformed theology produces a carelessness toward sin: "Oh well, I will always be forgiven." Penance fights this tendency by imposing consequences for sin. Third, the burden of guilt is lifted as forgiveness is granted during the sacrament of penance. This is profoundly liberating for some people.

CONFESSION AND SCRIPTURE

Given the historical turbulence regarding confession, it is important to look to Scripture to understand the proper practice of confession. Scripture describes two common uses of confession.[29] The first is the confession of faith, publicly declaring our allegiance to God. This is seen throughout the Bible. When Jesus sent out his disciples to spread the gospel, he cautioned them that they would be scorned and rejected, noting, "Everyone therefore who acknowledges me before others, I also will acknowledge before my Father in heaven; but whoever denies me before others, I also will deny before my Father in heaven" (Matt. 10:32-33). Jesus knew that some people would confess him and some would not. Later, the apostle Paul described confession of faith as an important goal of Christ's work of salvation: "Therefore God also highly exalted him and gave him the name that is above every name, so that at the name of Jesus every knee should bend, in heaven and on earth and under the earth, and every tongue should confess that Jesus Christ is Lord, to the glory of God the Father" (Phil. 2:9-11). Implicit in the confession of faith is a recognition of our need for God. We cannot reach God on our own—we must fall humbly at God's feet and ask for help.

Second, confession of sin is described throughout Scripture. When we sin, we are instructed to confess in various ways, depending on the circumstances involved. We must freely confess our sin to God. While reflecting on the goodness of God's forgiveness, King David remembered, "Then I acknowledged my sin to you, and I did not hide my iniquity; I said, 'I will confess my transgressions to the Lord,' and you forgave the guilt of my sin" (Ps. 32:5). And in 1 John 1:8-9 we are reminded of the same principle: "If we say that we have no sin, we deceive ourselves, and the truth is not in us. If we confess our sins, he who is faithful and just will forgive us our sins and cleanse us from all unrighteousness."

In addition to confessing to God, we are also obliged to confess sins to one another, especially those we have harmed. Jesus addressed this in the Sermon on the Mount when he told people not to offer sacrifices to God until relationship conflicts have been resolved with one another. "First be reconciled to your brother or sister, and then come and offer your gift" (Matt. 5:24). James gave more general instructions that encourage us to share our weaknesses and failures in the context of a loving, praying, supportive Christian community. "Therefore confess your sins to one another, and pray for one another, so that you may be healed. The prayer of the righteous is powerful and effective" (James 5:16).

WHAT IF THIS HAPPENED?

Now that Ms. Morse has confessed her adultery to her counselor, she wonders if she should also tell her husband. She looks to her counselor for advice.

This is a difficult situation, and no advice should be given reflexively without considering the implications and nuances of the specific situation. But these admonitions of Scripture should be remembered in formulating a response. Even if he does not know it, Ms. Morse's husband has been hurt, and the route to reconciliation may require Ms. Morse to confess her affair.

Scripture also refers to confessing sin to spiritual leaders. David confessed his sin to the prophet Nathan (2 Sam. 12); people confessed their sins and were baptized by John the Baptist (Matt. 3); and the believers at Ephesus confessed their sins to the apostle Paul (Acts 19). The scriptural practice of confession to spiritual leaders is always voluntary, an act of free will for the purpose of spiritual restoration. In contrast, the doctrine of penance that Calvin criticized so sharply had become obligatory: people confessed as part of a mechanized process of repentance.

Finally, we are instructed in Scripture to confess our sins to a local church body under some circumstances. If a sin affects an entire community of believers, then the sin is sometimes to be confronted or confessed publicly (see the example faced by the Corinthian church in 1 Cor. 5 and the resolution alluded to in 2 Cor. 2:6-8). In general, confession may be limited to the scope of those directly affected by the sin.

Throughout Scripture and church history, we see two common themes of confession. One is the confession of personal sin, sometimes done in the presence of a priest, the offended party, a trusted friend, or a community of believers, and sometimes offered secretly to God. The other is a general confession of faith—admitting the futility of our own attempts to grasp for meaning and acknowledging our need for God. Both types of confession require humility.

Spirituality

Confession requires humility, and humility is not easy. Often one's initial exposure to spiritual disciplines makes confession more difficult because we become so enthralled by the spiritual life that we mistakenly assume spirituality is a path to happiness rather than humility. There is often a sense of exhilaration, as if life's struggles have been immediately and permanently resolved by several weeks or months of spiritual disciplines. Confession is not appealing for those who see spiritual growth as a path to greater happiness and exuberance because confession requires us to acknowledge the chronic ache of human existence and our utter inability to transcend our sin nature with willpower alone. C. S. Lewis wrote that a "Christian's nostril is to be continually attentive to the inner cesspool." [30] The smell of sin is not a pleasant one, but it is a necessary one for Christians serious about spiritual growth.

We soon learn that the disciplines are not an end in themselves. They are not a panacea, and life's struggles continue. God calls us to a disciplined life not in order to make us feel good but to transform us by giving us a clearer understanding of ourselves and of God's character. Spiritual development causes us to be increasingly saddened by fallen human character, grieved by the effects of sin in the world, and surprised and overwhelmed by God's redemptive grace. This is the essence of humility—seeing ourselves and God accurately.

Humility must be distinguished from self-abasement. Jeremy Taylor, a seventh-century scholar, wrote that "humility does not consist in criticizing yourself, or wearing ragged clothes, or walking around submissively wherever you go. Humility consists in a realistic opinion of yourself, namely, that you are an unworthy person." [31] We are unworthy but not worthless. There is no value in seeing ourselves as utterly evil and loathsome. Rather, humility requires us to look at ourselves honestly and recognize that we are a convoluted mixture of motives, of good and bad, pure and impure, altruism and egocentrism. Humility means we understand human strengths as well as human weaknesses. We must not forget human potential and goodness because somewhere deep inside is always a glimmering urge to confess, to be restored and reconciled in meaningful relationships, to do what is right and abandon what is wrong. Dallas Willard calls this our "innate integrity." [32] We inwardly long to confess our sins to one another, to make restitution for our sins, and to find forgiveness. Confession draws us out of our secluded darkness and brings us into the light. Yet, we often resist inner urges for confession and forgiveness.

RESISTING CONFESSION

Confession involves sacrificing our good image for the sake of truth or a relationship with another. Because confession has a cost, we often resist it. There are at least two forms this resistance can take.

For some people, resistance takes the form of avoiding the spiritual life. If coming to Christ involves admitting need, then they prefer to stay away, surrounding themselves with a cloak of self-sufficiency and independence. Those who admit no need have nothing to confess.

For others, the spiritual life is appealing and rich, and the community of Christian believers is rewarding and fulfilling. Soon their spirituality becomes a source of secret pride. When churches are filled with people nursing spiritual pride, the blessings of community are overshadowed by ugly competition. Rather than being a place where Christians confess to one another, the church sometimes becomes a place where we compete with one another, trying to impress others with our spiritual maturity. Confession is difficult in this context because to confess is to shatter our fantasized persona of perfection.

WHAT IF THIS HAPPENED?

Mr. and Ms. Christensen are seeing a counselor for help with their marriage. Mr. Christensen is a deacon in the church, a pillar in the community, and an inattentive chauvinist at home. His success in life, his intentional practice of spiritual disciplines, and the respect he gets from others have made him a proud man. He resists any counseling efforts that suggest he may share some blame in the marriage problems.

Some would like to think of Mr. Christensen as a strong-willed hypocrite. Perhaps it is more accurate to see him as a vulnerable pilgrim, trying to ease his inner pain by avoiding blame and seeking approval from others.

The Christensens' counselor is wise enough to see Mr. Christensen's pain beneath his defensive and oppositional style. The counselor does two essential things: She supports Mr. Christensen by being accepting and nurturing, and she refuses to shield him or excuse him from the pain associated with his poor choices at home. As he feels accepted by his counselor, he becomes more honest with himself and his spouse. The pain of confrontation and insight is profound at times, but Mr. Christensen grows through the counseling experience.

Both those who resist confession by avoiding the spiritual life and those who resist because of secret pride are in need of the same two things that Mr. Christensen's counselor fostered: support and pain. Support draws lonely and isolated people into community. Pain draws those caught in the grip of self-sufficiency to a new understanding of need. Pain also weans us from our spiritual pride and allows us to look to God rather than reputation for strength.

Support and pain are both present in the spiritual life. In the sixteenth century, Saint John of the Cross wrote *The Dark Night of the Soul,* which describes how God walks with us on the path of spiritual growth. At first, we feel supported by God's presence— "nurtured and caressed by the Spirit" as we enter into the joy of knowing God.[33] We pray fervently, try new spiritual disciplines, and draw close to God. But with this newly discovered spiritual growth, spiritual impurities sprout and grow as well. Soon we become proud, like Mr. Christensen in the preceding example. Saint John of the Cross writes, "Such persons become too spiritual. They like to speak of 'spiritual things' all the time. They become content with their growth. They would prefer to teach rather than to be taught. They condemn others who are not as spiritual as they are. They are like the Pharisee who boasted in himself and despised the publican who was not as spiritual as he."[34] People at this stage of spiritual development fear confession because it will hurt their image. For this problem, God has a solution, though not a highly desirable one from a human perspective. The pain of the dark night of the soul draws us closer to God by removing impurities from our character.

Speaking of those on the spiritual path, Saint John continues, "There will come a time when God will bid them to grow deeper. He will remove the previous consolation from the soul in order to teach it virtue and prevent it from developing vice."[35] During this dark night, when the support and happiness we initially associated with spirituality has vanished, our character is gradually transformed. We learn to think less of ourselves and our religious piety and more about God's greatness. We learn about our spiritual pride and find paths to greater maturity. Humility—the capacity to see ourselves and God accurately—is the proper posture for confession, and our capacity for humility is forged in times of darkness, in confronting failures and weaknesses.

PSYCHOLOGICAL AND SPIRITUAL HEALTH

An accurate understanding of sin and confession does lead to humility and hope, not despair and shame. This is an essential distinction for Christian counselors because so many of those we work with feel shame instead of hope. They sometimes resist confession, assuming it will only bring greater shame.

When faced with the reality of fallen human nature, we come to a fork in the road and are left with three choices (shown in figure 5). One choice is to do nothing, to stand paralyzed in a state of shame and proclaim our worthlessness. Many people who seek counseling come in this condition. They need help to move ahead. The second choice is to confess our fallen nature, find ways of making restitution when appropriate, accept forgiveness, and be restored to healthy relationships. Confession brings psychological growth and spiritual renewal. It is "a means of healing and transforming the inner spirit."[36] Notice that this route takes time, humility, and diligence. The third choice is to seek comfort through means other than confession. For example, we can feel better by learning to tell ourselves that our faults really are not too bad or by finding unconditional acceptance in a counselor. Rather than confessing and seeking forgiveness, we attempt to ease our conscience through psychological tricks that affect our ways of thinking and feeling. This is a secularized version of what Dietrich Bonhoeffer called cheap grace: "No contrition is required, still less any real desire to be delivered from sin."[37]

FIGURE 5

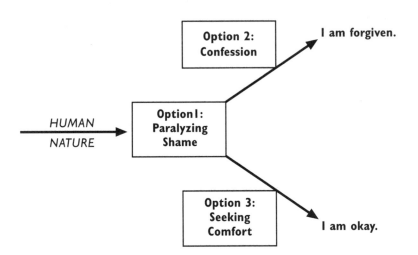

Some types of counseling, religious or not, are legitimate models of confession and forgiveness. At the end of these counseling relationships is the profound awareness, "I am forgiven." Other types of counseling are mostly ways of tricking people into feeling good again. At the end of these counseling relationships is the self-focused proclamation, "I am okay." Both routes make people feel better, but only confession brings humility and spiritual growth as well as emotional well-being.

By listing human nature as the problem in figure 5, I am not suggesting that all psychological problems are the direct result of personal sin. Many clients have problems that are more related to original sin than to personal sin. They carry scars of abandonment, rejection, abuse, and ridicule. They have learned faulty ways of adapting to life's demands or relating to others. But all psychological problems (as well as all other problems) are the direct or indirect result of fallen human nature. The questions we struggle with as counselors are, How do we understand the problem of fallenness? and How do we help our clients cope with the realities of living as fallen humans in a fallen world? Even when confession does not involve confessing specific misdeeds, an attitude of humility requires us to confess our inadequacy before God and our need for community with God and others.

Which counseling styles move clients toward healthy confession and forgiveness? This depends on the personal humility of the counselor and the nature of the counseling relationship more than the theory or specific technique the counselor uses. Some therapists— whether using behavioral, cognitive, psychodynamic, family systems, or other theories—are able to incorporate a worldview of humility and confession in their clinical work. Others are not. Some neglect confession. Some emphasize confession while neglecting to be humble. Others encourage confession and still remain humble, leading their clients to greater insight and maturity. To evaluate counseling styles that promote healing confession, we return to the same three questions asked in previous chapters. As each of the three questions is considered, it will be applied to the counseling case described here:

WHAT IF THIS HAPPENED?

Ron was sexually and emotionally abused by his parents during his childhood years. During adolescence he withdrew from his parents, began using drugs heavily, and was sexually irresponsible and promiscuous. In the mid-1970s he returned to college, became a Christian through a campus-ministry group, finished an undergraduate degree in economics, and started working. He has found it difficult to maintain steady employment over the past fifteen years, often because of personality conflicts with his supervisors. Ron has been married twice, divorced twice, and is now living on his own. His two children live with their mothers. He seeks counseling because of chronic feelings of emptiness and depression.

Ron is considering three counselors. Which should he choose?

Counselor A believes Ron's problems are caused by his childhood sexual abuse, which he has never dealt with adequately. As a child, Ron learned to think of himself as helpless and powerless, even over his own body. In counseling, he needs to be empowered, to explore and express his anger, and to rid himself of the guilt and shame he has carried with him for many years. What happened to Ron is not his fault. He needs to replace his shame with appropriate anger toward his abusers.

Counselor B believes Ron's problems are bitterness and a lack of repentance. Although Ron has been a Christian for more than fifteen years, he has not forgiven his parents and taken responsibility for his own immoral choices. Ron's bitterness toward his parents is obvious in his conflictual relationships with supervisors and his inability to stay married. Ron needs to confess his bitterness, forget what lies behind, and press on toward greater obedience and spiritual maturity.

Counselor C believes the sexual abuse that Ron experienced as a child is a tragic example of sin. Because of the abuse, Ron has carried shame feelings and has made poor choices for many years. To be liberated from his prison of shame, Ron must experience a new type of relationship with his counselor. In the context of a safe, nonjudgmental, honest counseling relationship, Ron will be free to explore his thoughts and feelings openly and to grieve the loss of a childhood. With time, and in the context of this safe relationship, Ron will be free to consider ways he has hurt others. Though not a sexual abuser, Ron has caused others pain just as his parents caused him pain. With this awareness, Ron will better understand his need for God's gracious redemption and will be freed from his prison of shame.

Counselor A and counselor C have much in common. Both value and emphasize a well-crafted, safe therapeutic relationship. Both believe Ron needs time and comfort to explore the losses of his past. They also have one important difference: Counselor A believes Ron can best replace his shame by understanding his anger toward his abusers, whereas counselor C believes Ron can best replace his shame with a sense of empathy for his abusers and by working through his grief about the past.

Will This Help Establish a Healthy Sense of Self?

COUNSELOR A

Counselor A neglects the role of confession in counseling. Counselor B emphasizes confession but does so in an aggressive manner that emphasizes power more than humility. Counselor C humbly supports Ron's need for confession in the context of a healing counseling relationship.

Using the scheme presented in figure 5, counselor A wants to bring Ron to the point where he believes, "I am okay." Counselor A sees no need for confession or forgiveness because Ron is the one who has been victimized. After seeing counselor A, Ron may feel relief from his depression, but his sense of identity may lack the humility that characterizes the spiritual life. If depression is anger turned inward, as Sigmund Freud believed, then counselor A will help Ron turn his anger outward where it belongs. But then what? Are abuse survivors destined for a life of anger? Each time Ron thinks of his parents, he may boil inside with anger. His anger frees him from the shame that has disabled him for years and may represent legitimate psychological progress, but he still lacks the empathy, insight, and humility of true spirituality.

Ron may correctly look to his childhood abuse as an explanation for what went wrong in his life. The trauma of abuse inevitably leaves emotional scars and psychological dysfunction. But what can be said of Ron's own choices that have hurt himself and others? Ron, like his parents, was damaged by a previous generation, and, like his parents, he has made choices that hurt the next generation. Yet the only confession that counselor A encourages Ron to consider is that of his parents' sin. This approach does not produce an accurate sense of self. Instead, it produces an identity of victimization that not only perpetuates anger, pride, and bitterness but also inhibits insight.

COUNSELOR B

Counselor B makes none of these errors but neglects humility. Using the scheme presented in figure 5, counselor B wants to bring Ron to the point where he believes, "I am forgiven." This is the proper goal for Christian counseling, but counselor B may not accomplish the goal as successfully as intended. By minimizing the impact of childhood sexual abuse and confronting Ron with his personal sin of bitterness, counselor B ignores the effects of shame in Ron's life. Indeed, this approach may add to Ron's shame. If Ron complies and appears to improve in counseling, it may be due only to Ron's desire to please and earn approval from his counselor. If Ron confesses his sin of bitterness and his counselor seems pleased with Ron's confession, then Ron will feel less depressed, and both will call the counseling successful. But is it really successful? Does Ron really feel forgiven by God, or does he feel okay because he has earned his counselor's approval?

Counselor B's approach resembles the sacrament of penance that the Reformers found objectionable. The counselor, an agent of God, hears the confession of a sinner, and the sinner is granted forgiveness. In centuries past, this arrangement gave the priest too much power, power that ultimately corrupted the effectiveness of the church and led to the religious revolt we call the Reformation. In this case, however, counselor B carries even more power than the priest who hears confession because the counselor not only accepts the confession but also points out the sin. By teaching Ron about the sin of bitterness and eliciting a confession and penitent attitude, counselor B assumes the problem is solved. But the power dynamic in the counseling relationship is overlooked. If Ron has confessed to please his counselor, it is not out of true understanding and conviction. Confession, unlike seeking approval, requires an honest look at oneself.

It is a mistake to assume that eliciting confession is a quick process. Many human burdens are buried beneath years of pain and layers of defense and will be understood only in the context of a safe counseling relationship that has lasted several weeks or months. "Confessions can be viewed as a multilayered reflection of self."[38] By being confrontive, counselor B may elicit an initial confession but will slam the door on honest self-exploration and further disclosure.

COUNSELOR C

Counselor C has the right idea. Counselor C believes that more than just admitting personal sin, confession involves acknowledging and grappling with our human limitations and our ache for intimacy with God and others. It is the confession of faith, which requires us to humbly acknowledge our need for God, that frees us from shame, brings us close to a gracious Redeemer, and makes us able to confess our sins.

By providing an honest, safe counseling environment, counselor C helps Ron to explore his past and present thoughts and feelings. Rather than viewing Ron as the product of his own selfish sin, counselor C sees Ron as immersed in the same flood of depravity as all other humans. Ron has been violated by others and has chosen his own evil, yet there is hope for Ron if he can see his need and reach beyond himself for help.

Counselor C wants Ron to come to a point of feeling forgiven but not just forgiven for specific personal sins. The goal is for Ron to recognize his need for someone beyond himself and to feel loved, accepted, and forgiven in the midst of growing relationship with

Christ. The counselor is not merely teaching Ron about forgiveness but is living out the essential quality of humility that gives forgiveness meaning and encourages honest self-exploration.

ENCOURAGING HONEST SELF-EXPLORATION

WHAT IF THIS HAPPENED?

During one session, Ron sighs, puts his head between his palms, and announces, "I feel so worthless. Yeah, my parents abused me, but I've done some bad things, too. I didn't abuse my kids, but I abandoned them. Is that any better?" Each of the counselors described here would respond differently.

Counselor A: "Ron, haven't you been hard enough on yourself? Is it really yourself you are angry with, or is it someone else?"

Counselor B: "You're asking an important question, Ron. God is stirring inside of you and asking you to answer. How do you suppose God would have you answer the question you are asking?"

Counselor C: "You're feeling surrounded by pain, Ron. Pain for what others have done to you, pain for what you have done to others, pain about how difficult life can be."

Whereas counselor A uses Ron's statement as a chance to externalize responsibility, and counselor B uses it to identify sin, counselor C uses it to establish empathy and encourage deeper exploration and sincere confession of need. Both counselor A and counselor B close the door on further self-exploration by asking for a specific response from Ron. In contrast, counselor C keeps the door open by communicating understanding and empathy without calling for a specific response. Counselor C might come from any of several theoretical persuasions that value insight—cognitive, psychodynamic, humanistic, family systems, or another—and is committed to attitudes of humility and empathy that free Ron to explore and understand his thoughts and feelings.

Will This Help Establish a Healthy Sense of Need?

COUNSELOR A

Counselor A communicates: "You are not a sinner but a victim of someone else's sin. You are okay." After counseling, Ron may feel better, but he may also struggle with the nagging doubts of unconfessed failure. A danger of externalizing blame is that clients sometimes stop considering their personal responsibilities and inadequacies. The impulses to confess feelings of loneliness, isolation, and guilt that bring clients to counseling are easily smothered by counselors who insist their clients are victims of the past. Clients learn to construct a facade of shame resistance but lack opportunities to explore the real sources of their shame because their counselors refuse to take confessions seriously.

COUNSELOR B

At the other extreme, when counselors encourage clients to internalize blame, psychopathology may worsen. Rather than producing a sincere awareness of need, this may produce a profound sense of helplessness and add to feelings of shame. This is illustrated by counselor B. Ron may learn to express remorse and exercise a surface-level form of confession, but he has not yet explored the depths and consequences of his childhood disappointment and anger. Confessing is not just listing our sins; it is letting another see who we really are. Ron is not prepared for true confession after seeing counselor B because he himself does not yet fully understand who he is.

COUNSELOR C

Counselor C helps Ron understand both internal and external attributions for his current situation. He has been hurt by people and situations beyond his control, and he has hurt others. Like every other human, he has sinned and has been sinned against. In a counseling context such as this, clients are freed to understand themselves accurately, to present themselves to a caring counselor without fear of reprimand or ridicule, and in the process, to recognize their need for others.

Will This Help Establish a Healing Relationship?

Though the counseling relationship is not spiritually redemptive in itself, it models our redemptive relationship with Christ. In the context of Christ's love and grace, we are freed to understand our human limits and needs and to reach upward for help. It is not our awareness of sin that comes first; it is only by God's prevenient grace (grace that comes before salvation) that we are able to see our sin and experience salvation (see Eph. 2:8-9). Grace comes first, then recognition of sin. We are freed to understand our weaknesses *after,* not *before,* we experience grace. This is the kind of relationship counselor C attempts to provide Ron.

Imagine the spiritual consequences if God related to us in a way similar to the way counselor A or counselor B did. If God were like counselor A, we would be saved because we are good people. Perhaps God would line us up, from best to worst, and then choose a dividing point. Those on one side are evil, abusive people, and those on the other side are powerless victims. Those who are abusers should confess, and those who are victims should feel angry at the abusers. Victims will be loved, and abusers will be punished. Does this sound right? Of course not. God does not rate our morality on a bell curve and then accept everyone who is above the median. God recognizes and grieves over our sin but extends grace regardless of our merit. "For there is no distinction, since all have sinned and fall short of the glory of God; they are now justified by his grace as a gift, through the redemption that is in Christ Jesus, whom God put forward as a sacrifice of atonement by his blood, effective through faith. He did this to show his righteousness, because in his divine forbearance he had passed over the sins previously committed; it was to prove at the present time that he himself is righteous and that he justifies the one who has faith in Jesus" (Rom. 3:22-26).

If God were like counselor B, our relationship with God would depend on our capacity to recognize and confess specific acts of personal sin. Christian faith would mutate to legalism, and we would all live in fear.

Thankfully, God loves us first, then draws us into a relationship where we are able to see the pervasive effects of personal and original sin. In the safety of God's loving arms, we are able to see ourselves honestly, confess our needs and sins to God, and savor the healing of redemptive grace.

None of us can replicate this perfectly in our counseling relationships or other relationships, but like counselor C, we can set this as our goal for a healing relationship. The interpersonal connection of counseling, or of caring community, is what makes confession bearable.[39]

FACING THE CHALLENGES

Challenge 1: Moving from Two Areas of Competence to Three

Most of us trained in psychology have learned a particular set of values regarding remorse and confession. We have learned to listen carefully to our clients' guilt feelings and self-condemning thoughts, then to help them reinterpret their story to relieve feelings of shame and often to externalize responsibility for their bad experiences and feelings. This is useful with many clients.

WHAT IF THIS HAPPENED?

Since childhood, Susan has blamed herself for all the bad in her life. Her mother, saddled with the excessive responsibility of four children and two jobs, often screamed at Susan, told her that she was worthless and that she should never have been born. Susan internalized those words and now berates herself frequently, reminding herself that she is worthless and would be better off dead.

A competent counselor, Christian or otherwise, will help Susan be kinder to herself. A cognitive therapist will help her change her self-talk to be less condemning and more affirming. A behaviorist might help her find success experiences and encourage Susan to reward her successes with positive self-statements. A psychodynamic therapist will help Susan unlock the shame of the past in order to understand the difference between her mother's words and her own view of herself. A humanistic therapist will provide a nurturing, safe, accepting relationship where Susan can learn to be nicer to herself. All these approaches have merit, and any will probably help Susan feel better and see herself more accurately.

Unfortunately, the popularization of psychology has resulted in good ideas being overapplied and misused. Counselors need to free clients like Susan from their shame, and sometimes we need to free people from excessive burdens of guilt. But too often we have also tried to free people from appropriate guilt and from acknowledging their need for God and others. The result is a popular psychology that promotes independence and self-sufficiency while it undermines the spiritual life. Though many competent psychotherapists, Christian and non-Christian, do not accept the prevailing dogma of guiltless individualism, popular psychology books have saturated society. As a result, many people have come to associate psychology with irresponsible freedom and self-centeredness.

If Susan reads a popular psychology book instead of seeing a competent therapist, she may rid herself of shame by taking on the identity of a self-sufficient, angry victim of past abusers. Susan needs to be freed of her shame, but not from all feelings of guilt because accurate guilt leads to greater self-understanding and ushers us into a healing process of confession, remorse, forgiveness, and redemption.

Competence in the spiritual life calls us to be critics of many contemporary popular psychology perspectives and invites us back to the ancient process of acknowledging human need, confessing, and finding forgiveness in the context of caring community. Saint

Augustine knew that healing was found not in self-centeredness but in confession and seeking God's favor: "Accept the sacrifice of my confessions from the ministry of my tongue, which Thou has formed and stirred up to confess unto Thy name. Heal Thou all my bones, and let them say, O Lord, who is like unto Thee?"[40] Spiritually sensitive counseling requires us to accept, even encourage, our clients' desires to cry out for help in the midst of their need. Crying out, confessing need, is a vital part of the healing process.

Challenge 2: Blurred Personal-Professional Distinctions

In the case of Ron, counselor B and counselor C were each committed to helping Ron come to a point of healthy confession, but only counselor C was effective. What was the difference? Humility. Humility is a product of personal training, not professional expertise. Christian counselors who personally practice the discipline of confession train themselves in humility and become more effective in the counseling office.

Christian counselors may exercise the personal discipline of confession in at least two ways. First, private confession to God helps us recognize our continual need for spiritual sustenance. This involves confession of sin, and it also involves ongoing confession of faith. We ought to remind ourselves every day, every opportunity we have, that we need wisdom and strength and mercy because our human abilities are limited and tainted by sin. In this continual confession, we remind ourselves that we are weak and that we long for God. We would prefer to be strong, but we are not. The apostle Paul asked God three times to remove a nagging problem, but the problem persisted. Paul's subsequent confession of need has been quoted many times through the intervening centuries: "So, I will boast all the more gladly of my weaknesses, so that the power of Christ may dwell in me. Therefore I am content with weaknesses, insults, hardships, persecutions, and calamities for the sake of Christ; for whenever I am weak, then I am strong" (2 Cor. 12:9-10).

Second, we can confess our needs and struggles to one another. Although personal needs can be discussed in the context of friendships, fellowship groups, and trusting marriages, professional difficulties often cannot be disclosed in these circles because of confidentiality concerns. Thus, many counselors seek help in the form of peer consultation, clinical supervision, or personal therapy.[41]

As counselors, our personal practice of confession affects our professional work. As humbling as it is to seek out personal therapy or to discuss counseling failures with a clinical supervisor, these risky acts of disclosure help us understand the role of confession in emotional and spiritual healing and make us more effective counselors.

Challenge 3: Expanded Definitions of Training

How do counselors train themselves for confession in counseling? The answer to this question depends on how one anticipates using confession in counseling.

CONFESSION AS A SPECIFIC COUNSELING TECHNIQUE

Some counselors may wish to use confession as a deliberate technique in counseling. For example, when working with couples, it may be helpful to take time during one or more counseling sessions for both spouses to confess their regrets and shortcomings to each other. Also, participants in many twelve-step recovery programs learn to confess misdeeds to those they have hurt in the past.

Most Christian counselors do not frequently use confession as a specific counseling technique. In a recent survey among members of the Christian Association for Psychological Studies (CAPS), respondents reported using instruction in repentance or confession with approximately one-third of their clients.[42] And when Christian counseling training program directors were surveyed, confession was found to have little or no emphasis in most curricula.[43]

Though Christian counselors use specific instruction in confession with only one-third of their clients, this need not be cause for alarm. Many clients come with problems that are unrelated or only marginally related to guilt feelings. To insist on repentance or confession might derail effective counseling in these instances. Also, many Christian counselors may value confession in counseling but do not attempt to reduce confession to specific counseling techniques.

CONFESSION AS A POSTURE FOR LIFE

Some views of confession, including the one presented in this chapter, do not lend themselves to specific counseling techniques. Instead, confession may be viewed as an effective posture for life and not just as expressions of remorse offered in the counseling office. From this perspective, counseling helps people learn to live humbly, admitting their weaknesses to another and drawing support from a safe counseling relationship and from knowing God. Counseling, because of its confessional nature, gives opportunity for clients to learn humility, what Andrew Murray calls the "root of every virtue." At best, confession becomes a way of life, a habit of holiness.

But this presents a problem: Counselors cannot simply walk into the office announcing that their clients need to be more humble and need to confess their sins. The very act of making such an announcement models arrogance and suppresses honest self-exploration. So how can counselors train themselves to promote honesty and humility in the counseling office? By becoming humble themselves.

Christian counselors, like clients, are healthiest when they view confession and humility as essential components of spiritual and emotional maturity. While some counselors practice autonomously, seemingly certain of their choices and techniques, others practice with humility, seeking advice from colleagues, praying for guidance, and even admitting uncertainty. This type of confessional posture is difficult to teach in the classroom, but it can nonetheless be included as part of counselor training.

In the Wheaton Doctor of Psychology program, students meet in small groups each week to discuss their clinical work with a faculty preceptor.[44] Clinical faculty members also meet together to discuss their private clinical work. In each of these groups we ask questions and confront our feelings of uncertainty. Should I refer this client to another counselor? Am I being sensitive to the cultural context of my client? What might happen if I pray aloud with this client? How do I deal with my feelings of anger or attraction toward this client? What should I do when I don't know what to say in the middle of a counseling session? Are there scriptural principles that should be applied in this situation? What happens when clients don't get better? Faculty do not have all the answers to these questions, but we are able to encourage students to keep refining the questions, find answers when available, and maintain a posture of authenticity and confession. After training is completed, counselors are wise to continue asking these questions. Finding a group of peers who are willing to adopt a confessional posture regarding their work is a useful way to find support and build a community of counselors who help one another. Whenever we are tempted to be complacent and satisfied with our knowledge or maturity, we should remember the wise words of Thomas à Kempis: "If it seemeth to thee that thou knowest many things, and understandest them well, know also that there are many more things which thou knowest not. Be not high-minded, but rather confess thine ignorance."[45]

Challenge 4: Confronting Dominant Views of Mental Health

In one sense, confession is quite compatible with contemporary views of mental health. The essence of counseling is confession. Clients cast off masks and disclose to counselors secrets they have locked away for years. With confession comes emotional release: feelings of guilt and remorse, and tears. After confession, clients often feel relieved and clean.[46] Unlike the topics discussed in previous chapters (Scripture, prayer, and confronting sin), confession is seen by most counselors, regardless of their religious persuasions, as a valuable part of counseling.

Are there differences between the prevailing use of confession in counseling and a Christian understanding of confession? I suspect there are more similarities than differences, but one potentially important difference is the one shown in figure 5. Whereas most forms of counseling are confessional in nature, the outcome of confession is different in Christian counseling. Redemption in traditional counseling is found in the counseling relationship itself. In Christian counseling, we try to live out a redemptive relationship while serving a greater Redeemer. One points toward "I am okay"; the other points toward "I am forgiven."

WHAT IF THIS HAPPENED?

Roger confesses a secret to his counselor. When he was sixteen, he screamed at his mother, "You're always complaining about how sick you are, but you don't care about anyone else! I wish I could just have a normal mother." She died of congestive heart failure three days later.

Roger's counselor listens carefully, allows Roger to express his pain and grief, and empathizes with how difficult his mother's death must have been. Roger feels a sense of relief from the shame and sadness that have haunted him for many years. During the following sessions, Roger feels better and rapidly moves toward termination. Roger started counseling believing that he was an ungrateful, evil, worthless person. He ends counseling believing that though he regrets some things about his past, he is okay and worthwhile. Roger has seen a competent counselor and feels better as a result.

Competent Christian counseling might look very similar to the counseling Roger received in this example. A Christian counselor would also listen empathically and intently to Roger's confession, allow him to express feelings of shame and remorse, and avoid judgmental or harsh statements. But in the sessions that follow the confession, the counseling may move in a slightly different direction. The first counselor moves Roger toward "I am okay," while the Christian counselor moves Roger toward "I am forgiven." These two examples illustrate the difference.

EXAMPLE 1

Roger: I feel glad that I told you about my mom a few weeks ago, and I have experienced a lot of relief during the past weeks. I really feel a lot better. But sometimes I start thinking about it again, and I just feel overwhelmed with shame *(tears form in his eyes).*

Counselor: What do you suppose the next step is? What will it take for you to feel okay about yourself?

From here, the session is focused on healthy forms of self-talk to help relieve the shame Roger feels. For example, "That was a long time ago. I'm sorry about what I said, but there is no use wallowing in guilt. Mom would want me to get on with my life."

EXAMPLE 2

Roger: I feel glad that I told you about my mom a few weeks ago, and I have experienced a lot of relief during the past weeks. I really feel a lot better. But sometimes I start thinking about it again, and I just feel overwhelmed with shame *(tears form in his eyes).*

Christian Counselor: What do you suppose the next step is? What will it take for you to feel forgiven?

From here, the session is focused on Roger's spiritual life and how he views God as harsh and punitive, just as he perceived his father. He and his counselor arrange some homework assignments using visualization, Scripture memory, and self-talk that help him see God more accurately.

In one case, the counseling relationship is an end in itself, and in the other case, the counseling relationship points Roger toward a closer connection with God. Not all clients are interested in considering their spiritual lives in counseling; but for those who are, Christian counselors can help them experience forgiveness as well as relief from shame.

Challenge 5: Establishing a Scientific Base

Unlike some other topics considered in this book, confession and the role of appropriate guilt in mental health appear to be of growing scientific interest. The studies that have been published to date, many of which were reviewed earlier in this chapter, suggest that confession promotes health and that some forms of guilt are helpful. Furthermore, people who are deeply committed to their religious values appear more likely than others to experience healthy forms of guilt and confession. Mounting scientific evidence suggests that Christian counselors should value confession as part of the counseling process.

Challenge 6: Defining Relevant Ethical Standards

An important ethical principle for health-care professionals, dating back to the Hippocratic oath, is to "treat people with respect for their dignity as human beings."[47] Christian counselors, and all health professionals, strive to treat people with kindness and courtesy.

Most Christian counselors are good about introducing a friendly, human touch into their counseling work. In a recent national survey of 500 Christian counselors, a colleague and I found that 94 percent use self-disclosure, at least rarely, in their counseling work; 98 percent call clients by first names; and 95 percent have clients address them by first name, at least on occasion. Though some ardent psychodynamic therapists believe any touch is threatening to a client, 99 percent of Christian counselors disagree and are willing to shake clients' hands.[48] This appears to be good news: Christian counselors are committed to treating people with friendliness and kindness.

Though the news is good, viewing confession as a vital part of therapy introduces at least two risks that Christian counselors ought to consider. First, if confession is viewed only as admitting personal sin, it is difficult for a counselor to maintain humility and, thus, a respect for the client's dignity. Counselors who believe their job is to help clients identify and repent of specific acts of disobedience are placing themselves in a position of arbitrary authority where arrogance is difficult to escape. Arrogance and respect for a client's dignity do not go well together. It seems better to view confession as a lifestyle that is practiced by a counselor and learned by clients because of the collaborative nature of counseling. Confession from this perspective is more often a confession of general need than a confession of specific sin. Counselor and client together acknowledge the limits, weaknesses, and needs associated with being human, and look for strength in Christian faith and community.

Second, some counselors may attempt to model humility and confession through excessive self-disclosure. By advocating an attitude of humility and a general posture of confession, I do not mean to imply that counselors should relate personal incidents of weakness and failure to clients. As discussed briefly in chapter 5, too much self-disclosure on the part of the counselor can muddle and interfere with the counseling process. This role reversal of the counselor-client relationship is inevitably harmful and is one of the predictors of sexualized counseling relationships.[49]

Self-talk, not self-disclosure, is the means by which a counselor can become humble and develop a posture of confession. Throughout a counseling session, we talk to ourselves, telling ourselves how we are doing and how the client is doing. An attitude of confession requires us to remind ourselves of our own weaknesses and vulnerabilities. As clients describe their feelings of fear, anger, shame, guilt, or loneliness, we remind ourselves that life is a struggle and that we all are vulnerable to pain. As clients confess mistakes, we remind ourselves that God has dealt graciously with us for past mistakes and that we can be ministers of that grace to our clients. This inward attitude of confession and humility helps create a counseling environment of respect for the client's dignity.

SUMMARY

Blaise Pascal wrote in the seventeenth century: "If man was not made for God, why is he only happy in God? If man was made for God, why is he so opposed to God?"[50] This observation is an apt summary of the contemporary practice of confession in counseling. On one hand, there seems to be an internal longing for God, what Pascal described as a "God-shaped vacuum." This longing is seen in our human desire to confess our misdeeds and our need for forgiveness. To be sure, this longing has become completely secularized for some people, even to the point that it is not recognized as God-directed. Though the changes of the Reformation, the Enlightenment, and postmodernism have taken the practice of confession away from the organized church and turned it over to psychotherapists, it is the inner, God-given urge for confession and forgiveness that makes both penance and therapy effective.

On the other hand, we have opposed God in our practice of confession. Some people have secularized the urge for confession by resisting God's call to humility and caring community. Psychotherapists do important work, but without religious substance they cannot replace the spiritual necessity of confessing our need for God. Others, often Christians, have opposed God more subtly, exhibiting personal pride and arrogance while calling clients to humility and confession.

Spiritually sensitive confession in Christian counseling calls us to a place of humility and compassion. All of us, clients and counselors together, are needy people crying to a gracious God for mercy. Confession gives voice to our cries and hope for forgiveness.

7/ FORGIVENESS

written with Katheryn Rhoads Meek

If the human body were not capable of repairing itself, by the time we reached adulthood, each of us would be an ugly mass of abrasions, bruises, incisions, and infections. Fortunately, each mosquito bite, scrape, and injury is healed by a sophisticated physiological repair system that restores us to health.

Similarly, if there were no way to repair injured interpersonal relationships, each of us would have a long list of enemies. People on the list would include both those who have treated us poorly and those we have hurt with insensitive words and actions. Fortunately, as with our physical bodies, we have been graciously granted an interpersonal healing mechanism so that we do not have to develop such a list. Forgiveness is God's gift, modeled perfectly in the work of Jesus Christ and reflected dimly but frequently in human interactions.

But there is an important difference. Physiological healing is autonomic and effortless; our body does the work in the background of consciousness. Interpersonal healing, in contrast, usually requires deliberate work, conscious effort, and often extraordinary courage. The work of forgiveness is arduous and difficult, and counselors are often called on for help.

WHAT IF THIS HAPPENED?

Ms. Hurt sees a counselor to help her deal with consequences of childhood sexual abuse. After a strong therapeutic relationship

has been built, she offers her counselor some of her memories,
horrific stories of being forced to have sexual intercourse during
her early teenage years. Her abuser, an uncle, still lives in the
same town and desires to have a relationship with Ms. Hurt.
Ms. Hurt has had no contact with him for three years.

Counselors encounter many clients like Ms. Hurt and face a
number of complex questions related to situations like these. Should
Ms. Hurt be encouraged to forgive her uncle? Should her anger be
encouraged? Is reconciliation an appropriate goal for Ms. Hurt and
her uncle? Should Ms. Hurt seek civil or criminal restitution, or
should she at least ask that her uncle pay for counseling?

This case illustrates the difficult questions surrounding the concept of forgiveness in Christian counseling. The questions are so
complex and the permutations of possible counseling situations so
numerous that no simple answers can be offered in a brief chapter
such as this. Rather, my goal is to raise pertinent issues and make
recommendations for Christian counselors to consider so that each
unique counseling situation can be carefully evaluated in a psychologically and spiritually sensitive manner.

Before discussing the nature of forgiveness in Christian counseling, it is important to distinguish forgiveness from several impostors
and related concepts. First, forgiving is sometimes confused with
excusing. Concluding that "it wasn't that big a deal" is not the same
as forgiveness. Excusing is casual and routine, but forgiveness requires sustained effort, usually over a long period of time. Any form
of interpersonal forgiveness that is portrayed as quick and easy
cannot be true forgiveness, though it is also true that forgiveness
becomes easier with practice and spiritual development.

Second, forgiveness is sometimes confused with denial or passive
acceptance. Remaining silent and refusing to confront in the presence of an offense is not the same as forgiving. Passive acceptance
emphasizes keeping peace at any cost, even if silent resentments are

harbored for years; whereas forgiveness first involves recognizing and grieving over the damage that has been done, then choosing to release the negative emotions associated with the offender.

Third, forgiveness is not self-blame. Forgiving another does not require us to accept responsibility for what went wrong. At times we may share responsibility for the problem, and at other times we may not. In either case, forgiveness is possible.

Fourth, forgiveness is not always associated with remorse and repentance on the part of the offending party. At times, people have successfully forgiven those who refuse to accept responsibility for their actions.

Fifth, forgiveness and reconciliation are not the same. Though reconciliation requires forgiveness, forgiveness does not always require reconciliation. At times, it is right to forgive yet unwise to enter back into a relationship with one who lacks remorse and is likely to offend again.

A clear understanding of forgiveness is an essential starting point for Christian counselors. We can begin to understand forgiveness by looking at the three foundations considered throughout this book: psychology, theology, and spirituality.

FOUNDATIONS

Psychology

Not many years ago it seemed that the psychological community had almost completely ignored the topic of forgiveness. Psychologists worked every day to help heal fragmented relationships and mend wounds from the past, yet they rarely discussed forgiveness with their clients. Between 1980 and 1984, psychology journals published only thirty-two articles related to forgiveness. Things have changed rapidly over the past decade, however, and now forgiveness is a burgeoning topic of discussion and debate within the field of psychology. Between 1990 and 1994, psychology journals published ninety articles related to forgiveness, almost a 300 percent increase from the same period in the previous decade.

Psychologists have strong and varying opinions about the place of forgiveness in psychology. There are at least three perspectives. First, some psychologists are opposed to any use of forgiveness in therapy.[1] Second, some see forgiveness as beneficial because it promotes the mental health of the forgiver. Here, forgiveness is essentially reduced to a clinical technique aimed at providing the client with relief from the often destructive consequences of relational struggles—consequences such as anger, bitterness, and resentment.[2] Third, some counselors consider forgiveness to be an extension of Christian duty.[3] Some in this third group also fit in the second group. That is, they see forgiveness as a response of obedience to God with personally beneficial consequences.

Because of the limited scope of this chapter, we will consider only these three perspectives. However, it is important to note that these categories do not adequately capture the entire forgiveness literature in psychology. Many other professionals have written about different aspects of forgiveness: granting and seeking forgiveness;[4] distinguishing forgiveness from other constructs;[5] developing methods of measuring interpersonal forgiveness;[6] the relationship between psychological theory and forgiveness;[7] the emotional process required for authentic forgiveness;[8] and ways to use forgiveness in counseling practice.[9]

OPPOSITION TO FORGIVENESS IN THERAPY

Although the gist of the forgiveness literature tends to focus on its power as a therapeutic technique, several authors either completely reject it or put rigid boundaries on its use. Psychodynamic therapist Alice Miller globally writes against the pursuit of any form of either forgiveness or reconciliation. In her book *Banished Knowledge,* she rebukes her colleagues who advocate forgiveness and makes every attempt to distance herself from them.[10] Miller believes that forgiveness is detrimental to patients and is almost always done out of a false sense of moral obligation.

Other authors address problems with forgiveness in discussing sexual abuse. Ellen Bass and Laura Davis devote a section of their best-selling book, *The Courage to Heal,* to the topic of forgiveness. They maintain that it is necessary for sexual abuse victims to forgive only themselves, never the perpetrators. The authors say to those who have religious convictions about forgiveness, "If you have strong religious ties, particularly Christian ones, you may feel it is your sacred duty to forgive. This just isn't true. If there is such a thing as divine forgiveness, it's God's job, not yours."[11] Bass and Davis argue that it is both "insulting" and "minimizing" to encourage an abuse victim to forgive an abuser.[12]

Returning to the example at the beginning of this chapter, if Ms. Hurt were to see a counselor who opposes forgiveness, she would be encouraged to explore her pain, grasp her anger, grieve her losses, and move ahead with her life. Forgiveness would never be discussed unless Ms. Hurt brought it up, and then the discussion might be quickly discouraged.

FORGIVENESS AS A CLINICAL TECHNIQUE

If Ms. Hurt saw a different counselor, one who encouraged her to work toward forgiveness, the counseling goals might be quite different. Ms. Hurt's counselor might help her release her feelings of bitterness and anger and ultimately forgive her uncle. Why? Because it will help Ms. Hurt feel better. Just as the abuse in her past has done her great harm, so the bitterness and resentment in the present continue to hurt her each day. By letting go of her resentment, she may help herself feel better.

Similarly, couples in conflict may function better after they forgive one another. Worthington and DiBlasio advocate "mutual forgiveness" in couples therapy.[13] These are good uses of forgiveness, but they sometimes result in an unfortunate separation of forgiveness and religion.

Those who use forgiveness in counseling because it helps people feel better often acknowledge the religious meaning of forgiveness, then attempt to separate forgiveness from its religious ties in order to incorporate it into their clinical work with both Christian and non-Christian clients. For example, Donald Hope advocates forgiveness as an effective tool with abuse victims. He portrays the healing benefits of forgiveness by describing a counseling case where a man, after becoming involved in an evangelical church group, forgave his alcoholic father for years of heartache, trauma, and abuse. After forgiving his father under the direction of a minister, dramatic changes took place in him: his current relationships improved; he became a more active and loving parent; and he thought less critically of himself.[14] Hope connects this moving transformation to the one act of forgiveness, failing to consider the possible life-changing effects of this man's new religious faith. Perhaps what prompted this client's act of forgiveness was a deep awareness of his own failings and need for forgiveness and mercy. His experience of grace might naturally have led him to adopt a humble attitude toward himself and others. His newly discovered Christian belief system may have caused this one act of forgiveness to produce the emotionally beneficial consequences.

Forgiveness, in its theological and spiritual context, is profound, life giving, and transforming. When we remove the religious context and think of forgiveness only as a clinical technique, we risk losing the essence of forgiveness. The Human Development Study Group, devoted to understanding forgiveness in psychology, warns: "A definition that exclusively emphasizes forgiveness as the reduction of negative emotions may lead clients away from resentment or hatred, but into a cold neutrality that is not forgiveness."[15] Forgiveness finds life and meaning in Christianity, but when the faith structure is removed, it can easily degenerate into this state of cold neutrality.

FORGIVENESS AS A CHRISTIAN DUTY

A third approach to forgiveness is to view it as an obligation for those who desire to live a Christian life. If Ms. Hurt's counselor embraced this perspective, the therapist might instruct Ms. Hurt that she has been forgiven by God and that her Christian obligation is to forgive her abuser. Her counselor recognizes that forgiveness may take time, honest exploration of her feelings of anger, and grief over what she has lost because of the abuse; but ultimately she has a duty to forgive.

Jared Pingleton suggests that therapists recognize and attempt to cultivate in clients an understanding of three essential elements of the forgiveness process: "(a) forgiveness can only be received from God if given to others, (b) forgiveness can only be given to others if received from self, and (c) forgiveness can only be given to self if received from God."[16] This model demonstrates that the ability to bestow forgiveness on self and others is inextricably linked to the ability to receive it from God.

Cultivating in our clients an awareness of the Christian duty to forgive requires balance. On one hand, if we resort to didactic techniques or attempt to rush the process of forgiveness, we risk interfering with the insight process and may communicate a lack of empathy or understanding. Though both counselors and clients have a Christian duty to forgive others, it is not usually effective for counselors to forcefully communicate this duty to clients. On the other hand, if we never introduce the concept of forgiveness, many clients will not think of it on their own. Contemporary society has been even more saturated with popular psychology than with Christian tradition, and forgiveness is often overlooked by those who have been taught to nurse their anger and attribute their weaknesses to past mistreatment.

Thus, the challenge facing Christian counselors is to introduce the concept of forgiveness without being forceful or simplistic. There is a forgiveness that involves intellect and another that also involves emotional release. If we are too directive in our counseling, we may produce only intellectualized forgiveness. If we avoid the topic altogether, neither type of forgiveness may occur. How can we produce a forgiveness that starts with the mind and also engages emotions?

TOWARD AN INTEGRATED PERSPECTIVE OF FORGIVENESS

In 1994, Michael McCullough and Everett Worthington, Jr., reviewed the forgiveness literature and concluded that "theological, philosophical, and psychological understandings of forgiveness have not been well integrated."[17] They went on to hypothesize that using forgiveness in a therapeutic context has the capacity for tremendous spiritual implications that potentially lead to beneficial psychological consequences as well. In order to realize the potential for forgiveness in Christian counseling, each counselor needs to work personally on the integration task that McCullough and Worthington call us to consider—a task that requires finding value in each of the three perspectives described here as well as carefully considering the theological and spiritual meanings of forgiveness.

At first glance, it may appear that Christian counselors have nothing to learn from those outspoken therapists who want nothing to do with forgiveness. A closer look may reveal some legitimate concerns in their perspectives. When counselors become strident in advocating forgiveness, they may elicit approval seeking in their clients. Because these clients want to please their counselors, they may go through the intellectual motions of forgiveness without gaining the insight and emotional release that accompany true forgiveness. Though their counselors may be satisfied that these clients have forgiven past offenses, the clients themselves may leave counseling less certain about what was accomplished, feeling confused, coerced, or misunderstood. Similarly, because forgiveness is often confused with reconciliation, even bringing up the topic of forgiveness may elicit fear of further harm in some, especially if their offenders have expressed no remorse. These clients may assume their counselors are suggesting that they should reconcile and enter into a relationship with their offenders, an assumption that may quickly generate feelings of shame and fear.

Like those who oppose forgiveness in counseling, those who view forgiveness as a clinical technique have also made important contributions that must be considered in an integrated view of forgiveness. For counseling to be useful, it must ultimately be practical, affecting the lives of those involved. Teaching specific skills of forgiveness can help make counseling practical by helping people repair damaged relationships.

Similarly, seeing forgiveness as Christian duty has value. At times we all need to be reminded of what we *ought* to do as a way to combat what we *want* to do. Dietrich Bonhoeffer wrote that "the call to follow Christ always means a call to share the work of forgiving men their sins. Forgiveness is the Christlike suffering which it is the Christian's duty to bear."[18] Though retaining anger and resentment builds strong walls of protection, our Christian values require us to tear down those walls and make ourselves vulnerable in forgiving others, even those who have hurt us. Forgiveness is not a natural act; it is a supernatural one. We learn forgiveness through Christ, then attempt to exercise it in our relationships with others.

Thus, we find value in all three perspectives: those who oppose forgiveness in counseling, those who use forgiveness as a clinical technique, and those who see forgiveness as a theological duty. Integrating these perspectives into a useful counseling style is a difficult task. Fortunately, we can find significant help by looking at theological and spiritual perspectives on forgiveness.

Christian Theology

Throughout the Old Testament and the New Testament, the Scriptures present a salvation story in which God continually redeems a wayward people, to offer them a relationship that is possible only through forgiveness.[19] It is exclusively through God's forgiveness that humanity heals. Without God's forgiveness, people remain in a broken and isolated state; with God's forgiveness they receive new life.

The sacrificial death of Jesus is the ultimate act of forgiveness. He was abused and ridiculed. Finally his blood was "poured out for many for the forgiveness of sins" (Matt. 26:28). His sacrificial death, in substitution for sinful humanity, appeased God's wrath against sin and brought peace.

But a Christian view of forgiveness does not stop with Jesus hanging on a cross; the New Testament instructs us to forgive one another as God has forgiven us. In one of several similar passages, the apostle Paul instructs, "Be kind to one another, tender-hearted, forgiving one another, as God in Christ has forgiven you" (Eph. 4:32). Paul's instructions imply a Christian duty to forgive one another, but they also suggest a way of life that exudes forgiveness. We are to *be* tender, kind, forgiving. Forgiveness is a quality of Christian character, not just an act of the will.

This subtle distinction between forgiveness as an act of the will and forgiveness as a reflection of character is illustrated in the following two examples.

EXAMPLE 1

In the context of Christian counseling, Ms. Hurt recognizes she has an obligation to forgive her uncle and decides to give it a try. After spending ample time understanding her anger and grieving the losses of the past, she begins to pray each day for her uncle, asking God to release her from the anger and bitterness she feels. Over time, God answers her requests, and soon she can think of her uncle without feeling burdened with bitterness.

These are healthy changes for Ms. Hurt—changes that were initiated by her sense of Christian duty and prompted by her counselor. As good and as promising as these changes are, an alternative approach might work even better.

EXAMPLE 2

During Christian counseling, Ms. Hurt works through her feelings of anger and her grief over the type of childhood and adulthood she will never experience. She also works to understand herself better and begins to acknowledge her faults and weaknesses in the context of her safe counseling relationship. As she recognizes her own vulnerabilities and weaknesses, she gives up trying to earn God's love and begins learning how to rest in God's love. In time, her anger gives way to tenderness, her resentment to kindness. Soon she realizes that she is less bitter toward her uncle. She senses an inner urge to forgive. Ms. Hurt works each day to release her pain, to rest in God's love, to confess her shortcomings, and to forgive those who have hurt her, including her uncle.

Though the differences between these two examples are subtle, the second illustrates forgiveness as a reflection of insight and character transformation rather than as an act of willpower. As we acknowledge our own predilection toward wrongdoing and how we are undeservedly and regularly forgiven, we can learn to respond in the same forgiving manner toward others. Forgiveness is humble submission to the one who continuously forgives us.

Thus, a Christian understanding of forgiveness begins with a recognition of the depravity inherent in humanity. I agree with Erickson that "our approach to the problems of society will . . . be governed by our view of sin."[20] If sin is ubiquitous, affecting every person, then we are all an active part of the human problem. As we comprehend human weakness and propensity for evil, both in their wider historical context and in our own individual lives, we recognize our need both to give and to receive forgiveness. With a mature understanding of our own sin and God's mercy, we are increasingly able to see ourselves as we view the wrongdoing of others. This is not to suggest that forgiveness is easy but that forgiveness is facilitated by empathy and humility. Lewis Smedes describes this phenomenon in *Forgive and Forget:* "With a little time, and a little more insight, we begin to see both ourselves and our enemies in humbler profiles. We are not really as innocent as we felt when we were first hurt. And we do not usually have a gigantic monster to forgive; we have a weak, needy, and somewhat stupid human being. When you see your enemy and yourself in the weakness and silliness of the humanity you share, you will make the miracle of forgiving a little easier." [21]

Spirituality

Forgiveness, then, is an act of compassion that comes from one person's identifying with another. It suggests that two people are equally fallible, one responding to the offense of the other in loving identification. Saint Francis of Assisi, a thirteenth-century monk, wrote of the personal lesson in humility to be gleaned from another person's offense. "Whom are we to count as our 'friends'? All those whose unjust actions and words cause us all manner of grief and trial. . . . How can I suggest that you should greatly love such people? For this reason: Their evil actions draw out and display to us our own evil responses—anger, gossip, slander, hatred and the like. Then we see our sin for what it is. And only then can we repent and forsake it."[22]

Healing comes as we see ourselves in those who hurt us. We come face-to-face with our own sin and can turn to God for cleansing. This type of insight and humility enables us to forgive. Forgiveness becomes an act of empathy, with one person saying to the other, "I may not have done exactly what you did, but I am also capable of doing evil. Just as I need forgiveness, so I forgive you."

When Peter asked Jesus if he should forgive one who sins against him as many as seven times, Jesus answered, "Not seven times, but, I tell you, seventy-seven times" (Matt. 18:22). He went on to tell a story of a king who called in a slave to settle an account. The slave owed the king an unimaginable amount of money, more than could ever be repaid with a lifetime's wages. The slave could not repay, so the king ordered him sold. When the slave begged for mercy, the king, in his mercy, forgave the debt. After leaving the king's presence, the forgiven slave went and found a fellow slave who owed him a small amount of money, grabbed him by the throat, and insisted on immediate payment. When the king heard of this, he called the first slave back, exclaiming, "You wicked slave! I forgave you all that debt because you pleaded with me. Should you not have had mercy on your fellow slave, as I had mercy on you?" The king handed the slave over to the torturer. After telling this disturbing story, Jesus announced: "So my heavenly Father will also do to every one of you, if you do not forgive your brother or sister from your heart" (Matt. 18:35).

Refusing to forgive another is placing ourselves above that person, as if we are in a state of moral superiority. Thomas à Kempis warned: "Count not thyself better than others, lest perchance thou appear worse in the sight of God, who knoweth what is in man."[23] As abhorrent as we may find the actions of sexual abusers, murderers, rapists, thieves, and psychopaths, we must acknowledge that we are all sinners whose only hope for redemption is found in a forgiving and gracious God.

Recognizing our condition as sinners places us in a position of humility before God and one another. Only from this position of humility can we fully understand forgiveness. The apostle Paul described this in his letter to the Colossian Christians: "As God's chosen ones, holy and beloved, clothe yourselves with compassion, kindness, humility, meekness, and patience. Bear with one another and, if anyone has a complaint against another, forgive each other; just as the Lord has forgiven you, so you also must forgive. Above all, clothe yourselves with love, which binds everything together in perfect harmony" (Col. 3:12-14).

In summary, Christian counselors who sensitively integrate psychological, theological, and spiritual perspectives on forgiveness are distinguished by several characteristics:

1. They recognize the potential damage of introducing forgiveness as a therapeutic goal too early in the treatment relationship.
2. They value techniques that emphasize forgiveness while recognizing that forgiveness requires inner transformation as well as behavioral change.
3. They recognize a Christian duty to forgive but do not use that duty to coerce or manipulate clients.
4. They remember that forgiveness was not invented by counselors or psychologists but by God, who chose to redeem humanity through the sacrificial work of Jesus Christ.
5. They see a connection between sin, confession, and forgiveness, understanding that forgiveness properly flows out of humble self-awareness and gratitude to a forgiving God.

PSYCHOLOGICAL AND SPIRITUAL HEALTH

Let us imagine that Ms. Hurt is cloned into four identical clients, each of whom sees a different Christian therapist for counseling. Each therapist helps Ms. Hurt, but each goes about it in a different way.

COUNSELOR A

Counselor A is a behavioral psychologist. She listens intently to Ms. Hurt's story of abuse, expresses empathy and concern, and works with Ms. Hurt to formulate a treatment plan that will help her function better in her daily life. As part of the treatment plan, counselor A teaches Ms. Hurt progressive relaxation and coping imagery. With practice, Ms. Hurt eventually learns to relax all the muscles in her body while imagining an interaction with her uncle. She sees herself acting assertively, setting appropriate boundaries, and telling her uncle how much damage the abuse has caused her. After imagining the interaction in the safety of a counseling session, she meets with her uncle and has a similar interaction in real life. Counseling continues, and Ms. Hurt continues her relaxation and imagination exercises. Eventually, she imagines forgiving her uncle, letting go of all the anger and bitterness, and looking to the future rather than the past. Her uncle never expresses remorse directly to her, and she never tells him of her choice to forgive. But she feels relief and peace after counseling.

COUNSELOR B

Counselor B sees Ms. Hurt and approaches the problem from a different theoretical perspective. Counselor B is a psychodynamically oriented psychiatrist who helps Ms. Hurt explore and uncover the emotional conflicts of her childhood. Early in therapy, Ms. Hurt discusses her memories of being sexually abused by her uncle. Counselor B listens intently and works to maintain enough warmth to communicate empathy yet enough distance to allow Ms. Hurt to experience her conflictual feelings. Counselor B puts no time pressure on Ms. Hurt, allowing her to explore and express feelings at her own pace. She begins feeling better. Eventually, after many months of successful treatment, Ms. Hurt brings up the topic of forgiveness. She has brought up the topic before, but only as a means of controlling her inner rage. This time is different. Counselor B realizes that Ms. Hurt is ready to consider forgiving her uncle.

COUNSELOR C

Counselor C is a biblical counselor. He listens carefully to Ms. Hurt's story, builds a good therapeutic relationship based on mutual respect, then begins to take a leadership role in the counseling process. He explains to Ms. Hurt that her wounds are deep and that her emotions are natural. He also explains that natural responses are not always helpful. The goal of counseling will be to help her respond to God's prompting rather than to the inner instincts of anger and bitterness. She will hear God's prompting through Scripture and prayer—the tools counselor C plans to use in counseling. Together, counselor C and Ms. Hurt explore the meaning and consequences of sin, the importance of forgiveness and repentance, and the essence of focusing on the future rather than the past. Ms. Hurt grows spiritually and emotionally, and she ultimately forgives her uncle.

COUNSELOR D

Counselor D is a cognitive therapist who helps people change their thoughts and beliefs in order to manage their emotions better. Because counselor D is a good listener and a caring person, she establishes good rapport with Ms. Hurt almost immediately. They begin exploring Ms. Hurt's beliefs and assumptions. Ms. Hurt emerged from her childhood believing that she is responsible for the actions of others. For years she has quietly blamed herself for being abused, believing that if she had been quieter or had dressed differently, then her uncle would have left her alone. She and her counselor look carefully at this belief until Ms. Hurt decides her belief is incorrect and acknowledges that her uncle is responsible for his choices. This cognitive change helps Ms. Hurt feel less depressed, but she becomes intensely angry. Her new belief is that her uncle is a terrible and awful person who should be punished and humiliated. This belief also subsides with continued therapy as Ms. Hurt begins to recognize how confused and lonely her uncle feels. The ache of past abuse will always be with her, but she decides to release her rage and choose forgiveness.

Fortunately, our four clients have seen good therapists. Each counselor has helped Ms. Hurt work through the tragedy of abuse and come to a point where she is willing to forgive her uncle. Each has taken a different theoretical route, but all the routes have been successful. Because of their different approaches to counseling, each of these therapists brings a unique set of strengths and weaknesses to the counseling work—qualities that affect the way forgiveness is perceived and handled in counseling. These strengths and weaknesses will be considered in the context of the familiar questions considered in previous chapters.

Will This Help Establish a Healthy Sense of Self?

COUNSELOR A

One strength of counselor A's approach is the increasing sense of self-efficacy that Ms. Hurt develops as counseling progresses. She learns to express her feelings forthrightly and assertively, even to the point of confronting her uncle. Before counseling, she was locked in the grips of shame and self-doubt. After counseling, she confidently expresses her feelings and opinions.

A potential weakness with behavioral approaches to forgiveness is the assumption that negative emotions can be changed by standard behavioral procedures such as the reciprocal-inhibition procedures used by counselor A. It may be that Ms. Hurt, because of her early life trauma, does not respond to treatment in the same ways as those who have not been abused. Most of us find it relieving to give up our negative emotions and forgive another. But the abuse victim has learned to associate giving up with being hurt. When she gives up her rights, someone takes advantage of her. So treatment might not go as quickly or as neatly as suggested in the brief vignette with counselor A and Ms. Hurt.

Before forgiveness techniques can be therapeutic, several prerequisites should be met: Ms. Hurt fully understands the extent of her injuries due to sexual abuse; she moves beyond her tendency toward self-blame; she honestly experiences appropriate anger toward her abuser; she feels empowered to set boundaries that keep her from being abused again; and she has a complex understanding of the abuser rather than a stereotyped and simplified view of him.[24] Many of these changes normally occur in the context of a trusting therapeutic relationship and cannot be rushed with behavioral techniques.

COUNSELOR B

Counselor B designs his treatment specifically to help Ms. Hurt develop a more robust sense of self. Individuation, the capacity to see oneself as an individual rather than as a symbiotic extension of another, is the goal of many psychodynamic therapies. By giving Ms. Hurt time and freedom to explore her inner feelings and conflicts, counselor B helps her individuate. Once she is comfortable with herself, she is in a better position to genuinely forgive her abuser.

Unfortunately, many psychodynamic therapists stop at the individuation stage and do not continue on to consider forgiveness. The topic of forgiveness is viewed suspiciously, ignored, or criticized by many psychodynamic therapists.

COUNSELOR C

Whereas some psychodynamic therapists may never get around to considering forgiveness with Ms. Hurt, that problem will not occur with biblical counselors. One advantage of counselor C's approach is its directness with regard to forgiveness. Counselor C helps Ms. Hurt see herself and her abuser as God sees them—needy, broken people searching for spiritual and interpersonal reconciliation.

A potential disadvantage to this approach is that the counselor might unwittingly step into the role of a dominant leader that preys on Ms. Hurt's need to please others. Even when Ms. Hurt reports feeling better and making good progress, it may be little more than her shame-based efforts to please her counselor. Clients who believe they must forgive in order to please a therapist or to fulfill a spiritual obligation have difficulty gaining the necessary insight for true forgiveness. This can lead to words and behaviors that reflect denial more than forgiveness, with the client choosing conflict-avoidance over direct and honest communication. David Augsburger warns, "Forgiveness happens as past resentments are owned, not disowned; are recognized, not repressed; are released, not retained; and are woven into new bonding relationships with others."[25]

COUNSELOR D

Counselor D, a cognitive therapist, helps Ms. Hurt establish a healthy sense of self by considering her beliefs and assumptions and helping her revise them. In the process of learning metacognition (the ability to think about her thoughts) she discovers that she has some personal control over her feelings, that she is not destined to respond out of shame or approval seeking. From this, she develops a healthy sense of autonomy and individuation.

Unfortunately, some cognitive therapists minimize the importance of emotions and focus on logic almost exclusively. For these counselors and their clients, forgiveness is reduced to an intellectual exercise that might best be described as pseudoforgiveness.[26] Authentic forgiveness is an emotionally intense process, and overly intellectualized forms of therapy tend to skip over important parts of the forgiveness process.[27]

Will This Help Establish a Healthy Sense of Need?

COUNSELOR A

Establishing a healthy awareness of one's need for God and others requires delicate balance. We might assume that recognizing our need is simply a matter of thinking less of ourselves, but for those who are already caught in the grips of shame, thinking less of themselves is not helpful. Just as teaching a codependent person that he or she needs others is futile at best and destructive at worst, so many need to feel more confident in themselves and their abilities before they are able to see their need for God and others. This is counselor A's approach: helping Ms. Hurt feel better about herself, more confident in her coping abilities, and more in control of her life. Once she has more confidence in herself, then she can begin to understand her need for others.

The risk is that counselor A will help Ms. Hurt feel strong, that her symptoms will improve, and that counseling will stop before she reaches a point of humble identification with her abuser. If a clinician employs behavioral forgiveness techniques without understanding the Christian theological foundation for forgiveness, the client may miss significant opportunities for insight and self-awareness.[28] This theologically deprived type of forgiving can create a mind-set of superiority in the forgiver, as if the client believes, "I will forgive you because I live on a higher plane than you, and I refuse to let you drag me down to your level."

COUNSELOR B

Though I am not a psychodynamic therapist, I am convinced that psychodynamic theory is the best available option for helping clients confront their need for God and others. While counselors A, C, and D are helping "patch up" Ms. Hurt with behavioral, cognitive, and spiritual techniques, counselor B is helping her stare intently at her deepest feelings of pain, loneliness, and isolation. Counselor B believes Ms. Hurt will grow only as she honestly looks at all aspects of herself, including the parts she has spent years avoiding. She will leave therapy recognizing her weaknesses as well as her strengths and will see her need for God and others.

Despite the cautious attitudes about forgiveness among psychodynamic counselors, a healthy understanding of forgiveness fits naturally into this model of therapy. Once we recognize our inner loneliness and longing for community, as well as our propensity toward selfishness and egocentrism, then we are ready to reach out to other imperfect humans with gestures of forgiveness and compassion. We best understand and experience forgiveness from this posture of humble identification with others.

COUNSELOR C

After establishing rapport, counselor C confronts Ms. Hurt with her need right away. Fortunately, counselor C helps Ms. Hurt find hope for her spiritual and emotional needs through Scripture and prayer. She sets her mind on the future and forgives her uncle for the past.

The risk counselor C introduces is that Ms. Hurt is not yet strong enough to face her state of need. Those overwhelmed with burdens of shame need to find ways to understand their shame before they are capable of seeing their shortcomings and faults accurately. Rather than producing a healthy state of humility, counselor C may be unwittingly encouraging an unhealthy state of humiliation that only deepens the shame of his client.[29]

COUNSELOR D

Before counseling with counselor D, Ms. Hurt believed that she was responsible for her childhood abuse. In the process of examining and evaluating her beliefs and assumptions, she grew to realize that her uncle was responsible and she was not. This discovery helped liberate her from years of depression.

Even the best changes sometimes have unwanted side effects. Because Ms. Hurt learned in counseling to attribute events of the past to external causes (her uncle) rather than internal (herself), she may continue to use her new attributional style and resist any notion that she has faults. Rather than accepting responsibility for the ongoing struggles of life, she may settle comfortably into the victim role and attribute her problems to the villains who have caused them. Counselor D needs to watch for this tendency and help her find a middle ground where she can make either internal or external attributions, depending on the circumstances involved.

Will This Help Establish a Healing Relationship?

Counselor A assumes that the active ingredients in her work with Ms. Hurt are the behavioral techniques used to teach new coping skills. She sees the relationship as an important mechanism for transfusing these techniques.

Counselor B sees the relationship itself as the active ingredient. Ms. Hurt will learn to be caring toward herself by observing and interacting with a caring therapist. Her capacity to see herself accurately, and thus to forgive, requires insights that can be generated only in the context of a healthy relationship.

Counselor C sees God's Word as the active ingredient in change. The counseling relationship is important because it is the vehicle through which Ms. Hurt will be exposed to Christian principles, Scripture, and prayer.

Counselor D sees the counseling relationship as one important way to counter Ms. Hurt's faulty assumptions. In addition to the techniques of cognitive therapy, she uses a caring therapeutic relationship to help Ms. Hurt feel valued and worthwhile.

Though each counselor places slightly different emphasis on the therapeutic relationship, it is important to all of them. I suspect the counseling relationship is the common factor that makes each form of therapy effective.[30] Forgiveness is not so much a skill that is taught as it is a worldview that is caught.

A good counselor helps a client recognize a past offense, making sure that the client does not excuse, condone, or dismiss the offense. The therapist then walks the client through periods of anger, grief, and loneliness. The client learns to trust again by relying on the therapist to legitimize the undeserved anguish and by seeing that the therapist will not leave the client in an unresolved state of bitterness and anger. Clinicians are already teaching forgiveness, consciously or not, when they treat their clients in this way. One psychologist put it this way: "Perhaps it is this experience of being valued in the present despite obvious shortcomings and failures in the past that provokes clients into forgiving their pasts, developing a more forgiving attitude in the present, releasing judgments and grievances, and thus creating more options for the future."[31]

FACING THE CHALLENGES

Challenge 1: Moving from Two Areas of Competence to Three

If the capacity to forgive is a character quality requiring humble identification with an offender and if the treatment relationship is an important ingredient in change, then counselors should evaluate their own capacity to forgive and humbly identify with their clients. For many counselors this necessitates a conceptual shift that requires us to give up much of our sense of power and importance, as illustrated in the following three examples.

First, humble identification requires us to see our clients as similar to ourselves. Therapists who have sought counseling themselves are familiar with the struggle of taking on the client role. We want to think of ourselves as better adjusted, healthier, more spiritual than our clients, so we often resist getting personal therapy. When circumstances force us into personal therapy, we can no longer maintain the myths of superiority. We, like our Christian clients, are pilgrims along a spiritual path—pilgrims who fail frequently and are often stunned by the pain and difficulty of life.

A second example is found in dealing with angry clients. Good therapists draw out emotions in counseling, and those emotions usually spill over their proper boundaries and are directed at the counselor. Thus, virtually all effective counselors deal frequently with their clients' anger.

WHAT IF THIS HAPPENED?

Joe is working to forgive his absent father, whom he rarely saw during his childhood years. After spending several sessions discussing his father, he looks his counselor in the eye and blurts out: "You're just like him. You sit there and don't say anything. You're probably not even listening. What, are you thinking about your golf game this afternoon?"

Which response should the counselor choose?

Response 1: "I am listening to you, not thinking about golf."

Response 2: "These are painful feelings for you—as if you are here but not here. And you've had these feelings before."

Response 3: "I don't appreciate those accusations. They are not true, and you are out of place to suggest they are."

Joe and his counselor have talked about the goal of forgiveness, but now the counselor has an opportunity for something much better than talking about forgiveness. The counselor can embody the quality of forgiveness by humbly identifying with Joe. The second response, obviously the best, is nondefensive and encourages Joe to explore his feelings while modeling interpersonal humility.

Third, humble identification with clients requires counselors to monitor their own self-talk during counseling sessions. At times, the stressful work of counseling causes us to be cynical. Even when we are kind in our overt responses, we sometimes think critical or harsh thoughts about our clients. Humble identification involves a willingness to release our own frustrations and disappointments about a counseling session and to remain prayerfully supportive of our clients in our thoughts as well as our words. A counselor's spiritual life is routinely tested in the counseling office and is evident in the inner experiences and attitudes of the counselor.

Challenge 2: Blurred Personal-Professional Distinctions

In counseling, our professional activities are transacted at a personal level. These interactions reflect more than business practices; they also reflect our capacity for humility, forgiveness, and setting appropriate boundaries.

For instance, dealing with missed counseling appointments is often a matter of professional policy, established by a group of counselors sharing office space. However, implementing the policy is more than a business decision and is usually at the personal discretion of the counselor.

WHAT IF THIS HAPPENED?

On a particularly bad day, a counselor has two consecutive missed appointments. The first, Mr. Greggs, has never missed an appointment before. He calls two hours later from a hotel room across the country, apologizing that he neglected to check his personal schedule before going on a brief business trip. The second, Mr. Thom, has missed three of the last seven sessions.

Instances like these two provide counselors with personal opportunities to model what forgiveness is and is not. Although the counselor has the right, according to the stated office policy, to charge Mr. Greggs for his missed appointment, choosing not to charge communicates a personal willingness to forgive. The counselor may recognize that she also forgets things occasionally, and in humble identification with her client, she chooses to forgive the missed appointment. This is the essence of forgiveness: choosing to identify with Mr. Greggs, then releasing him from the rightful consequences of his actions.

The situation with Mr. Thom is different. His counselor has already demonstrated a willingness to forgive, not charging him for his first two missed appointments. But Mr. Thom appears unaware or unconcerned about the consequences of his continued irresponsibility. Forgiving is not the same as excusing, overlooking, or condoning. The counselor is concerned that Mr. Thom is taking advantage of her forgiving spirit. This is analogous to what Dietrich Bonhoeffer calls "cheap grace," misunderstanding God's forgiveness as justification for self-centered living. Bonhoeffer describes cheap grace as "the deadly enemy of the church."[32] Something similar to cheap grace seems to be a detriment for Mr. Thom, who has difficulty maintaining stable employment, remaining committed in relationships, and following through on financial responsibilities. Because of her concern that Mr. Thom learn to respect her boundaries and his responsibilities, the counselor chooses to charge for the missed session. In both cases the counselor makes a personal choice regarding professional policy.

Counselors often have opportunities to live out the essence of forgiveness, but it requires carefully balancing a forgiving spirit with a commitment to justice and personal responsibility. If we lean too far in one direction, we become harsh and unforgiving in our professional manner and policies, making it difficult to model a forgiving spirit for our clients, many of whom are working to forgive others. If we lean too far in the other direction, we risk being naive and gullible, and we unwittingly model excusing or condoning rather than true forgiveness.[33]

Challenge 3: Expanded Definitions of Training

As with other topics considered in this book, learning how to handle forgiveness in the counseling office is not typically included in graduate school curricula.[34] In spite of this, forgiveness is one of the most frequently used religious interventions among Christian counselors. Members of the Christian Association for Psychological Studies (CAPS) report using concepts of forgiveness with more than half their clients.[35] This probably means that most Christian counselors use on-the-job-training to learn the best ways to implement forgiveness in their counseling work.

Counselors who find successful ways to implement forgiveness in their counseling sometimes report their ideas in journals and books. For example, Everett Worthington, Jr., and Frederick DiBlasio reported their idea of a specific forgiveness session in their work with couples.[36] Both spouses prepare for the session several weeks in advance, concentrating on their own errors and need for forgiveness. In the forgiveness session, each confesses wrongdoing and seeks forgiveness from the other. Worthington and DiBlasio illustrate the technique with a case example. Several others have also reported their forgiveness counseling methods in writing, an investment that helps other counselors in their work.[37]

In addition to reading what other counselors do, counselors can grow in their ability to use forgiveness in counseling as they grow spiritually. The idea of forgiveness seems strange and foreign to those who have not experienced God's forgiveness. But for those who know God's grace, forgiveness is a vital part of spiritual maturity. To model forgiveness to our clients and to understand forgiveness in our own lives, we must first understand how much we have been forgiven.

Perhaps the best training for forgiveness in our personal and professional lives is found in the spiritual discipline of confession. Honest confession brings us to that place of humility where we understand how much we need forgiveness and how much we have been forgiven. Without confession, we minimize our faults and sometimes even feel smug about our capacity to forgive others. Those who understand forgiveness the best have stared intently at their sin, cried out to God in their need, and been amazed at the miracle of God's grace.

The discipline of confession brings counselors to a point of personal humility. Though counselors do not bring their confessions to the counseling office, they do bring their humility, a quality that promotes trust and rapport and safety in counseling relationships and makes clients willing to confess their needs and struggles. Forgiveness and counseling go together well when the counseling office is a safe place for clients to confess their struggles, bitterness, troubling emotions, and nagging sins. Confession promotes humility, and humility promotes interpersonal forgiveness.

Challenge 4: Confronting Dominant Views of Mental Health

Though religious counselors discuss forgiveness with their clients more frequently than nonreligious counselors, dominant views of mental health appear to be shifting toward greater acceptance of forgiveness regardless of the counselor's religious orientation.[38] Several important articles about forgiveness have been published in *Psychotherapy,* a journal published by a division of the American Psychological Association (APA). A number of therapists are writing about the benefits of forgiveness, though they are not themselves religious. This is good news! Or is it?

The current trend in the psychological literature is to abandon the religious significance of forgiveness so that it might be more acceptable to nonreligious clients and therapists. Unfortunately, this sometimes results in subtle but important changes in one's understanding of forgiveness. In Christian tradition, forgiveness is extended from one person to another out of gratitude for God's forgiveness. In contemporary psychology, forgiveness is often a way for the forgiver to feel better, an unloading of emotional baggage. One psychotherapist describes forgiveness as a logical decision: "To opt for a forgiving attitude is to see that while on the level of immediate experience there is some catharsis in venting feelings of anger and vengeance, to hold onto these feelings and fantasies, to cathect them with energy, over the long term is self-defeating."[39]

To the secular psychotherapist, forgiveness may be logical, but to the Christian, forgiveness is not logical at all. Forgiveness originates in the surprise of history: the incredible, stunning, miraculous act of a divine Savior hanging on a cross and dying for sinful humans. All Christian virtue, including the capacity to forgive, emanates from this illogical event. Edwin Zackrison, a theologian, describes this well: "Just as nothing in us motivates God to forgive, so nothing in others motivates us to forgive. Such an attitude can only be born in the heart of one who has experienced such forgiveness."[40]

One form of forgiveness, the type that is becoming popular in counseling, is based on logic and self-protection: "I will forgive you because I refuse to let your offenses hurt me anymore." The other, the type we see in Christianity, is based on personal insight and humble identification: "I will forgive you because I also have been forgiven of much." Though we call both forgiveness, they are different enough to warrant different names.

Challenge 5: Establishing a Scientific Base

Before we can study forgiveness well, we need precise ways to measure forgiveness. Several researchers have been working on ways to measure forgiveness, most of them interested in whether or not people are willing to seek and grant interpersonal forgiveness.[41] Given the variety of perspectives that are found in the mental health field, it may be equally important to know why some people are willing to forgive.

Katheryn Rhoads Meek, a doctoral student at Wheaton College, is developing a scale to assess why some people choose to forgive. The Reasons for Forgiveness Scale, which must be administered by computer, first gives respondents scenarios in which interpersonal forgiveness is one possible response. The scenarios are adapted from the Willingness to Forgive scale that was developed and described by Hebl and Enright.[42] Those respondents who choose forgiveness as their response are then asked why they would forgive. Respondents rate each of the following motives on a four-point scale, ranging from not at all important to extremely important.

REASONS FOR FORGIVENESS SCALE

1. Forgiveness helps me get on with my life. Otherwise I would think about it all the time.
2. I want to keep peace in our relationship.
3. I understand why he/she did it (going through a rough time, personal issues, etc.).
4. I've done bad things too and have been forgiven.
5. I love this person.
6. It's not that big a deal.
7. If I had behaved differently, it wouldn't have happened.
8. Forgiveness is the right thing to do.

Some of these motives reflect self-blame, excusing, or condoning more than forgiveness. Some reflect self-serving reasons for forgiveness, and others reflect humble identification. An initial reliability study has provided promising support for the Reasons for Forgiveness Scale, and additional studies are being planned. Understanding various motives for forgiveness may help other researchers design helpful studies in the future.

If Christians understand forgiveness differently from others in the mental health field, it seems reasonable to expect that forgiveness in Christian counseling may take a different form and have results that are different from the way forgiveness is used in other forms of counseling. To date, no research comparing Christian and non-Christian forms of forgiveness has been reported. The Reasons for Forgiveness Scale is an important step in this direction.

Challenge 6: Defining Relevant Ethical Standards

Counselors have an ethical obligation to provide cost-effective services for their clients. Short treatment protocols are preferred by insurance companies and by most people seeking help. This creates an ethical tension for counselors interested in forgiveness.

On one hand, if counselors hurry their work, especially work related to forgiveness, they may settle for a superficial, intellectualized form of forgiveness rather than one based on deep understanding. I remember helping one client write a letter of forgiveness to a parent; then several months later she began to uncover repressed memories of sexual abuse by the same parent. She was not ready to forgive fully because she had not yet fully understood what she was forgiving. Hurried forgiveness carries the risk of being shallow and temporary.

On the other hand, if therapists wait until clients bring up the topic of forgiveness, therapy may take longer than necessary. Some clients seem to flourish in the patient role, especially if they are encouraged to see themselves as victims. Some clients will even unconsciously fabricate "repressed" memories in order to maintain the comfort of the counseling relationship. In these cases, the counselor must gently nudge the client toward forgiveness. Striking a balance between patience and goal directedness is a challenging part of forgiveness counseling.

A related ethical challenge comes in recognizing that not all clients have the emotional ability to forgive, at least not until significant emotional growth occurs. Often those who have the most to forgive, because they have been victimized as young children, are vulnerable to the phenomenon of splitting. With splitting, they neatly divide the world into two groups: the good people and the bad people. Good people can do no wrong, and bad people can do no right. Those prone to splitting find forgiveness virtually impossible.[43] If a counselor pushes forgiveness onto a client prone to splitting, the counselor ends up being viewed as bad and the client terminates counseling. Thus, a competent counseling approach requires helping these clients grow beyond their primitive defenses before attempting to work on forgiveness.

SUMMARY

Forgiveness is an increasingly popular topic among counselors. Although this is an encouraging trend, it is important to remember that a Christian understanding of forgiveness may differ from the ways others understand forgiveness. When forgiveness techniques are used in Christian counseling, they should be considered in the context of self-awareness, empathy, humility, and insight, and not just as a way for a client to experience emotional relief. Our capacity to forgive one another depends, at least to some extent, on our capacity to understand both our need for forgiveness and God's gracious gift of forgiveness. This type of healing brings a person into a deeper relationship with God and others.

8/ REDEMPTION

Throughout this book I have referred to religious interventions in Christian counseling, but I have rarely discussed how they might be applied in working with those who are not Christians. For example, non-Christian clients will have an understanding of sin and confession that is different from that of Christian clients. Forgiveness may seem unnecessary to those who have not experienced the bliss of Christ's grace. Praying routinely with non-Christian clients might raise the clients' defenses and suspicions. So what, if anything, is distinct about Christian counseling when working with those who are not Christians?

Furthermore, some Christian clients come to counseling with problems that have little to do with their religious values or beliefs. Just as their non-Christian counterparts do, Christian counselors may use systematic desensitization to treat phobias, cognitive restructuring to treat dysthymia, and schema-oriented treatments for personality disorders. Does Christian counseling for these clients look different from other forms of counseling? Other than specifically religious interventions, as described in previous chapters, I suggest there are two distinctive elements of Christian counseling: identification and a redemptive worldview. These two distinctives cut across all client problems and religious values.

The first is simple: Christian counselors identify themselves as Christians. If religious values affect the process and outcome of counseling, as we believe they do, then we ought to fully inform those seeking our services of our Christian values.[1] I include the following statement as part of a longer informed-consent form that all clients read and sign before beginning treatment:

AN EXAMPLE OF INFORMED CONSENT REGARDING RELIGIOUS VALUES

I will use a form of cognitive therapy. We will carefully examine your personal history and current circumstances in order to find and revise faulty thinking patterns and beliefs that contribute to your symptoms. Both your personal values and mine will affect the ways your beliefs are evaluated. Thus, it is important that you know something about my values and that you are free to question me about my value assumptions at any time. I believe many biological, psychosocial, and emotional factors contribute to psychological problems. As a Christian psychologist, I believe that some psychological problems result from the evil embedded in human nature and in our culture. People often experience problems as a result of being hurt by others (past or present), making poor choices, undervaluing things that are truly important, and overvaluing things that are unimportant. It is not essential that you share my Christian beliefs, but you have the right to know my value assumptions and are free to discuss them with me at any time.

In addition to providing opportunity for informed consent, a statement such as this opens an opportunity for Christian truth to be incarnated in the therapy relationship. If the relationship with the therapist is healing and inviting, then the client may come to think of Christianity as healing and inviting. Though evangelism leading to spiritual conversion is rarely a part of counseling, a healthy Christian-counseling relationship often encourages clients to explore religious values and faith during and after counseling.

Furthermore, an overt statement about the counselor's Christian values makes spirituality and religion a legitimate topic for the client to discuss. Often clients will not discuss their religious beliefs if they are unsure of their counselor's values.

The second distinction of Christian counseling that applies to all clients and all counseling situations is our understanding of redemption, the topic of this final chapter. The central experience of a Christian's life is a redemptive relationship with Jesus Christ—a relationship that transforms our understanding of human encounters, including those in the counseling office.

Redemption means the act of buying back, or recovering by paying a price. For example, not many years ago people collected green stamps that could be *redeemed* for merchandise. These stamps, worthless on their own, were given value with their purchasing power. In the spiritual and interpersonal realms, redemption means that humans, broken and battered by life's trials, have value and meaning restored to their lives.

Only God offers eternal redemption. Humans confess their sin and find forgiveness, hope, and meaning in God's grace. Though spiritual redemption is the most important type of redemption to find, humans are also able to offer a form of interpersonal redemption to one another. This human-to-human redemption is a common part of Christian mercy and Christian counseling.

For the purposes of this chapter, a redemptive worldview in counseling is defined as a set of beliefs, values, and assumptions that cause us not only to reflect humbly and gratefully on how God is drawing us out of our captivity to sin but also to motivate us to help restore others to hope and wholeness. Notice that spiritual redemption and human redemption are closely related. When we are redeemed by Christ, rescued from our self-destructive and futile ways, we become more interested in living out our faith in redemptive relationships with others. We are God's hands and feet in a world that needs to be rescued from the pervasive effects of human depravity. Some people believe that human acts of redemption will ultimately improve the world and bring God's kingdom to earth. Others believe that human acts of redemption are important insofar as they point others toward a redemptive relationship with God. In either case, the redemptive nature of the counseling relationship is a practical way of responding to God's transforming mercy.

WHAT IF THIS HAPPENED?

Dawn Trodden is in counseling with Ms. Hope, a lay counselor in a church-based ministry. Dawn has had a hard life. She was abused as a child, was abandoned in her first marriage, and has bounced from job to job over the last several years. Dawn has complicated her life with some bad choices, including promiscuity and alcohol abuse. She came for counseling feeling depressed and hopeless.

Ms. Hope is a caring Christian counselor who listens well and cares deeply for her clients. She likes Dawn and feels confident that Dawn will eventually begin feeling better and making better decisions.

Dawn cannot explain it, but she often feels a foreign sense of optimism and energy after leaving her counseling sessions. For the first time in her life she feels understood and valued. Shame is loosening its grip on her life because of the counseling relationship. Ms. Hope is spending time and energy buying Dawn back from the dehumanizing forces of her past.

Redemption is found not primarily in counseling techniques but in the nature of a caring counseling relationship. Thus, learning to be a redemptive counselor requires more than learning a set of skills that can be taught in a classroom or listed in a book. Rather, the capacity to engage in redemptive counseling relationships comes with psychological, theological, and spiritual insight and growth.

FOUNDATIONS

Psychology

Redemptive psychotherapy relationships can be viewed from a number of psychological perspectives, depending on one's theoretical preferences. Though human acts of redemption can be viewed as an important part of psychotherapy within any theoretical framework, we will consider these three: object-relations, Adlerian, and cognitive therapy.

OBJECT RELATIONS

From an object-relations perspective, our capacity to see value in ourselves depends on how others have treated us in the past. Some, like Ms. Trodden in the previous example, come to counseling without ever knowing a redemptive human relationship based on grace and acceptance.

Object-relations theorists believe that we internalize roles from early life relationships and carry them with us by treating ourselves and others the same ways we have been treated and have responded.[2] An abused child, such as Ms. Dawn Trodden, internalizes the role of abuser from interactions with her abusive parent and may grow up to abuse herself or others. She also internalizes the role of victim and may frequently cast herself or others in a victim role as an adult. For clients like Dawn, a therapy relationship built on trust and respect is radically new and initially difficult to accept, but the relationship is ultimately transforming.

People with a number of relatively healthy relationships in their past are able to affirm, encourage, and love themselves; they have learned these skills by being affirmed, encouraged, and loved by others. Sadly, some have not had access to healthy relationships and therefore have not learned appropriate ways of caring for themselves. For these clients, the nature of the therapeutic relationship is paramount. As they learn to find grace and acceptance from their counselor, they also learn to be nicer to themselves.[3] They are learning a new skill from a therapist, then applying it to their

244 / **Psychology, Theology, and Spirituality in Christian Counseling**

self-image. This is the essence of good counseling and of human redemption, buying back people's dignity by investing in their lives, treating them with respect and affirmation.

Counselors serve as "transitional objects," providing a temporary relationship that helps clients gain insight and relate better to others in relationships that are more permanent than counseling relationships. In this sense, Christian counselors help their clients understand God by demonstrating redemption. This is not to say we teach redemption as a professor teaches a class or a pastor teaches a congregation, but we live out a redemptive relationship in the counseling office.

ADLERIAN PSYCHOLOGY

Alfred Adler postulated that humans are consumed with a drive toward selfishness and superiority because they are plagued with an underlying sense of weakness and inferiority. The goal of therapy is to help clients gain insight into feelings of inferiority, be freed from futile methods of seeking dominance and superiority, and adopt a more empathetic, altruistic style of life. Adler described this capacity for empathy and altruism as "social interest."

Adler wrote about successfully treating a schizophrenic patient. For the first three months, the patient was silent in treatment. Adler kept meeting him week after week. After the silence broke, the patient abruptly raised his hand to hit Adler. Adler did not defend himself. On another occasion, the patient smashed a window during a session. Adler helped him bandage his bleeding hand, maintaining a kind and friendly attitude. The patient improved, and Adler asked him why treatment was successful. He responded, "That is quite simple. I had lost all courage to live. In our consultations I found it again."[4] This patient was redeemed from schizophrenia through a counseling relationship with Adler.

Adlerian psychotherapists attempt to bring people back from a life of selfish ambition by displaying social interest in the therapy relationship. This is analogous to the Christian concepts of redemption and grace: the goal of counseling is redemption, and the mechanism for change is grace.[5] Grace requires the counselor to be unconditionally kind and nonauthoritarian, freeing the client to break the bonds of shame and inferiority. Empowering grace is redemptive.

COGNITIVE THERAPY

Recent developments in cognitive therapy have affirmed the importance of a redemptive therapeutic relationship. Though some counselors still practice cognitive therapy as an exercise in logic and argument, most contemporary cognitive therapists recognize the importance of the therapeutic alliance.[6]

Cognitive therapists want to change the underlying beliefs of their clients. For example, let us imagine that Ms. Trodden has the belief that she will ultimately be rejected by everyone. This belief shapes her feelings and specific thoughts in any relationship, including her relationship with her counselor, Ms. Hope. Because she believes she will be rejected, Dawn tries pushing Ms. Hope away at several points during counseling. In the fifth session Dawn explodes in anger, screaming that she will never come back for another session. She misses the eighth session entirely, hoping her counselor will call to see where she was. In the twentieth session she tries to manipulate Ms. Hope into loaning her money. All these efforts are tests to see if her belief is correct: Will my counselor reject me?

How successful will it be for Ms. Hope to try to dissuade Dawn of her rejection belief with logic alone? It will not be successful because Dawn did not arrive at her belief with logic; it was the product of deep emotional scars and childhood losses that occurred before she was capable of adult logic. Her beliefs will be changed the same way they were established—through relationships.

Contemporary cognitive therapists assess clients' beliefs and assumptions and then deliberately live out roles that defy those assumptions. To clients who believe they must be perfect to be loved, the cognitive therapist is nonchalant when the client shows up ten minutes late for an appointment and may even see it as a sign of progress. To clients who believe they are worthless and unimportant, the cognitive therapist is unusually attentive and affirming. To clients who believe they must maintain control at all costs, the cognitive therapist is assertive and bold. In each case the nature of the therapeutic relationship is specifically chosen to be redemptive for the specific client with a specific set of dysfunctional beliefs.

CAVEATS

Two warnings are in order. First, although discussing redemptive therapeutic relationships creates a pleasant picture of counseling, we must be careful not to become overconfident or arrogant in our role of living out redemption. Many of the abuses of counseling occur when counselors begin confusing themselves with God. We are human and can offer nothing of eternal significance without God. Second, counselors are people too and come into the counseling office with their own damage from past relationships. For example, a national survey of clinical and counseling psychologists revealed that two-thirds of the women and one-third of the men had been abused physically or sexually.[7] Those who have not been sexually or physically abused have faced other problems that affect their abilities to perceive others accurately and treat them with respect and kindness. Even counselors who have gone through prolonged personal therapy continue to have blind spots; we are all affected by personal and universal sin. This suggests that counselors cannot model redemption perfectly. We need to keep looking beyond ourselves to understand redemption.

Christian Theology

A REDEMPTIVE FUNNEL

In Scripture we see what we might call a redemptive funnel, as shown in figure 6. Near the beginning of the Old Testament, redemption is a general concept, but by the end of the New Testament it has become quite specific and focused.[8] In the general sense, we see God redeeming people from various types of corporate and personal distress, including slavery, poverty, plague, and oppression. In most cases, God provided this type of general redemption through other humans. For example, God raised up Moses to redeem the Hebrews from a life of slavery. God used Rahab to redeem the life of two of Joshua's spies (Josh. 2); then God used Joshua to redeem Rahab's life (Josh. 6). As the Old Testament progresses, we see increasing emphasis on God redeeming people from sin, calling them out of a life of darkness and self-deception into a life of obedience and faithfulness. David, king of Israel and psalmist, proclaimed, "Bless the Lord, O my soul, and do not forget all his benefits—who forgives all your iniquity, who heals all your diseases, who *redeems* your life from the Pit, who crowns you with steadfast love and mercy, who satisfies you with good as long as you live so that your youth is renewed like the eagle's" (Ps. 103:2-5, italics added). This type of redemption comes directly from God— only God heals our diseases and offers full forgiveness for sins.

FIGURE 6

GENERAL ACTS OF REDEMPTION
God redeems people from
various hardships.

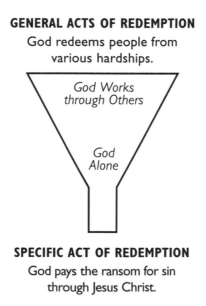

SPECIFIC ACT OF REDEMPTION
God pays the ransom for sin
through Jesus Christ.

In the New Testament, redemption becomes even more specific as it is personified in Jesus Christ. Jesus paid the ransom for human sin and thereby redeemed us. "Christ redeemed us from the curse of the law by becoming a curse for us—for it is written, 'Cursed is everyone who hangs on a tree'—in order that in Christ Jesus the blessing of Abraham might come to the Gentiles, so that we might receive the promise of the Spirit through faith" (Gal. 3:13-14).

The climax of Scripture is seen in the ending point of this redemptive funnel: God redeemed us through the sacrificial work of Jesus. Redemption through Christ is the central theme of a Christian's spiritual life, delivering us from the curse of eternal death and freeing us to live an abundant life in Christ. The apostle Paul described redemption vividly: "You were dead through the trespasses and sins. . . . But God, who is rich in mercy, out of the great love with which he loved us even when we were dead through our trespasses, made us alive together with Christ" (Eph. 2:1, 4-5).

SEEING BOTH ENDS OF THE FUNNEL

Recognizing Christ's redemption is essential for Christian faith, but it is also important to remember both ends of this redemptive process. Throughout history God has used humans as ambassadors of redemption. The narrative of Scripture tells an important story of God's sustaining a nation through both divine and human acts of provision and grace.

The story of every Christian ought to be similar. The climax of our individual lives is found in the redemptive work of Christ, but as we look on our personal histories, we see much more. It is not just that God saved all humanity from sin two thousand years ago and then stopped acting redemptively. God continually redeems people from poverty, isolation, loneliness, emptiness, depression, alienation, and sin. These general acts of redemption are showered on us as we see God working through circumstances and other people to sustain us through difficult times and times of prosperity. God is with us.[9]

Humans are often God's agents for this general type of redemption. Of course, we can never provide redemption at the narrow end of the funnel, where Christ redeems us from our sins, but when redemption is seen as freeing people from hardships, humans can participate with God. As each of us recalls God's sustaining, redemptive work in our lives, we recall people—those who have given an encouraging word, an exhortation, an act of kindness at strategic moments. God is doing the redeeming, but he often works through people. Recognizing God's sustaining and redeeming presence, seen through relationships with others, encourages us to be agents of redemption in a needy world.

The tragedy of the split between social-gospel Christians and fundamentalist Christians early in the twentieth century is that one group seemed determined to view only one end of the funnel, insisting that the redemptive work of Christ deserves our exclusive attention, while the other group seemed equally determined to view only the other end of the funnel, often equating salvation with human acts of kindness. In Scripture we see both ends of this funnel. Redemption culminates in the work of Christ; it is the only way to God. Yet Christ's redemption calls us to action in the world around us.

Both ends of the funnel are essential. A decade before the fundamentalism–social gospel split, J. Stuart Holden, author of *Redeeming Vision,* preached that "the Gospel of Christ is the gospel of action. It not only calls upon men to believe a statement but also to follow a Saviour. Its genius is not adherence to a plan but obedience to a Man. It emphasizes doings rather than doctrines, and offers a creed only as the foundation of a character."[10]

John Wesley saw religious affections as the common denominator between God's act of redemption in Christ and human acts of mercy and kindness.[11] When we understand that Christ died to redeem us from sin, our affections are turned toward God in loving appreciation. Old ways of thinking are burst apart as we see God's kindness and grace. These same affections also engage us in the world around us as we are led to acts of mercy.

In the eighteenth century, Jonathan Edwards observed, "A person who has a knowledge of doctrine and theology only—without religious affection—has never engaged in true religion."[12] What is true religion? "Religion that is pure and undefiled before God, the Father, is this: to care for orphans and widows in their distress, and to keep oneself unstained by the world" (James 1:27).

Once we understand the flow of God's redemption through history, culminating in the work of Christ, and once we let this understanding saturate our affections and passions, we also recognize that the process of redemption calls us to redemptive relationships with others.

Spirituality

It is clear from the preceding section that the theological meaning of redemption is multifaceted. Redemption is at once a historical reality culminating in Christ's atoning work, a personal event that occurs at the moment of salvation, and a lifelong process of spiritual growth leading to personal piety and social action. Though all of these are essential parts of redemption, the disciplines of spiritual formation are primarily focused on the process of redemption and purification to which Christ calls us. It is not that we become more redeemed as we grow spiritually but that we become more aware of our Redeemer, more deeply burdened by the persistent sins that visit us, more passionate about finding his will, and more comfortable in granting him control of our circumstances. With time, we see that Christ continually redeems us, delivering us again and again from our foolish ways and drawing us to himself.

REDEMPTION AND SPIRITUAL DISCIPLINES

Several of the spiritual disciplines serve to remind us of God's ongoing redemption. Meditation brings us back to the feet of our Savior after we have wandered away, chasing the demands and attractions of the day. It is often useful to meditate on God's grace through our personal histories. We can all recall times of being stuck in painful circumstances when, perhaps in the depths of our despair,

God graciously provided a way of escape. Fasting can be used as a metaphor of our need for God. With each sensation of hunger or each impulse to eat, we remember that we are people with a deep need for intimacy with God, just as we need food. Reading the spiritual classics allows us to see God's methods of redeeming others who have gone before us. In corporate worship, we gather to encourage one another along the path of redemption, sharing our common weaknesses and celebrating our gracious Savior. With confession, we name our sins, weaknesses, and vulnerabilities as we plead with God to continue transforming us. With each of these disciplines we are brought back to Christ, redeemed from our waywardness.

REDEMPTION AND HUMILITY

Redemption is closely related to confession and forgiveness, discussed in the two preceding chapters. Richard Foster refers to the doctrine of redemption as the "ground upon which we can know that confession and forgiveness are realities that transform us."[13] In the chapters on confession and forgiveness, I emphasized the role of personal humility. Humility is also an important part of understanding redemption.

Humans are lost if left to their own resources, and that is bad enough. But to make matters worse, many people are confident that they are not lost. When I am in a strange city and want to disregard my wife's suggestion that I stop for directions, I assure her that I know where I am going, that I can make it on my own. Of course, I do not find my way until I admit my need and ask for help. No one can be ransomed from lostness before recognizing his or her need. The posture of redemption is one of humility. Like stopping at a service station for directions, we must fall on our face before God and admit we are lost.

Another analogy of our need for humility is found in the rat laboratory. Animal researchers have located in rodent brains a "hot spot" that provides a pleasurable physiological stimulus. If rats have an electrode inserted in the hot spot, they will spend all day pressing the bar that delivers the pleasurable sensation. They ignore food, water, and hygiene in their pursuit of pleasure. In the same way, the pleasures of sin usurp our affections and attention and naturally draw us toward that which is pleasurable but ultimately futile and harmful. We need to be redeemed, bought back from our propensity toward pleasure seeking and drawn closer to Christ, who sees our deepest needs even while we are preoccupied with our urgent desires.

Andrew Murray describes humility as the "secret, the hidden root of thy redemption." He goes on to instruct, "Sink down into it deeper day by day."[14] We go deeper into a life of humility and redemption by practicing the disciplines that remind us of our inclination toward sin and our need for God.

From these discussions of the psychology, theology, and spirituality of redemption, several important conclusions can be derived:

1. Spiritual redemption can be found only in Christ, who provided the ransom to free us from our captivity to sin. In this sense, redemption is a one-time work fulfilled in Christ's atonement.

2. Spiritual redemption is also a process whereby God draws us closer and saves us from addiction to the pleasures of sin. This process of redemption both requires and produces humility as we recognize our desperate need for a gracious God.

3. God not only redeems us spiritually but also delivers us from many perils and hardships, often through the kindness of others.

4. As God's redemption transforms our affections, we are motivated to be God's agents of redemption, helping those in need find hope and relief from trials.

5. Counseling provides opportunities to be redemptive agents in a fallen and needy world.

6. A redemptive worldview in counseling calls us not necessarily to specific techniques or theoretical frameworks
but to counseling relationships that reflect the grace and
kindness we understand through God's redemptive love.

PSYCHOLOGICAL AND SPIRITUAL HEALTH

In an address entitled "Psychotherapy and Redemption," given at the
American Psychological Association (APA) meetings in 1990,
Hendrika Vande Kemp, a psychologist at Fuller Theological Seminary,
illustrated the many challenges of redemptive psychotherapy with a
fascinating case study.[15] Her client, whom she called Deborah, was
raised by a violent, abusive father and an emotionally aloof mother.
Deborah recalled being sexually assaulted twice during her adolescent
years, once by a boy she was dating and once by a middle-aged
exhibitionist. Yet her mother told her she had only imagined both
incidents. These contradictory experiences confused Deborah and later
caused her to question the validity of other experiences.

Deborah married a man much like her father—abusive and
aggressive. After raping her on the second night of their marriage,
an act that resulted in both emotional and physical damage, the man
caused four years of sexual and emotional conflict. Eventually he
insisted that Deborah get psychological treatment. The marriage
ended soon thereafter.

By the time Deborah reached a counselor, she was a troubled
woman with symptoms of various personality disorders, an eating
disorder, depression, confused thinking, and suicidal desires. It
would be nice if the story ended happily with a counselor helping
her overcome these various symptoms. Unfortunately, she bounced
from therapist to therapist, with two of her counselors damaging
her more by sexually exploiting her. By the time Deborah came to
Dr. Vande Kemp's attention, she had seen six different therapists.

Dr. Vande Kemp became acquainted with Deborah in two ways:
she supervised a practicum student who provided therapy for
Deborah, and she sometimes had direct contact with Deborah

through her consultative role. Both Dr. Vande Kemp and the practicum student supported Deborah through the difficult and arduous process of filing ethics charges against a former therapist. Deborah developed with Dr. Vande Kemp a strong bond, which she expressed appropriately through several thank-you notes and cards.

When Deborah was attacked while jogging and the hospital staff did not want her to return home alone, she called Dr. Vande Kemp. With some discomfort about the therapeutic boundary issues, Dr. Vande Kemp allowed Deborah to stay with her for a short time, then made sure that Deborah and her therapist worked through whatever confusion this stirred up for Deborah.

Some time later Deborah's emotional health improved, she moved out of town and married again, and had children. She appeared content in her role as a mother and sent holiday greeting cards to Dr. Vande Kemp each year. In one card she mentioned that she had been diagnosed with breast cancer. At the time of Dr. Vande Kemp's APA address, Deborah's second husband had left her. She was living with a family that had "adopted" her, and she was about to die. Despite the tragic ending, this case study illustrates several important components of a redemptive counseling relationship.

Will This Help Establish a Healthy Sense of Self?
Through relationships with Dr. Vande Kemp and her practicum student, Deborah developed a stronger, more accurate sense of herself. In this sense, her counseling was redemptive, drawing her out of a state of helpless victimization to one of empowerment. The greatest evidence for this change is seen in her willingness to bring charges against a former therapist who had sexually exploited her.

Deborah learned early in life that her proper role was one of compliance and conformity. She tried to prevent her father's violent outbursts by not "rocking the boat." She married a man very similar to her father and again tried to cope by losing her own identity. Two therapists took advantage of her desire to comply and had sexual relationships with her in the guise of helping her. One therapist left the state before Deborah was strong enough to bring charges. After several months of therapy with Dr. Vande Kemp's student, Deborah was strong enough to bring charges against the second therapist.

How did Deborah move from being passive and overly compliant to being empowered to stand for justice? Through a redemptive counseling relationship. Vande Kemp observed that redemption often involves reconnection, binding together the fragments of a shattered life into a recovered sense of self. Redemption occurred not by the counselor's insisting that Deborah seek justice but by helping Deborah reconnect her feelings with reality, by binding her up until she was strong enough to make a good decision on her own.

Notice that a strong sense of self does not necessarily produce selfishness. Ultimately Deborah decided to seek justice because she did not want other women to be hurt as she had been hurt. Her own experience with redemption caused her to reach out redemptively to others.

Will This Help Establish a Healthy Sense of Need?

In one sense, Deborah was overwhelmed with her need even before counseling with Dr. Vande Kemp's student. She had attempted suicide twenty times, seen six different therapists, and viewed herself as wretched and worthless. She knew a great deal about need but not much about a healthy sense of need.

As she became stronger in the context of therapy, she learned to approach need in a healthier way, as revealed in her call to Dr. Vande Kemp from the hospital. Earlier in Deborah's life, she had coped with need by clinging to aggressive and demanding men, by trying to find symbiotic relationships with dominating people, or by suicide attempts. When she called Dr. Vande Kemp from the hospital, she was reaching out to someone who had proven herself to be caring and nurturing. It was a healthy response to need.

This shows the interconnectedness of self, need, and healing relationships. If Deborah had not developed a stronger sense of self in counseling or if there had not been a healing bond between the two of them, she would not have taken the risk of calling Dr. Vande Kemp.

WHAT IF THIS HAPPENED?

Both counselor A and counselor B are convinced that contemporary American society places too great an emphasis on individuality and self-sufficiency. They both believe that many of their clients need to develop a more accurate understanding of interdependency, including an awareness of their need for others.

Counselor A addresses this in the first counseling session. She often says something like this: "Counseling is an interaction between people. If I am going to help you, it will be because you recognize you need me. We can't do everything on our own. We all need help sometimes."

Counselor B approaches need differently. In the first session, she commonly asks, "Tell me how it feels for you to be here today." She listens carefully to the client's response but does not discuss the idea of need any further unless the client invites the discussion.

I prefer counselor B's approach because it gives the counseling relationship time to develop. Eventually there may be overt discussions of need in counseling but only after the therapeutic relationship is established and the client has developed a strong enough sense of self to speak assertively about need. Counselor A seems to be inviting excessive dependence, which may cause the client to be either clingy or wary. A healthy awareness of need is best established in conjunction with a healthy sense of self in the context of a safe relationship.

Will This Help Establish a Healing Relationship?

Redemptive counseling is relationally sensitive counseling. It cannot be reduced to a set of clinical techniques. It was the character of the therapist and the supervisor, as well as their relationships with Deborah, that provided Deborah with redemption and hope. In her APA address, Vande Kemp emphasized that the redemptive therapist affirms a client's longing for salvation. The counselor becomes a conduit for distributing God's grace.

Redemptive Christian counselors value their opportunities to be ministers of God's grace to others. They see character—not their own natural character, but the character that God is producing and renewing in their lives—as the greatest tool they offer in counseling.

Though the relational aspects of counseling carry great healing power, we should be realistic about their limitations. Often the people who need redemptive relationships the most are also the ones who are most resistant to entering into such a relationship and who gain the least from it when they do enter in. For instance, a recent study of sexually abused Christian women demonstrated that childhood sexual abuse interferes with adult capacity to feel loved and accepted by God and others.[16] Even Deborah, after doing well in therapy, continued to have relational problems. She married and divorced a second time and unwisely conformed to her husband's demands that she not get medical treatment for breast cancer.

The sobering reality is that we cannot completely transform our clients, even with the best counseling relationships. The best we can hope for is that we initiate a spark in the process of redemption—a spark that produces the warmth of feeling loved and illuminates a future where all human liabilities will be set aside and redemption will be fully accomplished.

FACING THE CHALLENGES

Challenge 1: Moving from Two Areas of Competence to Three
The methods of psychology and theology are steeped in intellectual and rational traditions. Psychological theories are developed by carefully observing human behavior, formulating specific hypotheses, testing these hypotheses with double-blind studies, and then

revising the theories accordingly. Similarly, Christian theological perspectives are shaped by a careful analysis of Scripture in light of other academic disciplines such as philosophy, history, and anthropology. We need the academic contributions of psychology and theology in order to be effective Christian counselors, but we also need to understand spirituality.

The methods of spirituality are different. Although one can study spiritual formation from academic perspectives, the primary value of Christian spirituality is experiential. We look to God for daily sustenance, not because we can prove God with a double-blind study or because of the ontological or teleological arguments that God exists, but because we have met God personally and have become people of faith. It is precisely this amorphous, experiential nature of spirituality that often raises our suspicions and concerns about spiritual formation. It all seems so boundless, so infinitely prone to human distortion. We need theological boundaries in order to maintain orthodox and scripturally sound views of redemption, yet we also need the experiential depth of a personal spiritual journey.

The capacity for Christians to integrate a redemptive worldview into their counseling work is both facilitated and limited by their faith experience.

WHAT IF THIS HAPPENED?

What if the prevailing values of mental health professionals were to change suddenly and everyone became interested in redemption as part of the counseling process? Training programs would start offering courses in redemptive therapy. Clinical supervisors would teach supervisees how to implement redemption in their clinical work. A few new doctoral programs would spring up, each offering degrees in redemptive psychotherapy. Continuing education workshops, Yellow Pages advertisements, and national conventions all would point toward redemption.

> I create this far-fetched scenario to ask a question: Who would be best prepared to offer counseling services in this new mental health environment? Christians would be. We have reflected deeply on redemption, and more important we have experienced profound redemption in the spiritual realm. No amount of classroom experience or continuing education could provide the same background that we have learned experientially.

This illustrates how spiritual experience prepares Christian counselors to think redemptively in the counseling office. Redemption in counseling is not a technique learned in the classroom but a worldview that wells up in those who walk close to Christ and then spills over into every relationship, including those in the counseling office. Of course, if we accept this premise, then we must also acknowledge that the extent to which we incorporate a redemptive worldview in our counseling work is limited by the depth of our spiritual experience with redemption.

Desiring a redemptive worldview calls us to the spiritual journey and bids us to draw closer to our Redeemer.

Challenge 2: Blurred Personal-Professional Distinctions

When Sigmund Freud infused psychoanalysis with his passion for scientific objectivity, he cast the therapist as a value-free professional observer of the patient. Though many of Freud's ideas have withstood the challenges of the past century, this one has not. Far from being an objective observer, the therapist is an active agent in a therapeutic transaction. A counselor is both professional and personal; the roles cannot be neatly divided.

WHAT IF THIS HAPPENED?

Pastor Karing has seen Stormy Ann Dempty for several sessions, helping Ms. Dempty deal with anger control, feelings of sadness, and spiritual apathy. On the fourth session, Ms. Dempty looks questioningly at Pastor Karing and asks, "What kinds of things do you do to keep your spiritual vision going?" Pastor Karing hears two voices in his head.

> ***Voice 1 (a deeply resonant, professional voice):*** She is trying to get me to cross over into a personal relationship that might cloud my objectivity, add to transference and countertransference difficulties, and displace her responsibility for change onto me. I should simply respond by saying, "The question is more interesting than any answer I might give. I'm wondering what it might mean that you ask that."

> ***Voice 2 (a tentative, personal voice):*** This may be a good opportunity to share with Stormy some of my methods of meditating and praying from Scripture. She may find them as helpful as I have.

Neither of Pastor Karing's two options are clearly right or clearly wrong. He may be correct that Ms. Dempty's request for information could improperly confuse the counseling roles. He may also be correct that a specific personal disclosure regarding devotional techniques could be helpful to Ms. Dempty. The important point is that he feels inner conflict, as he should. The boundaries between professional and personal are difficult to define for those with a redemptive worldview.

The same observation could be made for Dr. Vande Kemp's decision to allow Deborah to stay at her home for several days. Though I am impressed with her decision, I am more impressed with the inner conflict she felt in making the decision. If it were an easy decision in either direction, then either her understanding of professional ethics or her capacity for a redemptive worldview would have to be questioned.

Challenge 3: Expanded Definitions of Training
Though I have emphasized the importance of personal spiritual training throughout this book and this chapter, it is important to remember

that most forms of Christian counseling require both professional and personal training. It would be a mistake, for example, to assume that redemption through Christ is sufficient to make one competent in dealing with the variety of situations faced by professional counselors.

A careless attitude toward professional training might lead one to the conclusion that counselors with redemptive worldviews are nice people who spend an hour every week being nice to each of their clients. This is no more accurate than saying God redeems us by being nice to us. God understands us perfectly, so the process of redemption looks different for each person and each situation. At times we experience God's wrath and justice. At times God is merciful and kind. Sometimes God seems distant and hard to find. During each of these times, God is trying to purify our faith and deliver us from the snares of self-deception and evil.[17]

Similarly, effective counselors are warm and affirming at times, assertive and confrontive at other times, and occasionally distant and aloof. Any of these strategies can be effective or damaging, depending on the circumstances of counseling. Because we are not God, we are prone to imperfect judgments, misunderstandings about our clients, and self-serving biases. This calls all counselors to a place of humility and reminds us of the importance of good training, ongoing consultation and supervision, high ethical standards, and reliance on the Holy Spirit's guidance as we navigate the murky waters of counseling.

Challenge 4: Confronting Dominant Views of Mental Health

At the beginning of this chapter I suggested two distinctions of Christian counselors: we identify ourselves as Christians, and we maintain a redemptive worldview in our counseling work. Both of these distinctions conflict with dominant assumptions of mental health.

Most counselors, regardless of their personal religious orientation, see themselves as sensitive to the varying religious values of their clients. Such sensitivity has recently been mandated for psychologists by the APA.[18] Although this is generally good news for religious clients, it reduces the perceived need for counselors to describe their personal religious values. Because counselors perceive themselves to be sensitive to a wide range of religious values, they do not see a need to be explicit about their personal beliefs.

If sensitivity to religious beliefs means not ridiculing or undermining a client's beliefs, then it is probably true that most counselors are sensitive to religious differences and there is little need to disclose personal religious values. But if religious beliefs transform the way we see human problems and provide insights for the way those problems are treated, then the personal religious values of the counselor are relevant to treatment and are important to identify. Even if other counselors are not doing so, Christian counselors who believe their values affect the way they counsel can demonstrate a commitment to ethical excellence by disclosing their personal religious values to new clients.

A redemptive worldview in Christian counseling also challenges recent mental health traditions that emphasize redemption from within oneself. Contemporary counseling theory emphasizes personal freedom through cleaning out psychic conflicts, changing irrational beliefs, modifying ineffective behavior patterns, and finding self-fulfillment. All these interventions can be useful in various situations, but they tend to overvalue individualism and self-discovery. The Christian message of redemption, a vital part of counseling theory until the twentieth century, calls us to redemption in relation to others.[19] Most important, we are called out of our sinful ways to community with God and into caring community with one another. Christian counselors emerge from this caring community to live out their redemptive worldview in a variety of vocational and professional contexts.

In his book *Redemptive Intimacy,* philosopher Dick Westley describes the redemptive nature of Christian communities: "As Church, we form a counter culture to our world, but a counter culture of a most ironic sort. We seek not to coerce and badger our neighbors, but to live our lives of intimacy in trusting openness to them, always hoping that they may see in us something of the 'parable of God' and finally get the point of it all."[20]

Challenge 5: Establishing a Scientific Base

As psychotherapy and counseling-outcome research has progressed, there has been increasing interest in the common factors that all forms of therapy share. Many hundreds of studies have looked at the level of specific counseling interventions, as illustrated in figure 7, and the general conclusion is that "no psychotherapy is superior to any other, although all are superior to no treatment."[21] Weinberger has recently suggested it is time to focus on the five common factors listed in figure 7, all of which he believes are "eminently measurable."[22]

FIGURE 7

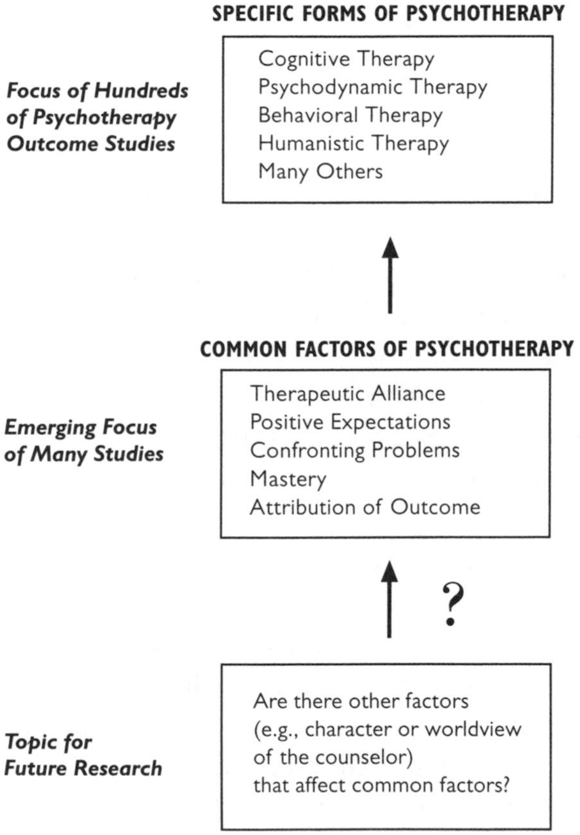

SPECIFIC FORMS OF PSYCHOTHERAPY

Focus of Hundreds of Psychotherapy Outcome Studies

Cognitive Therapy
Psychodynamic Therapy
Behavioral Therapy
Humanistic Therapy
Many Others

COMMON FACTORS OF PSYCHOTHERAPY

Emerging Focus of Many Studies

Therapeutic Alliance
Positive Expectations
Confronting Problems
Mastery
Attribution of Outcome

Topic for Future Research

Are there other factors (e.g., character or worldview of the counselor) that affect common factors?

Common-factors research is important as the next step in understanding the mystery of the counseling process, yet I suspect there may be another level of inquiry that lies ahead. Could it be that the character and worldview of the counselor have a meaningful impact on the common factors? Testing this assertion poses monumental scientific challenges because of measurement problems. Although several good scales for common factors already exist, there are no good ways to measure concepts as difficult to grasp as character. And how do we get beyond traditional attitude measures to assess a counselor's worldview, such as the redemptive worldview described here? These preliminary measurement tasks will have to be addressed before the relationship between character and common factors can be systematically evaluated.

Challenge 6: Defining Relevant Ethical Standards

At the heart of counseling ethics are two key principles: do good, and do no harm. Though the nuances are complex and the implications numerous, if counselors could consistently abide by these two standards, there would be few ethics violations.

These same two principles form the ethical foundation for a redemptive worldview in counseling. Clients often come to us feeling oppressed by the forces of evil in the world, tired of the struggle for inner and interpersonal peace. They are feeling vulnerable and weak, and they are looking to a counselor for help and hope. It is their vulnerability that makes it so important that we value doing good and not harm.

At times, the redemptive counselor takes risks, but not excessive risks. It was risky for Dr. Vande Kemp to allow Deborah to stay in her home for several days while recovering from being attacked. I, along with many counselors, feel an immediate and automatic sense of discomfort with such an arrangement, assuming that this type of multiple-role relationship with a supervisee's client pushes ethical boundaries and may result in harm to the client. Yet it may have been this risky act of compassion that most clearly communicated

God's grace to Deborah. Vande Kemp was careful to note that therapists must maintain ethical boundaries and recognize their own limits and vulnerabilities. I am convinced that Dr. Vande Kemp would not have invited Deborah to stay at her home if she had been the therapist rather than the supervisor or if she had any feelings other than altruistic compassion for Deborah. Deborah's early therapists also crossed ethical boundaries, but with impure motives, and they ended up harming Deborah. Some risk, for the sake of redemption, is wise. Excessive risk without carefully considering our personal vulnerabilities and the ethical implications of our actions can harm those we are claiming to help.

When Deborah first came for counseling, she was beaten down by past relationships and oppressed by her view of herself and her future. Two therapists took Deborah in her vulnerable state, pretended they were doing good, then did harm by sexually exploiting her. One therapist, a Christian with a commitment to a redemptive worldview, did good, empowering Deborah to make better decisions and reach out for help.

SUMMARY

The problem with sin is that it separates us from God; the wonder of redemption is that we are brought back into relationship with God. This is living truth that ushers us into a rich spiritual life of communion with Christ. Christian counselors with a redemptive worldview respond to others with humility because they recognize that from which they have been redeemed, with compassion because they experience God's grace, and with gratitude because of God's sustaining presence.

Discussing redemption in counseling is a fitting conclusion for this book because redemption is a rich and complex topic requiring an understanding of the other topics considered: Scripture, sin, confession, forgiveness, and prayer. Christians learn about redemption by understanding the general and specific themes of *Scripture*.

Scripture describes a redemptive God, longing to draw people out of the grips of sin and rebellion to the bliss of fellowship with the divine. Picture Jesus, surrounded by cynical Pharisees, proclaiming these words of redemption, mingled with sorrow and frustration: "Jerusalem, Jerusalem, the city that kills the prophets and stones those who are sent to it! How often have I desired to gather your children together as a hen gathers her brood under her wings, and you were not willing!" (Matt. 23:37). Understanding *sin* gives meaning to redemption. Those who deny sin see no need for spiritual redemption—"I'm okay; you're okay." A Christian view of sin forces us beyond popular psychology to a point of understanding our need to be ransomed from the forces of evil that pervade our world. With *confession,* we acknowledge our sin and our need for help. Graciously, God grants *forgiveness* as we experience the wonder of being redeemed, bought back from captivity to sin to an abundant life in Christ. Once we experience redemption, especially as we allow it to seep into our affections, our understanding of *prayer* can never be the same. Prayer ushers us to the throne of a gracious God who brings us out of slavery to human folly and into a land of spiritual abundance. This God is to be honored and praised and served in work and every part of life.

CONCLUSION

THE MULTITASKING COUNSELOR

We began this journey, in chapter 1, by considering Jill, a depressed woman looking for a spiritually sensitive counselor. Her task of selecting a Christian counselor is both important and difficult. It is important because her values and perspectives will change as a result of counseling. It is difficult because Jill is looking for a rare counselor capable of multitasking. (*Multitasking* is a term used to describe computers that can process more than one job at a time). The most effective Christian counselors are able to process several ideas simultaneously.

Counselors who are not capable of multitasking end up treating only part of the problem. If her counselor understands the psychological world while ignoring the theological and spiritual, Jill's deep longings for God may never be understood and valued in the counseling process. If her counselor emphasizes the spiritual life but overlooks psychology and theology, she may be led in a futile search inward—looking desperately for an inner child or an inner guide or an inner light but avoiding the true self-understanding that comes from humbly loving a sovereign God. If her counselor emphasizes theology alone, she may leave with a stronger sense of what she *ought* to do while feeling powerless as to *how* she should make necessary changes.

What does multitasking look like in Christian counseling? Throughout this book I have suggested three essential categories that must be considered simultaneously: psychology, theology, and spirituality.

From a psychological perspective, effective counselors are able to participate fully in a treatment relationship while simultaneously stepping outside the relationship to view the problems of the client and the nature of the counseling relationship from a more objective vantage point. At the same time, as counselors empathize and reflect emotions within the counseling relationship, they are also evaluating and assessing from outside the counseling relationship—noticing voice tone, nonverbal gestures, facial expressions, and styles of relating. This type of psychological multitasking requires excellent training, cultural sensitivity, and supervised experience to master. But there is more.

Effective Christian counselors also consider theological perspectives at the same time that they engage in the various psychological tasks of counseling. Historical and systematic theology, biblical understanding, and Christian tradition are all valued and considered essential components of counseling. These tasks require a basic working knowledge of the Bible, Christian history, and theological systems. But there is still more.

Multitasking for the Christian counselor also involves an understanding of the spiritual life of the client. How are the client's problems related to spiritual development? When is a problem simply a behavioral habit to be eliminated or reshaped, and when is a problem a reflection of deep, inner yearnings for intimacy with God and others? How can a treatment relationship be crafted to foster qualities of humility and insight? When, if ever, should prayer or Scripture memory be used in counseling or prescribed to a client? These are the types of questions that most mental health practitioners rarely consider, but Christian counselors regularly encounter questions such as these. Training for spiritual sensitivity may begin in the classroom or by reading spiritual classics, but it must continue in the private lives of counselors. The spiritual disciplines help us understand God's grace and our own fallenness and give us opportunities to glean fragments of wisdom from our omniscient God.

Multitasking in the counseling office is an exhausting process. It is no wonder that many counselors feel emotionally depleted by the end of a long day at work! May God guide us each to the deep, still waters of life where we find energy, hope, courage, humility, compassion, and peace.

ENDNOTES

Acknowledgments

1. Portions of chapter 7 are drawn from an article Katheryn and I wrote: "Forgiveness: More than a Therapeutic Technique," *Journal of Psychology and Christianity* (in press).

2. Portions of chapter 1 are condensed from an article Jim and I wrote: "Psychology, Theology, and Spirituality: Challenges for Spiritually Sensitive Counseling," *Christian Counseling Today* (winter 1996).

Chapter 1: Religion in the Counseling Office

1. Stephen Quackenbos, Gayle Privette, and Bonnel Klentz, "Psychotherapy: Sacred or Secular?" *Journal of Counseling and Development* 63 (1985): 290–293.

2. Mark R. McMinn, "Religious Values, Sexist Language, and Perceptions of a Therapist," *Journal of Psychology and Christianity* 10 (1991): 132–136.

3. Stanton L. Jones, "A Constructive Relationship for Religion with the Science and Profession of Psychology: Perhaps the Boldest Model Yet," *American Psychologist* 49 (1994): 184–199.

4. Albert Ellis, *The Case against Religion: A Psychotherapist's View* (New York: Institute for Rational Living, 1971).

5. Research contradicting the evidence of the atheists includes Allen E. Bergin, "Religiosity and Mental Health: A Critical Reevaluation and Meta-analysis," *Professional Psychology: Research and Practice* 14 (1983): 170–184; Allen E. Bergin, "Values and Religious Issues in Psychotherapy and Mental Health," *American Psychologist* 46 (1991): 394–403; Allen E. Bergin, Randy D. Stinchfield, Thomas A. Gaskin, Kevin S. Masters, and Clyde E. Sullivan, "Religious Life-Styles and Mental Health: An Exploratory Study," *Journal of Consulting and Clinical Psychology* 35 (1988): 91–98; Michael J. Donahue, "Intrinsic and Extrinsic Religiousness: Review and Meta-analysis," *Journal of Personality and Social Psychology* 48 (1985): 400–419. Evidence of caution can be found in Albert Ellis, *The Case against Religiosity* (New York: Institute for Rational Living, 1983); Albert Ellis, "Do I Really Hold that Religiousness Is Irrational and Equivalent to Emotional Disturbance?" *American Psychologist* 47 (1992): 428–429; Albert Ellis, "My Current Views of Rational-Emotive Therapy

(RET) and Religiousness," *Journal of Rational-Emotive & Cognitive-Behavior Therapy* 10 (1992): 37–40.

6. Albert Ellis, "The Advantages and Disadvantages of Self-Help Therapy Materials," *Professional Psychology: Research and Practice* 24 (1993): 336.

7. For critiques of postmodernism, see M. Brewster Smith, "Selfhood at Risk: Postmodern Perils and the Perils of Postmodernism," *American Psychologist* 49 (1994): 405–411.

8. Ronald Rapee and David Barlow, "Panic Disorder: Cognitive-behavioral Treatment," *Psychiatric Annals* 18 (1988): 473–477.

9. Task Force on Promotion and Dissemination of Psychological Procedures, "Training in and Dissemination of Empirically Validated Psychological Treatments: Report and Recommendations," *The Clinical Psychologist* 48 (1995): 3–23.

10. Everett L. Worthington, Jr., "A Blueprint for Intradisciplinary Integration," *Journal of Psychology and Theology* 22 (1994): 79–86.

11. Gary R. Collins, "Moving through the Jungle: A Decade of Integration," *Journal of Psychology and Theology* 11 (1983): 5.

12. Worthington, Jr., "Blueprint," *Journal of Psychology and Theology* 22 (1994): 80.

13. Dallas Willard, *The Spirit of the Disciplines* (San Francisco: HarperCollins, 1988), 18.

14. Gary R. Collins, "The Puzzle of Popular Spirituality," *Christian Counseling Today* (winter 1994): 10–14.

15. Mark R. McMinn and James C. Wilhoit, "Psychology, Theology, and Spirituality: Challenges for Spiritually Sensitive Counseling," *Christian Counseling Today*, (fall 1995).

16. Michael J. Lambert and Allen E. Bergin, "The Effectiveness of Psychotherapy," *Handbook of Psychotherapy and Behavior Change,* 4th ed., ed. Allen E. Bergin and Sol L. Garfield (New York: Wiley, 1994), 143–189; Mary Lee Smith, G. V. Glass, and R. L. Miller, *The Benefits of Psychotherapy* (Baltimore: Johns Hopkins Press, 1980).

17. Jerome D. Frank, "Therapeutic Factors in Psychotherapy," *American Journal of Psychotherapy* 25 (1971): 350–361.

18. Susan C. Whiston and Thomas L. Sexton, "An Overview of Psychotherapy Outcome Research: Implications for Practice," *Professional Psychology* 24 (1993): 43–51.

19. McMinn, "Religious Values," *Journal of Psychology and Christianity*: 132–136.

20. Allen E. Bergin, "Psychotherapy and Religious Values," *Journal of Consulting and Clinical Psychology* 48 (1980): 95–105; Timothy A. Kelly and Hans H. Strupp, "Patient and Therapist Values in Psychotherapy: Perceived Changes, Assimilation, Similarity, and Outcome," *Journal of Consulting and Clinical Psychology* 60 (1992): 34–40; Frank I. Martinez, "Therapist-client

Convergence and Similarity of Religious Values: Their Effect on Client Improvement," *Journal of Psychology and Christianity* 10 (1991): 137–143; Dominic O. Vachon and Albert A. Agresti, "A Training Proposal to Help Mental Health Professionals Clarify and Manage Implicit Values in the Counseling Process," *Professional Psychology: Research and Practice* 23 (1992): 509–514; Everett L. Worthington, Jr., ed., *Psychotherapy and Religious Values* (Grand Rapids: Baker, 1993).

21. Dominic O. Vachon and Albert A. Agresti, "A Training Proposal to Help Mental Health Professionals Clarify and Manage Implicit Values in the Counseling Process," *Professional Psychology: Research and Practice* 23 (1992): 509.

22. Richard J. Foster, *Celebration of Discipline: The Path to Spiritual Growth* (San Francisco: HarperCollins, 1988); Willard, *Disciplines.*

23. Gary W. Moon, Judy W. Bailey, John C. Kwasny, and Dale E. Willis, "Training in the Use of Christian Disciplines as Counseling Techniques within Christian Graduate Training Programs," *Psychotherapy and Religious Values,* ed. Everett L. Worthington, Jr. (Grand Rapids: Baker, 1993), 191–203.

24. Ibid., 200.

25. Ibid., 201.

26. Samuel A. Adams, "Spiritual Well-being, Religiosity, and Demographic Variables as Predictors of the Use of Christian Counseling Techniques." Poster presented at the annual meetings of the American Psychological Association. Los Angeles: August 1994.

27. Eugene H. Peterson, *A Long Obedience in the Same Direction: Discipleship in an Instant Society* (Downers Grove, Ill.: InterVarsity Press, 1980).

28. Stanton L. Jones and Richard E. Butman, *Modern Psychotherapies: A Comprehensive Christian Appraisal* (Downers Grove, Ill.: InterVarsity Press, 1991).

29. Raymond A. DiGiuseppe, Mitchell W. Robin, and Wendy Dryden, "On the Compatibility of Rational-Emotive Therapy and Judeo-Christian Philosophy: A Focus on Clinical Strategies," *Journal of Cognitive Psychotherapy: An International Quarterly* 4 (1990): 355–368; Paul Hauck, *Reason in Pastoral Counseling* (Philadelphia: Westminster, 1972); Paul Hauck, "Religion and RET: Friends or Foes?" *Clinical Applications of Rational-Emotive Therapy,* ed. Albert Ellis and M. E. Bernard (New York: Plenum Press, 1985), 237–255; W. Brad Johnson, "Rational-Emotive Therapy and Religiousness: A Review," *Journal of Rational-Emotive & Cognitive-Behavioral Therapy* 10 (1992): 21–35; W. Brad Johnson, "Christian Rational-Emotive Therapy: A Treatment Protocol," *Journal of Psychology and Christianity* 12 (1993): 254–261; W. Brad Johnson and Charles R. Ridley, "Brief Christian and Non-Christian Rational-Emotive Therapy with Depressed Christian Clients: An Exploratory Study," *Counseling and*

Values 36 (1992): 220–229; Constance Lawrence, "Rational-Emotive Therapy and the Religious Client," *Journal of Rational-Emotive Therapy* 5 (1987): 13–20; Constance Lawrence and Charles H. Huber, "Strange Bedfellows?: Rational-Emotive Therapy and Pastoral Counseling," *The Personnel and Guidance Journal* 61 (1982): 210–212; John Powell, *Fully Human, Fully Alive* (Niles, Ill.: Argus, 1976); Sandra D. M. Warnock, "Rational-Emotive Therapy and the Christian Client," *Journal of Rational-Emotive & Cognitive-Behavior Therapy* 7 (1989): 263–274.

30. Constance Lawrence and Charles H. Huber, "Strange Bedfellows?: Rational-Emotive Therapy and Pastoral Counseling," *The Personnel and Guidance Journal* 61 (1982): 210.

31. Mark R. McMinn, "RET, Constructivism, and Christianity: A Hermeneutic for Christian Cognitive Therapy," *Journal of Psychology and Christianity* 13 (1994): 342–355.

32. Thomas A. Harris, *I'm OK—You're OK: A Practical Guide to Transactional Analysis* (New York: Harper & Row, 1967).

33. Ellis, *The Case against Religion,* 3; see also Albert Ellis and Eugene Schoenfeld, "Divine Intervention and the Treatment of Chemical Dependency," *Journal of Substance Abuse* 2 (1990): 459–468.

34. Everett L. Worthington, Jr., Philip D. Dupont, James T. Berry, and Loretta A. Duncan, "Christian Therapists and Clients' Perceptions of Religious Psychotherapy in Private and Agency Settings," *Journal of Psychology and Theology* 16 (1988): 282–293.

35. Ibid., 292.

36. Robert A. Ball, and Rodney K. Goodyear, "Self-reported Professional Practices of Christian Psychotherapists," *Psychotherapy and Religious Values,* ed. Everett L. Worthington, Jr. (Grand Rapids: Baker, 1993), 171–182.

37. W. Brad Johnson, "Outcome Research and Religious Psychotherapies: Where Are We and Where Are We Going?" *Journal of Psychology and Theology* 21 (1993): 297–308.

38. W. Brad Johnson, Ronald DeVries, Charles R. Ridley, Donald Pettorini, and Deland R. Peterson, "The Comparative Efficacy of Christian and Secular Rational-Emotive Therapy with Christian Clients," *Journal of Psychology and Theology* 22 (1994): 130–140; W. Brad Johnson and Charles R. Ridley, "Brief Christian and Non-Christian Rational-Emotive Therapy with Depressed Christian Clients: An Exploratory Study," *Counseling and Values* 36 (1992): 220–229; David Richard Pecheur and Keith J. Edwards, "A Comparison of Secular and Religious Versions of Cognitive Therapy with Depressed Christian College Students," *Journal of Psychology and Theology* 12 (1984): 45–54.

39. L. Rebecca Propst, "The Comparative Efficacy of Religious and Non-religious Imagery for the Treatment of Mild Depression in Religious

Individuals," *Cognitive Therapy and Research* 4 (1980): 167–178; L. Rebecca Propst, Richard Ostrom, Philip Watkins, Terri Dean, and David Mashburn, "Comparative Efficacy of Religious and Nonreligious Cognitive-behavioral Therapy for the Treatment of Clinical Depression in Religious Individuals," *Journal of Consulting and Clinical Psychology* 60 (1992): 94–103.

40. L. Rebecca Propst, Richard Ostrom, Philip Watkins, Terri Dean, and David Mashburn, "Comparative Efficacy of Religious and Nonreligious Cognitive-behavioral Therapy for the Treatment of Clinical Depression in Religious Individuals," *Journal of Consulting and Clinical Psychology* 60 (1992): 94–103.

41. Daniel R. Somberg, Gerald L. Stone, and Charles D. Claiborn, "Informed Consent: Therapists' Beliefs and Practices," *Professional Psychology: Research and Practice* 24 (1993): 153–159; Therese Sullivan, William Martin, Jr., and Mitchel M. Handelsman, "Practical Benefits of an Informed-consent Procedure: An Empirical Investigation," *Professional Psychology: Research and Practice* 24 (1993): 160–163.

42. Everett L. Worthington, Jr., "Religious Counseling: A Review of Published Empirical Research," *Journal of Counseling and Development* 64 (1986): 421–431.

43. Enrico E. Jones and Steven M. Pulos, "Comparing the Process in Psycho-dynamic and Cognitive-behavioral Therapies," *Journal of Consulting and Clinical Psychology* 61 (1993): 306–316; Whiston and Sexton, "An Overview of Psychotherapy Outcome Research," *Professional Psychology,* 43–51.

44. Propst et al., "Comparative Efficacy of Religious and Nonreligious Cognitive-behavioral Therapy," *Journal of Consulting and Clinical Psychology,* 94–103.

45. Ibid.

46. Ibid.

47. Propst, "The Comparative Efficacy of Religious and Non-religious Imagery," *Cognitive Therapy and Research,* 167–178; Propst et al., "Comparative Efficacy of Religious and Nonreligious Cognitive-behavioral Therapy," *Journal of Consulting and Clinical Psychology,* 94–103.

Chapter 2: Toward Psychological and Spiritual Health

1. Jerome D. Frank, "Psychotherapy: The Restoration of Morale," *American Journal of Psychiatry* 131 (1974): 271–274; David E. Orlinsky, Klaus Grawe, and Barbara K. Parks, "Process and Outcome in Psychotherapy—Noch Einmal," *Handbook of Psychotherapy and Behavior Change* (4th ed.), ed. Allen E. Bergin and Sol L. Garfield (New York: Wiley, 1994), 270–376.

2. Mark R. McMinn, *Cognitive Therapy Techniques in Christian Counseling* (Waco, Tex.: Word).

3. Enrico E. Jones and Steven M. Pulos, "Comparing the Process in Psychodynamic and Cognitive-behavioral Therapies," *Journal of Consulting and Clinical Psychology* 61 (1993): 306–316.

4. Aaron T. Beck, Arthur Freeman, and Associates, *Cognitive Therapy of Personality Disorders* (New York: Guilford, 1990); Richard C. Bedrosian and George D. Bozicas, *Treating Family of Origin Problems: A Cognitive Approach* (New York: Guilford, 1994); Jeffrey E. Young, *Cognitive Therapy for Personality Disorders: A Schema-focused Approach,* rev. ed. (Sarasota, FL: Professional Resource Press, 1994).

5. Erik H. Erikson, *Childhood and Society* (New York: Norton, 1963).

6. Ibid.

7. Timothy Beougher and Lyle Dorsett, eds., *Accounts of a Campus Revival: Wheaton College 1995.* (Wheaton, Ill.: Harold Shaw, 1995).

8. Marsha M. Linehan, *Cognitive-behavioral Treatment of Borderline Personality Disorder* (New York: Guilford, 1993).

9. Michael J. Lambert, "Psychotherapy Outcome Research: Implications for Integrative and Eclectic Therapists," *Handbook of Psychotherapy Integration,* ed. John C. Norcross and Marvin R. Goldfried (New York: Basic Books, 1992), 94–129; Kenneth S. Pope, Janet L. Sonne, and Jean Holroyd, *Sexual Feelings in Psychotherapy* (Washington, D.C.: American Psychological Association, 1993).

10. Gordon Allport, *Pattern and Growth in Personality* (New York: Holt, Rinehart and Winston, 1961); Carl G. Jung, "On the Psychology of the Unconscious," *Two Essays on Analytical Psychology* (Princeton, N.J.: Princeton University Press, 1972), 3–119; Harry S. Sullivan, *Conceptions of Modern Psychiatry* (New York: Norton, 1953).

11. Albert Bandura, "Self-efficacy Mechanism in Human Agency," *American Psychologist* 37 (1982): 122–147.

12. Mark R. McMinn, "RET, Constructivism, and Christianity: A Hermeneutic for Christian Cognitive Therapy," *Journal of Psychology and Christianity* 13 (1994): 342–355.

13. William P. Henry, Hans H. Strupp, Thomas E. Schacht, and Louise Gaston, "Psychodynamic Approaches," *Handbook of Psychotherapy and Behavior Change,* 4th ed., ed. Allen E. Bergin and Sol L. Garfield (New York: Wiley, 1994), 467–508.

14. Jay E. Adams, *The Christian Counselor's Manual* (Grand Rapids: Baker, 1973).

15. For an interesting discussion of this, see David G. Myers and Malcolm A. Jeeves, *Psychology through the Eyes of Faith* (San Francisco: Harper & Row, 1987), 129–136.

16. Maslow was critical of organized religion, showing the same misunderstandings of a vital Christian faith that many psychologist authors

demonstrate. See Abraham H. Maslow, *Religions, Values, and Peak-Experiences* (New York: The Viking Press, 1964).

17. Richard J. Foster, *Celebration of Discipline: The Path to Spiritual Growth* (San Francisco: HarperCollins, 1988), 33.

18. Benedict of Nursia, "Excerpts from *The Rule*," in *Devotional Classics,* ed. Richard J. Foster and James Bryan Smith (San Francisco: HarperCollins, 1993), 178–183.

19. Mark R. McMinn, "Religious Values and Client-therapist Matching in Psychotherapy," *Journal of Psychology and Theology* 12 (1984): 24–33.

20. Hans H. Strupp, "The Psychotherapist's Skills Revisited," *Clinical Psychology* 2 (1995): 70.

21. Kenneth S. Pope and J. C. Bouhoutsos, *Sexual Intimacy between Therapists and Patients* (New York: Praeger, 1986).

22. American Psychological Association, "Ethical Principles of Psychologists and Code of Conduct," *American Psychologist* 47 (1992): 1605.

23. Charles R. Carlson, Panayiota E. Bacaseta, and Dexter A. Simantona, "A Controlled Evaluation of Devotional Meditation and Progressive Relaxation," *Journal of Psychology and Theology* 16 (1988): 362–368.

Chapter 3: Prayer

1. Margaret M. Poloma and George H. Gallup, Jr., *Varieties of Prayer: A Survey Report* (Philadelphia: Trinity Press International, 1991), 26.

2. Michael E. McCullough, "Prayer and Health: Conceptual Issues, Research Review, and Research Agenda," *Journal of Psychology and Theology* 23 (1995): 15–29.

3. Ralph W. Hood, Jr., Ronald J. Morris, and P. J. Watson, "Religious Orientation and Prayer Experience," *Psychological Reports* 60 (1987): 1201–1202.

4. Robert A. Ball and Rodney K. Goodyear, "Self-reported Professional Practices of Christian Psychotherapists," *Psychotherapy and Religious Values,* ed. Everett L. Worthington, Jr. (Grand Rapids: Baker, 1993), 171–182; Marc Galanter, David Larson, and Elizabeth Rubenstone, "Christian Psychiatry: The Impact of Evangelical Belief on Clinical Practice," *American Journal of Psychiatry* 148 (1991): 90–95.

5. Frederic C. Craigie and Siang-Yang Tan, "Changing Resistant Assumptions in Christian Cognitive-behavioral Therapy," *Journal of Psychology and Theology* 17 (1989): 93–100. See also Marc Galanter, David Larson, and Elizabeth Rubenstone, "Christian Psychiatry: The Impact of Evangelical Belief on Clinical Practice," *American Journal of Psychiatry* 148 (1991): 90–95.

6. Shawn W. Hales, Randall Sorenson, Joan Jones, and John Coe, "Psychotherapists and the Religious Disciplines: Personal Beliefs and Professional Practice," paper presented at the conference of the Christian Association for Psychological Studies, Virginia Beach, April 1995.

7. Craigie and Tan, "Changing Resistant Assumptions," *Journal of Psychology and Theology,* 98.

8. Sylvia Fleming Crocker, "Prayer as a Model of Communication," *Pastoral Psychology* 33 (1984): 83.

9. For example, see this study of family physicians and their reasons for praying with older adult patients: Harold G. Koenig, Lucille B. Bearon, and Richard Dayringer, "Physician Perspectives on the Role of Religion in the Physician–Older Patient Relationship," *The Journal of Family Practice* 28 (1989): 441–448.

10. Craigie and Tan, "Changing Resistant Assumptions," *Journal of Psychology and Theology,* 98.

11. For an article about meditation in counseling, see Joseph D. Driskill, "Meditation as a Therapeutic Technique," *Pastoral Psychology* 38 (1989): 83–103.

12. Charles R. Carlson, Panayiota E. Bacaseta, and Dexter A. Simantona, "A Controlled Evaluation of Devotional Meditation and Progressive Relaxation," *Journal of Psychology and Theology* 16 (1988): 362–368.

13. L. Rebecca Propst, "The Comparative Efficacy of Religious and Non-religious Imagery for the Treatment of Mild Depression in Religious Individuals," *Cognitive Therapy and Research* 4 (1980) 167–178.

14. Susanne Schneider and Robert Kastenbaum, "Patterns and Meanings of Prayer in Hospice Caregivers: An Exploratory Study," *Death Studies* 17 (1993): 471–485.

15. John R. Finney and H. Newton Malony, "An Empirical Study of Contemplative Prayer as an Adjunct to Psychotherapy," *Journal of Psychology and Theology* 13 (1985): 284–290.

16. Hales et al., "Psychotherapists and the Religious Disciplines."

17. J. C. Lambert, "Prayer," *The International Standard Bible Encyclopedia,* ed. James Orr, John L. Nuelsen, Edgar Y. Mullins, Morris O. Evans, and Melvin Grove Kyle (Grand Rapids: Eerdmans, 1956), 2430.

18. Millard J. Erickson, *Christian Theology* (Grand Rapids: Baker, 1985), 405–406.

19. Ibid., 406.

20. Richard J. Foster, *Celebration of Discipline: The Path to Spiritual Growth* (San Francisco: HarperCollins, 1988), 33.

21. See, for example, David A. Seamands, *Healing of Memories* (Wheaton, Ill.: Victor Books, 1985) and Agnes Sanford, *The Healing Light* (New York: Ballantine Books, 1972).

22. Richard J. Foster, *Prayer: Finding the Heart's True Home* (San Francisco: HarperCollins, 1992).

23. Carlson et al., "A Controlled Evaluation of Devotional Meditation," *Journal of Psychology and Theology,* 362–368.

24. For an overstated criticism, see Dave Hunt and T. A. McMahon, *The Seduction of Christianity* (Eugene, Ore.: Harvest House, 1985).

25. Foster, *Prayer,* 1.

26. Foster, *Celebration of Discipline,* 33.

27. Ole Hallesby (translated by Clarence J. Carlsen), *Prayer* (Minneapolis: Augsburg, 1931), 12.

28. Dallas Willard, *The Spirit of the Disciplines* (San Francisco: HarperCollins, 1988), 186.

29. Bill Hybels, *Too Busy Not to Pray: Slowing Down to Be with God* (Downers Grove, Ill.: InterVarsity Press, 1988).

30. Hallesby, *Prayer,* 17.

31. Hybels, *Too Busy Not to Pray;* for additional ideas of prayer exercises, see Anthony Bloom, *Beginning to Pray* (New York: Paulist Press, 1970).

32. Hales et al., "Psychotherapists and the Religious Disciplines."

33. Carlson et al., "A Controlled Evaluation of Devotional Meditation," *Journal of Psychology and Theology,* 362–368.

34. Dave Hunt and T. A. McMahon, *The Seduction of Christianity* (Eugene, Ore.: Harvest House, 1985).

35. Propst, "The Comparative Efficacy of Religious and Non-religious Imagery," *Cognitive Therapy and Research,* 167–178. See also Mark R. McMinn, *Cognitive Therapy Techniques in Christian Counseling* (Waco, Tex.: Word, 1991), 126–127.

36. Hales et al., "Psychotherapists and the Religious Disciplines."

37. Marc Galanter, David Larson, and Elizabeth Rubenstone, "Christian Psychiatry: The Impact of Evangelical Belief on Clinical Practice," *American Journal of Psychiatry* 148 (1991): 90–95.

38. Crocker, "Prayer," *Pastoral Psychology,* 83–92.

39. Hallesby, *Prayer,* 17.

40. For a helpful discussion of this, see Gary W. Moon, "Spiritual Directors, Christian Counselors: Where Do They Overlap?" *Christian Counseling Today* (winter 1994), 29–33.

41. Foster, *Prayer,* 34.

42. Gary W. Moon, Judy W. Bailey, John C. Kwasny, and Dale E. Willis, "Training in the Use of Christian Disciplines as Counseling Techniques within Christian Graduate Training Programs," *Psychotherapy and Religious Values,* ed. Everett L. Worthington, Jr. (Grand Rapids: Baker, 1993), 191–203.

43. Kenneth S. Pope and J. C. Bouhoutsos, *Sexual Intimacy between Therapists and Patients* (New York: Praeger, 1986), 38–43.

44. AAMFT Code of Ethics (Washington, D.C.: American Association of Marriage and Family Therapy, 1991), 4.

45. Code of Ethics of the National Association of Social Workers (Washington, D.C.: National Association of Social Workers, 1993), 3.

282 / **Psychology, Theology, and Spirituality in Christian Counseling**

46. "Ethical Principles of Psychologists and Code of Conduct," *American Psychologist* 47 (1992): 1601.
47. Ethical Standards (Alexandria, Va.: American Counseling Association, 1988), 1.
48. See Foster, *Celebration of Discipline* and Foster, *Prayer*.
49 Willard, *Disciplines*.
50. Don Postema, *Space for God: The Study and Practice of Prayer and Spirituality* (Grand Rapids: CRC Publications, 1983).
51. Hallesby, *Prayer*.
52. For the encouraging trends, see Stanton L. Jones, "A Constructive Relationship for Religion with the Science and Profession of Psychology: Perhaps the Boldest Model Yet," *American Psychologist* 49 (1994): 184–199. For a discussion of self-determination in counseling, see Paul C. Vitz, *Psychology as Religion: The Cult of Self-Worship* (Grand Rapids: Eerdmans, 1977).
53. Allen E. Bergin, "Values and Religious Issues in Psychotherapy and Mental Health," *American Psychologist* 46 (1991): 394–403.
54. Moon et al., "Use of Christian Disciplines," *Psychotherapy and Religious Values,* 191–203.
55. "Ethical Principles," 1600.

Chapter 4: Scripture

1. Jerry Gladson and Charles Plott, "Unholy Wedlock? The Peril and Promise of Applying Psychology to the Bible," *Journal of Psychology and Christianity* 10 (1991): 54–64.
2. There are many such books. For example, Gary R. Collins, *The Biblical Basis of Christian Counseling for People Helpers* (Colorado Springs, Colo.: NavPress, 1993); Gary R. Collins, *Christian Counseling: A Comprehensive Guide* (Waco, Tex.: Word, 1980); Lawrence J. Crabb, Jr., *Effective Biblical Counseling: A Model of Helping Caring Christians Become Capable Counselors* (Grand Rapids: Zondervan, 1977); Roger Hurding, *The Bible and Counselling* (London: Hodder & Stoughton, 1992).
3. Daniel S. Sweeney and Garry Landreth, "Healing a Child's Spirit through Play Therapy: A Scriptural Approach to Treating Children," *Journal of Psychology and Christianity* 12 (1993): 351–356.
4. For example, Del Myra Carter, "An Integrated Approach to Pastoral Therapy," *Journal of Psychology and Theology* 14 (1986): 146–154; Siang-Yang Tan, "Cognitive-Behavior Therapy: A Biblical Approach," *Journal of Psychology and Theology* 15 (1987): 103–112. For discussions about RET, see Paul Hauck, "Religion and RET: Friends or Foes?" *Clinical Applications of Rational-Emotive Therapy,* ed. Albert Ellis and M. E. Bernard (New York: Plenum Press, 1985), 237–255; W. Brad Johnson, "Christian Rational-Emotive Therapy: A Treatment Protocol," *Journal of Psychology and Christianity* 12 (1993): 254–261; Constance Lawrence and Charles H.

Huber, "Strange Bedfellows?: Rational-Emotive Therapy and Pastoral Counseling," *The Personnel and Guidance Journal* 61 (1982): 210–212; Sandra D. M. Warnock, "Rational-Emotive Therapy and the Christian Client," *Journal of Rational-Emotive & Cognitive-Behavior Therapy* 7 (1989): 263–274.

5. Constance Lawrence, "Rational-Emotive Therapy and the Religious Client," *Journal of Rational-Emotive Therapy* 5 (1987): 19.

6. For example, Ed Bulkley, *Why Christians Can't Trust Psychology* (Eugene, Ore.: Harvest House, 1993); Dave Hunt and T. A. McMahon, *The Seduction of Christianity* (Eugene, Ore.: Harvest House, 1985); Jay E. Adams, *Competent to Counsel* (Grand Rapids: Baker, 1970).

7. I have argued elsewhere that one must critically evaluate the worldview differences between RET and Christianity before accepting RET as a tool for Christian therapy. See Mark R. McMinn, "RET, Constructivism, and Christianity: A Hermeneutic for Christian Cognitive Therapy," *Journal of Psychology and Christianity* 13 (1994): 342–355.

8. For discussions of Scripture used to confront codependency, see Richard J. Riodan and Diane Simone, "Codependent Christians: Some Issues for Church-Based Recovery Groups," *Journal of Psychology and Theology* 21 (1993): 158–164; for use of Scripture in addressing sexual affairs, see J. Lee Jagers, "Putting Humpty Together Again: Reconciling the Post-Affair Marriage," *Journal of Psychology and Christianity* 8 (1989): 63–72; for suggestions for using Scripture in play therapy, see Elaine D. Stover and Mark Stover, "Biblical Storytelling as a Form of Child Therapy," *Journal of Psychology and Christianity* 13 (1994): 28–36; for use of Scripture to confront irrational beliefs, see W. Brad Johnson, "Christian Rational-Emotive Therapy: A Treatment Protocol," *Journal of Psychology and Christianity* 12 (1993): 254–261; for suggestions for using Scripture as homework in cognitive therapy, see Mark R. McMinn, *Cognitive Therapy Techniques in Christian Counseling* (Waco, Tex.: Word).

9. Shawn W. Hales, Randall Sorenson, Joan Jones, and John Coe, "Psychotherapists and the Religious Disciplines: Personal Beliefs and Professional Practice," paper presented at the conference of the Christian Association for Psychological Studies, Virginia Beach, April 1995.

10. Robert A. Ball and Rodney K. Goodyear, "Self-reported Professional Practices of Christian Psychotherapists," *Psychotherapy and Religious Values,* ed. Everett L. Worthington, Jr. (Grand Rapids: Baker, 1993), 171–182.

11. Albert Ellis, "The Advantages and Disadvantages of Self-help Therapy Materials," *Professional Psychology: Research and Practice* 24 (1993): 336.

12. Eric L. Johnson, "A Place for the Bible within Psychological Science," *Journal of Psychology and Theology* 20 (1992): 346–355.

13. David H. Kelsey, *The Uses of Scripture in Recent Theology* (Philadelphia: Fortress Press, 1975), 1.
14. Ibid.
15. Millard J. Erickson, *Christian Theology* (Grand Rapids: Baker, 1985), 30–33.
16. Ibid., 256.
17. John Calvin, "Book 1: On the Knowledge of God the Creator," *John Calvin on the Christian Faith*, ed. John T. McNeill (New York: The Liberal Arts Press, 1957), 3–41.
18. Ibid., 19.
19. For a useful introduction to hermeneutics, see Gary R. Collins, *The Biblical Basis of Christian Counseling for People Helpers* (Colorado Springs, Colo.: NavPress, 1993), 41–59.
20. Richard J. Foster, *Celebration of Discipline: The Path to Spiritual Growth* (San Francisco: HarperCollins, 1988), 29.
21. Ibid.
22. For example, see Thomas Merton, *Praying the Psalms* (Collegeville, Minn.: Liturgical Press, 1956).
23. Foster, *Celebration of Discipline,* 29.
24. For a helpful discussion on this, see Gary R. Collins, "The Puzzle of Popular Spirituality," *Christian Counseling Today* (winter 1994): 10–14.
25. Bonnie Horrigan, "Christiane Northrup, MD: Medical Practice as a Spiritual Journey," *Alternative Therapies in Health and Medicine* 1 (1995): 64–71.
26. Stanton L. Jones, "Tentative Reflections on the Role of Scripture in Counseling," presentation made to psychology graduate students at Wheaton College, April, 1994.
27. See Philippians 4:8-9.
28. These potential problems were originally observed by my colleague and good friend Stanton L. Jones, "Tentative Reflections on the Role of Scripture in Counseling," presentation made to psychology graduate students at Wheaton College, April, 1994. Stan also discussed several helpful aspects of using Scripture in counseling, including the opportunity to consider both psychological and spiritual growth, glorifying God by valuing Scripture, trusting in a source more credible than human wisdom, and encouraging the client to look to Scripture for continued guidance.
29. Gary W. Moon, Judy W. Bailey, John C. Kwasny, and Dale E. Willis, "Training in the Use of Christian Disciplines as Counseling Techniques within Christian Graduate Training Programs," *Psychotherapy and Religious Values,* ed. Everett L. Worthington, Jr. (Grand Rapids: Baker, 1993), 191–203.
30. Ball and Goodyear, "Self-reported Professional Practices," *Psychotherapy and Religious Values,* 171–182.

31. For three examples of this, see W. Brad Johnson, "Christian Rational-Emotive Therapy: A Treatment Protocol," *Journal of Psychology and Christianity* 12 (1993): 254–261; Mark R. McMinn, *Cognitive Therapy Techniques in Christian Counseling* (Waco, Tex.: Word); Charles R. Barr, "Panic Disorder: 'The Fear of Feelings,'" *Journal of Psychology and Christianity* 14 (1995): 112–125.

32. Louis N. Gruber, "True and False Spirituality: A Framework for Christian Behavioral Medicine," *Journal of Psychology and Christianity* 14 (1995): 140. Italics are Dr. Gruber's.

33. Dallas Willard, *The Spirit of the Disciplines* (San Francisco: HarperCollins, 1988), 176.

34. Foster, *Celebration of Discipline,* 71.

35. Willard, *Disciplines,* 177.

36. Stanley R. Graham, "Desire, Belief, and Grace: A Psychotherapeutic Paradigm," *Psychotherapy: Theory, Research, and Practice* 17 (1980): 370.

37. Siang-Yang Tan, "Religious Values and Interventions in Lay Christian Counseling," *Journal of Psychology and Christianity* 10 (1991): 173–182.

38. W. Brad Johnson, "Outcome Research and Religious Psychotherapies: Where Are We and Where Are We Going?" *Journal of Psychology and Theology* 21 (1993): 297–308.

39. W. Brad Johnson, Ronald DeVries, Charles R. Ridley, Donald Pettorini, and Deland R. Peterson, "The Comparative Efficacy of Christian and Secular Rational-Emotive Therapy with Christian Clients," *Journal of Psychology and Theology* 22 (1994): 130–140.

40. W. Brad Johnson and Charles R. Ridley, "Brief Christian and Non-Christian Rational-Emotive Therapy with Depressed Christian Clients: An Exploratory Study," *Counseling and Values* 36 (1992): 220–229; David Richard Pecheur and Keith J. Edwards, "A Comparison of Secular and Religious Versions of Cognitive Therapy with Depressed Christian College Students," *Journal of Psychology and Theology* 12 (1984): 45–54.

41. L. Rebecca Propst, "The Comparative Efficacy of Religious and Non-religious Imagery for the Treatment of Mild Depression in Religious Individuals," *Cognitive Therapy and Research* 4 (1980): 167–178; L. Rebecca Propst, Richard Ostrom, Philip Watkins, Terri Dean, and David Mashburn, "Comparative Efficacy of Religious and Nonreligious Cognitive-behavioral Therapy for the Treatment of Clinical Depression in Religious Individuals," *Journal of Consulting and Clinical Psychology* 60 (1992): 94–103.

42. See Siang-Yang Tan, "Ethical Considerations in Religious Psychotherapy: Potential Pitfalls and Unique Resources," *Journal of Psychology and Theology* 22 (1994): 389–394; also see Alan C. Tjeltveit, "The Ethics of Value

Conversion in Psychotherapy: Appropriate and Inappropriate Therapist Influence on Client Values," *Clinical Psychology Review* 6 (1986): 515–537.

43. David W. Holling, "Pastoral Psychotherapy: Is It Unique?" *Counseling and Values* 34 (1990): 96–102.

Chapter 5: Sin

1. Richard Lederer, *Anguished English* (New York: Dell, 1987), 22.
2. Albert Ellis, "There Is No Place for the Concept of Sin in Psychotherapy," *Journal of Counseling Psychology* 7 (1960): 192.
3. Jay E. Adams, *Competent to Counsel* (Grand Rapids: Baker, 1970), 29. Dr. Adams has received a great deal of unfair, uninformed criticism from the Christian counseling community. Though I do not share Dr. Adams's opinion on confronting sin in counseling, I do respect his pioneering work in biblical counseling. Contemporary biblical counselors demonstrate both an awareness of sin in human problems and a commitment to empathy and compassion that is often overlooked by those criticizing their work. Most Christian counselors have distinct differences from most biblical counselors, as I myself do, but our common Christian bond calls us to work together and look for ways we can help one another in our work and ministries.
4. O. Hobart Mowrer, "Integrity Groups: Basic Principles and Objective," *The Counseling Psychologist* 3 (1972): 7–32.
5. O. Hobart Mowrer, "'Sin,' the Lesser of Two Evils," *American Psychologist* 15 (1960): 303.
6. See James D. Smrtic, "Time to Remove Our Theoretical Blinders: Integrity Therapy May Be the Right Way," *Psychotherapy: Theory, Research, and Practice* 16 (1979): 185–189; O. Hobart Mowrer and A. V. Veszelovszky, "There May Indeed Be a 'Right Way': Response to James D. Smrtic," *Psychotherapy: Theory, Research, and Practice* 17 (1980): 440–447.
7. Karl Menninger, *Whatever Became of Sin?* (New York: Hawthorne Books, 1973).
8. Several articles have appeared recently in *Pastoral Psychology:* Donald Capps, "The Deadly Sins and Saving Virtues: How They Are Viewed by Clergy," *Pastoral Psychology* 40 (1992): 209–233; Michael E. Cavanagh, "The Concept of Sin in Pastoral Counseling," *Pastoral Psychology* 41 (1992): 81–87; Andrew D. Reisner and Peter Lawson, "Psychotherapy, Sin, and Mental Health," *Pastoral Psychology* 40 (1992): 303–311.
9. Dr. Bernard Weiner has theorized various implications for viewing people either as sick or as sinners. See Bernard Weiner, "On Sin Versus Sickness: A Theory of Perceived Responsibility and Social Motivation," *American Psychologist* 48 (1993): 957–965.

10. Lyn Y. Abramson, Martin E. P. Seligman, and John D. Teasdale, "Learned Helplessness in Humans: Critique and Reformulation," *Journal of Abnormal Psychology* 87 (1978): 49–70.

11. Millard J. Erickson, *Christian Theology* (Grand Rapids: Baker, 1985), 578.

12. Edwin Zackrison, "A Theology of Sin, Grace, and Forgiveness," *Journal of Psychology and Theology* 11 (1992): 147–159.

13. The psychological implications of the universal nature of sin are discussed in John D. Carter, "Psychopathology, Sin and the DSM: Convergence and Divergence," *Journal of Psychology and Theology* 22 (1994): 277–285.

14. For a more complete discussion of this, see Mark R. McMinn and Gordon N. McMinn, "Complete Yet Inadequate: The Role of Learned Helplessness and Self-Attribution from the Writings of Paul," *Journal of Psychology and Theology* 11 (1983): 303–310.

15. It should also be noted that these claims are not supported by empirical research. See, for example, Allen E. Bergin, "Values and Religious Issues in Psychotherapy and Mental Health," *American Psychologist* 46 (1991): 394–403.

16. Richard J. Foster, *Celebration of Discipline: The Path to Spiritual Growth* (San Francisco: HarperCollins, 1988), 4–5.

17. This quotation comes from *The Imitation of Christ,* a classic either written or edited by Thomas à Kempis. It is included (on page 185), along with passages from many other devotional classics, in Richard J. Foster and James Bryan Smith (eds.), *Devotional Classics* (San Francisco: HarperCollins, 1993).

18. Thomas Merton, *Life and Holiness* (New York: Herder and Herder, 1963), 65.

19. This is a paraphrase of James 4:8.

20. Augustine, "The Confessions of St. Augustine," *The Treasury of Christian Spiritual Classics* (Nashville: Thomas Nelson, 1994), 1-156. Quotation from page 13.

21. Foster, *Celebration of Discipline,* 6.

22. CAPS members in one survey reported confronting sin with approximately 35 percent of their clients. See Shawn W. Hales, Randall Sorenson, Joan Jones, and John Coe, "Psychotherapists and the Religious Disciplines: Personal Beliefs and Professional Practice," paper presented at the conference of the Christian Association for Psychological Studies, Virginia Beach, April 1995. In another survey of CAPS members, confrontation was rarely used. Only one percent of the reported spiritual interventions involved confrontation. See Robert A. Ball and Rodney K. Goodyear, "Self-reported Professional Practices of Christian Psychotherapists," *Psychotherapy and Religious Values,* ed. Everett L. Worthington, Jr. (Grand Rapids: Baker, 1993), 171–182.

23. See David K. Clark, "Interpreting the Biblical Words for the Self," *Journal of Psychology and Theology* 18 (1990): 309–317.
24. C. S. Lewis, *Mere Christianity* (New York: Macmillan, 1952), 167.
25. For a helpful discussion of this distinction, see the writings from *Theologia Germanica,* included in Richard J. Foster and James Bryan Smith (eds.), *Devotional Classics* (San Francisco: HarperCollins, 1993), 147–153.
26. See American Psychiatric Association, *Diagnostic and Statistical Manual of Mental Disorders,* 4th ed. (Washington, D.C.: American Psychiatric Association, 1994), 629–673.
27. Mark R. McMinn and Nathaniel G. Wade, "Beliefs about the Prevalence of Dissociative Identity Disorder, Sexual Abuse, and Ritual Abuse among Religious and Non-religious Therapists," *Professional Psychology: Research and Practice* 26 (1995): 257–261.
28. A. W. Tozer, *The Pursuit of God* (Camp Hill, Penn: Christian Publications, 1993), 111.
29. Weiner, "On Sin Versus Sickness," *American Psychologist,* 957–965.
30. Blaise Pascal, *Pensées* (New York: Viking Penguin, 1966 translation), 77.
31. Benedict of Nursia, "Excerpts from *The Rule,*" in *Devotional Classics,* ed. Richard J. Foster and James Bryan Smith (San Francisco: HarperCollins, 1993), 180.
32. Foster, *Celebration of Discipline,* 55.
33. Dallas Willard, *The Spirit of the Disciplines* (San Francisco: HarperCollins, 1988), 166.
34. This suggestion also comes from Richard Foster. See Richard J. Foster and James Bryan Smith (eds.), *Devotional Classics* (San Francisco: HarperCollins, 1993), 182. Foster concludes, "Pray it often, and let it soften your heart."
35. Kenneth L. Woodward, "What Ever Happened to Sin?" *Newsweek* (6 February, 1995): 23.
36. See, for example, Albert Ellis, *The Case against Religion: A Psychotherapist's View* (New York: Institute for Rational Living, 1971). Similarly, Sigmund Freud described religion as a neurosis.
37. Allen E. Bergin, "Religiosity and Mental Health: A Critical Reevaluation and Meta-analysis," *Professional Psychology: Research and Practice* 14 (1983): 170–184; Allen E. Bergin, "Values and Religious Issues in Psychotherapy and Mental Health," *American Psychologist* 46 (1991): 394–403
38. Andrew D. Reisner and Peter Lawson, "Psychotherapy, Sin, and Mental Health," *Pastoral Psychology* 40 (1992): 303–311.
39. Allen E. Bergin, "Values and Religious Issues in Psychotherapy and Mental Health," *American Psychologist* 46 (1991): 394–403
40. I discuss this in more detail elsewhere. See Mark R. McMinn, "RET, Constructivism, and Christianity: A Hermeneutic for Christian Cognitive Therapy," *Journal of Psychology and Christianity* 13 (1994): 342–355.

41. I am not alone in suggesting a need for such a model. See, for example, Will Friesen and Al Dueck, "Whatever Happened to Law?" *Journal of Psychology and Christianity* 7 (1988): 13–22.

42. See Reisner and Lawson, "Psychotherapy, Sin, and Mental Health," *Pastoral Psychology*, 303–311.

Chapter 6: Confession

1. Kenneth L. Woodward, "What Ever Happened to Sin?" *Newsweek* (6 February 1995): 23.

2. Sharon Hymer, *Confessions in Psychotherapy* (New York: Gardner Press, 1988), 2–3.

3. Bernard Weiner, Sandra Graham, Oli Peter, and Mary Zmuidinas, "Public Confession and Forgiveness," *Journal of Personality* 59 (1991): 281–312.

4. James W. Pennebaker, Cheryl F. Hughes, and Robin C. O'Heeron, "The Psychophysiology of Confession: Linking Inhibitory and Psychosomatic Processes," *Journal of Personality and Social Psychology* 52 (1987): 781–793.

5. James W. Pennebaker and Robin C. O'Heeron, "Confiding in Others and Illness Rate Among Spouses of Suicide and Accidental Death Victims," *Journal of Abnormal Psychology* 93 (1984): 473–476.

6. For an article comparing psychotherapy with Roman Catholic confession, see Valerie Worthen, "Psychotherapy and Catholic Confession," *Journal of Religion and Health* 13 (1974): 275–284.

7. See Elizabeth Todd, "The Value of Confession and Forgiveness according to Jung," *Journal of Religion and Health* 24 (1985): 42.

8. Worthen, "Psychotherapy and Catholic Confession," *Journal of Religion and Health,* 283.

9. Richard C. Erickson, "Morality and the Practice of Psychotherapy," *Pastoral Psychology* 43 (1994): 81–91.

10. Allen E. Bergin, "Psychotherapy and Religious Values," *Journal of Consulting and Clinical Psychology* 48 (1980): 95–105.

11. Ibid., 100.

12. Ibid.

13. It should be noted that not all psychologists appreciated Bergin's dichotomy between theistic and clinical-humanistic values. Albert Ellis and Gary Walls both wrote critical responses to Bergin's article. See Albert Ellis, "Psychotherapy and Atheistic Values: A Response to A. E. Bergin's 'Psychotherapy and Religious Values,'" *Journal of Consulting and Clinical Psychology* 48 (1980): 635–639; Gary B. Walls, "Values and Psychotherapy: A Comment on 'Psychotherapy and Religious Values,'" *Journal of Consulting and Clinical Psychology* 48 (1980): 640–641.

14. Portions of this section are condensed from Katheryn Rhoads Meek, Jeanne S. Albright, and Mark R. McMinn, "Religious Orientation, Guilt, Confession, and Forgiveness," *Journal of Psychology and Theology,* (fall 1995).

15. Albert Ellis, "There Is No Place for the Concept of Sin in Psychotherapy," *Journal of Counseling Psychology* 7 (1960): 188–192.

16. O. Hobart Mowrer and A. V. Veszelovszky, "There May Indeed Be a 'Right Way': Response to James D. Smrtic," *Psychotherapy: Theory, Research, and Practice* 17 (1980): 440–447; June Price Tangney, "Moral Affect: The Good, the Bad, and the Ugly," *Journal of Personality and Social Psychology* 61 (1991): 598–607.

17. P. Scott Richards, "Religious Devoutness in College Students: Relations with Emotional Adjustment and Psychological Separation from Parents," *Journal of Counseling Psychology* 38 (1991): 189–196.

18. Richard Gramzow and June Price Tangney, "Proneness to Shame and the Narcissistic Personality," *Personality and Social Psychology Bulletin* 18 (1992): 369–376; June Price Tangney, "Moral Affect: The Good, the Bad, and the Ugly," *Journal of Personality and Social Psychology* 61 (1991): 598–607; June Price Tangney, Patricia E. Wagner, and Richard Gramzow, "Proneness to Shame, Proneness to Guilt, and Psychopathology," *Journal of Abnormal Psychology* 103 (1992): 469–478.

19. June Price Tangney, Patricia Wagner, Carey Fletcher, and Richard Gramzow, "Shamed into Anger? The Relation of Shame and Guilt to Anger and Self-Reported Aggression," *Journal of Personality and Social Psychology* 62 (1992): 669–675.

20. This study is reported in more detail elsewhere: Meek, Albright, and McMinn, "Religious Orientation," *Journal of Psychology and Theology* (fall 1995).

21. S. Bruce Narramore, *No Condemnation* (Grand Rapids: Zondervan, 1984).

22. Richards, "Religious Devoutness in College Students," *Journal of Counseling Psychology,* 194.

23. Janice Lindsay-Hartz, "Contrasting Experiences of Shame and Guilt," *American Behavioral Scientist* 27 (1984): 689–704.

24. David Belgum, *Guilt: Where Psychology and Religion Meet* (Englewood Cliffs, N. J.: Prentice-Hall, 1963), 52. Italics his.

25. See Ludwig Bieler, *The Works of St. Patrick* (New York: Newman Press, 1953); Augustine, "The Confessions of St. Augustine," *The Treasury of Christian Spiritual Classics* (Nashville: Thomas Nelson, 1994), 1–156.

26. John Calvin, *Institutes of the Christian Religions,* ed. John T. McNeill (Philadelphia: Westminster Press, 1960), 670.

27. From *Great Catechism.* Cited in Dietrich Bonhoeffer, *The Cost of Discipleship* (New York: Macmillan, 1959), 325.

28. These values of the sacrament of penance are pointed out by Richard J. Foster, a Protestant writer, in *Celebration of Discipline: The Path to Spiritual Growth* (San Francisco: HarperCollins, 1988), 148.

29. These two aspects of confession, including the specific confession models that follow, are discussed in H. E. Jacobs, "Confession," *The International Standard Bible Encyclopedia,* ed. James Orr et al., (Grand Rapids: Eerdmans, 1956), 699–700.

30. From *Letters to Malcolm.* Cited in Richard J. Foster, *Prayer: Finding the Heart's True Home* (San Francisco: HarperCollins, 1992), 43.

31. Jeremy Taylor "Excerpts from The Rule and Exercises of Holy Living," *Devotional Classics,* ed. Richard J. Foster and James Bryan Smith, (San Francisco: HarperCollins, 1993), 269.

32. Dallas Willard, *The Spirit of the Disciplines* (San Francisco: HarperCollins, 1988), 186.

33. Saint John of the Cross, "Excerpts from *The Dark Night of the Soul,*" *Devotional Classics,* ed. Richard J. Foster and James Bryan Smith, (San Francisco: HarperCollins, 1993), 33.

34. Ibid., 34.

35. Ibid.

36. Foster, *Celebration of Discipline,* 144.

37. Bonhoeffer, *Discipleship,* 325.

38. Hymer, *Confessions,* 174.

39. Willard, *Disciplines,* 188.

40. Augustine, "The Confessions of St. Augustine," *The Treasury of Christian Spiritual Classics* (Nashville: Thomas Nelson, 1994), 54.

41. For a more thorough discussion of these forms of professional development, see Mark R. McMinn and Katheryn Rhoads Meek, "Training Programs," *Ethics and the Christian Mental Health Professional,* ed. Randolph Saunders (Downers Grove, Ill.: InterVarsity Press 1996).

42. Shawn W. Hales, Randall Sorenson, Joan Jones, and John Coe, "Psychotherapists and the Religious Disciplines: Personal Beliefs and Professional Practice," paper presented at the conference of the Christian Association for Psychological Studies, Virginia Beach, April 1995.

43. Gary W. Moon, Judy W. Bailey, John C. Kwasny, and Dale E. Willis, "Training in the Use of Christian Disciplines as Counseling Techniques within Christian Graduate Training Programs," *Psychotherapy and Religious Values,* ed. Everett L. Worthington, Jr. (Grand Rapids: Baker, 1993), 191–203.

44. These groups are in addition to clinical supervision, which students obtain at their training sites.

45. Thomas à Kempis, "The Imitation of Christ," *The Treasury of Christian Spiritual Classics* (Nashville: Thomas Nelson, 1994), 433-554. Quote from page 444.

46. Hymer, *Confessions,* 5–7.

47. For a discussion of this principle, as well as psychologists' views of specific behaviors, see: Kenneth S. Pope, Barbara G. Tabachnick, and Patricia Keith-Spiegel, "Ethics of Practice: The Beliefs and Behaviors of Psychologists as Therapists," *American Psychologist* 42 (1987): 993–1006.

48. These results are reported in detail elsewhere: Mark R. McMinn and Katheryn Rhoads Meek, "Ethics Among Christian Counselors: A Survey of Beliefs and Behaviors," *Journal of Psychology and Theology*.

49. See Kenneth S. Pope and Jacqueline C. Bouhoutsos, *Sexual Intimacy between Therapists & Patients* (New York: Praeger, 1986), 3–6.

50. Blaise Pascal, *Pensées* (New York: Viking Penguin, 1966 translation), 146.

Chapter 7: Forgiveness

1. For example, see Ellen Bass and Laura Davis, *The Courage to Heal: A Guide for Women Survivors of Child Sexual Abuse* (New York: HarperCollins, 1992): Alice Miller, *Banished Knowledge* (New York: Doubleday, 1990).

2. See, for example, Donna S. Davenport, "The Functions of Anger and Forgiveness: Guidelines for Psychotherapy with Victims," *Psychotherapy* 28 (1991): 140–144; John H. Hebl and Robert D. Enright, "Forgiveness as a Psychotherapeutic Goal with Elderly Females," *Psychotherapy* 30 (1993): 658–667; Donald Hope, "The Healing Paradox of Forgiveness," *Psychotherapy* 24 (1987): 240–244; Human Development Study Group, "Five Points on the Construct of Forgiveness within Psychotherapy," *Psychotherapy,* 28 (1991): 493–496; Everett L. Worthington, Jr., and Frederick A. DiBlasio, "Promoting Mutual Forgiveness within the Fractured Relationship," *Psychotherapy* 27 (1990): 219–223.

3. For example, see Frederick A. DiBlasio and Brent B. Benda, "Practitioners, Religion, and the Use of Forgiveness in the Clinical Setting," *Journal of Psychology and Christianity* 10 (1991): 166–172; Robert D. Enright and Robert L. Zell, "Problems Encountered When We Forgive One Another," *Journal of Psychology and Christianity* 8 (1989): 52–60; Jared P. Pingleton, "The Role and Function of Forgiveness in the Psychotherapeutic Process," *Journal of Psychology and Christianity* 17 (1989): 27–35.

4. Michael E. McCullough and Everett L. Worthington, Jr., "Models of Interpersonal Forgiveness and Their Applications to Counseling," *Counseling and Values* 39 (1994): 2–14; Michael E. McCullough and Everett L. Worthington, Jr., "Encouraging Clients to Forgive People Who Have Hurt Them: Review, Critique, and Research Prospectus," *Journal of Psychology and Theology* 22 (1994): 3–20; Steven J. Sandage, Everett L. Worthington, Jr., and William Smith, "Seeking Forgiveness: Toward an Integration of Psychology and Theology," paper presented at the annual meetings of the Christian Association for Psychological Studies, Virginia Beach, April 1995.

5. Glenn Veenstra, "Psychological Concepts of Forgiveness," *Journal of Psychology and Christianity* 11 (1992): 160–169.

6. Paul A. Mauger, Tom Freeman, Alicia G. McBride, Jacqueline Escano Perry, Dianne C. Grove, and Kathleen E. McKinney, "The Measurement of Forgiveness: Preliminary Research," *Journal of Psychology and Christianity* 11 (1992): 170–180; Michael J. Subkoviak, Robert D. Enright, and Ching-Ru Wu, "Current Developments Related to Measuring Forgiveness," paper presented at the annual meeting of the Mid-Western Educational Research Association, Chicago, October 1992; Michael J. Subkoviak, Robert D. Enright, Ching-Ru Wu, Elizabeth A. Gassin, Suzanne Freedman, Leanne M. Olson, and Issidoros Sarinopoulos, "Measuring Interpersonal Forgiveness," paper presented at the annual meetings of the American Educational Research Association, San Francisco, April 1992.

7. There are many such articles. For example, see Cyde A. Bonar, "Personality Theories and Asking Forgiveness," *Journal of Psychology and Christianity* 8 (1989): 45–51; Emily F. Carter, Michael E. McCullough, Steven J. Sandage, and Everett L. Worthington, Jr., "What Happens When People Forgive? Theories, Speculations, and Implications for Individual and Marital Therapy," paper presented at the meetings of the American Psychological Association, Los Angeles, August 1994; Robert D. Enright, "Piaget on the Moral Development of Forgiveness: Identity or Reciprocity?" *Human Development* 37 (1994): 63–80; John Gartner, "The Capacity to Forgive: An Object Relations Perspective," *Journal of Religion and Health* 27 (1988): 313–320; Elizabeth A. Gassin and Robert D. Enright, "The Will to Meaning in the Process of Forgiveness," *Journal of Psychology and Christianity* 14 (1995): 38–49; Elizabeth DesPortes Dreelin and H. Newt Malony, "Religious Functioning and Forgiveness," paper presented at the meetings of the American Psychological Association, Los Angeles, August 1994.

8. Educational Psychology Study Group, "Must a Christian Require Repentance before Forgiving?" *Journal of Psychology and Christianity* 9 (1990): 16–19; Robert D. Enright, David L. Eastin, Sandra Golden, Issidoros Sarinopoulos, and Suzanne Freedman, "Interpersonal Forgiveness within the Helping Professions: An Attempt to Resolve Differences of Opinion," *Counseling and Values* 36 (1992): 84–103; Robert D. Enright and Robert L. Zell, "Problems Encountered When We Forgive One Another," *Journal of Psychology and Christianity* 8 (1989): 52–60.

9. Colleen K. Benson, "Forgiveness and the Psychotherapeutic Process," *Journal of Psychology and Christianity* 11 (1992): 76–81; Kenneth Cloke, "Revenge, Forgiveness, and the Magic of Mediation," *Mediation Quarterly* 11 (1993): 67–78; Donna S. Davenport, "The Functions of Anger and Forgiveness: Guidelines for Psychotherapy with Victims," *Psychotherapy* 28

(1991): 140–144; Frederick A. DiBlasio, "The Role of Social Workers' Religious Beliefs in Helping Family Members Forgive," *Families in Society: The Journal of Contemporary Human Services* (March, 1993): 163–170; Frederick A. DiBlasio, "Forgiveness in Psychotherapy: Comparison of Older and Younger Therapists," *Journal of Psychology and Christianity* 11 (1992): 181–187; Frederick A. DiBlasio and Brent B. Benda, "Practitioners, Religion, and the Use of Forgiveness in the Clinical Setting," *Journal of Psychology and Christianity* 10 (1991): 166–172; Frederick A. DiBlasio and Judith Harris Proctor, "Therapists and the Clinical Use of Forgiveness," *The American Journal of Family Therapy* 21 (1993): 175–184; John H. Hebl and Robert D. Enright, "Forgiveness as a Psychotherapeutic Goal with Elderly Females," *Psychotherapy* 30 (1993): 658–667; Human Development Study Group, "Five Points on the Construct of Forgiveness within Psychotherapy," *Psychotherapy* 28 (1991): 493–496; Jared P. Pingleton, "The Role and Function of Forgiveness in the Psychotherapeutic Process," *Journal of Psychology and Theology* 17 (1989): 27–35; Charlotte M. Rosenak and G. Mack Harnden, "Forgiveness in the Psychotherapeutic Process: Clinical Applications," *Journal of Psychology and Christianity* 11 (1992): 188–197; Everett L. Worthington, Jr., and Frederick A. DiBlasio, "Promoting Mutual Forgiveness within the Fractured Relationship," *Psychotherapy* 27 (1990): 219–223.

10. Alice Miller, *Banished Knowledge* (New York: Doubleday, 1990).

11. Bass and Davis, *The Courage to Heal,* 150.

12. Ibid.

13. Everett L. Worthington, Jr., and Frederick A. DiBlasio, "Promoting Mutual Forgiveness within the Fractured Relationship," *Psychotherapy* 27 (1990): 219–220.

14. Donald Hope, "The Healing Paradox of Forgiveness," *Psychotherapy* 24 (1987): 240–244.

15. Human Development Study Group, "Five Points on the Construct of Forgiveness within Psychotherapy," *Psychotherapy* 28 (1991): 494.

16. Jared P. Pingleton, "The Role and Function of Forgiveness in the Psychotherapeutic Process," *Journal of Psychology and Christianity* 17 (1989): 33.

17. Michael E. McCullough and Everett L. Worthington, Jr., "Encouraging Clients to Forgive People Who Have Hurt Them: Review, Critique, and Research Prospectus," *Journal of Psychology and Theology* 22 (1994): 3.

18. Dietrich Bonhoeffer, *The Cost of Discipleship* (New York: Macmillan, 1959), 100.

19. See Jerry A. Gladson, "Higher than the Heavens: Forgiveness in the Old Testament," *Journal of Psychology and Christianity* 11 (1992): 125–135; see also Madelynn Jones-Haldeman, "Implications from Selected Literary

Devices for a New Testament Theology of Grace and Forgiveness," *Journal of Psychology and Christianity* 11 (1992): 136–146.

20. Millard J. Erickson, *Christian Theology* (Grand Rapids: Baker, 1985), 563.

21. Lewis B. Smedes, *Forgive and Forget: Healing the Hurts We Don't Deserve* (San Francisco, Harper and Row, 1984), 104.

22. This writing of Saint Francis can be found in D. Hazard, *A Day in Your Presence: A 40-Day Journey in the Company of Francis of Assisi* (Minneapolis: Bethany House, 1992), 86.

23. Thomas à Kempis, "The Imitation of Christ," *The Treasury of Christian Spiritual Classics* (Nashville: Thomas Nelson, 1994), 447.

24. These prerequisites are described in detail in Donna S. Davenport, "The Functions of Anger and Forgiveness: Guidelines for Psychotherapy with Victims," *Psychotherapy* 28 (1991): 141–142.

25. David Augsburger, *Caring Enough to Forgive* (Ventura, Calif.: Regal Books, 1981), 95.

26. The term *pseudoforgiveness* is used by the Human Development Study Group, "Five Points on the Construct of Forgiveness within Psychotherapy," *Psychotherapy,* 28 (1991): 493–496.

27. For a helpful article on the process of forgiveness, see Charlotte M. Rosenak and G. Mack Harnden, "Forgiveness in the Psychotherapeutic Process: Clinical Applications," *Journal of Psychology and Christianity* 11 (1992): 188–197.

28. Counselors need to begin with a proper definition of forgiveness. For more discussion of this point, see Human Development Study Group, "Five Points on the Construct of Forgiveness within Psychotherapy," *Psychotherapy,* 28 (1991): 493–494.

29. For a discussion of humility vs. humiliation, see Bobby B. Cunningham, "The Will to Forgive: A Pastoral Theological View of Forgiving," *The Journal of Pastoral Care* 39 (1985): 141–149.

30. For several perspectives on the common factors that make various forms of therapy effective, see the articles in the spring 1995 issue of *Clinical Psychology: Science and Practice.*

31. Hope, "Healing Paradox," *Psychotherapy,* 241.

32. Bonhoeffer, *Discipleship,* 45.

33. For a discussion of excusing or condoning behavior, as opposed to true forgiveness, see Veenstra, "Psychological Concepts," *Journal of Psychology and Christianity,* 161–166.

34. Gary W. Moon, Judy W. Bailey, John C. Kwasny, and Dale E. Willis, "Training in the Use of Christian Disciplines as Counseling Techniques within Christian Graduate Training Programs," *Psychotherapy and Religious Values,* ed. Everett L. Worthington, Jr. (Grand Rapids: Baker, 1993), 191–203.

35. Shawn W. Hales, Randall Sorenson, Joan Jones, and John Coe, "Psychotherapists and the Religious Disciplines: Personal Beliefs and Professional Practice," paper presented at the conference of the Christian Association for Psychological Studies, Virginia Beach April, 1995.

36. Worthington, Jr., and DiBlasio, "Promoting Mutual Forgiveness," *Psychotherapy,* 219–223.

37. Davenport, "Functions of Anger and Forgiveness," *Psychotherapy,* 140–144; John H. Hebl and Robert D. Enright, "Forgiveness as a Psychotherapeutic Goal with Elderly Females," *Psychotherapy* 30 (1993): 658–667; Hope, "Healing Paradox," *Psychotherapy,* 240–244.

38. DiBlasio and Benda, "Practitioners, Religion, and the Use of Forgiveness in the Clinical Setting," *Journal of Psychology and Christianity,* 166–172.

39. Hope, "Healing Paradox," *Psychotherapy,* 242.

40. Edwin Zackrison, "A Theology of Sin, Grace, and Forgiveness," *Journal of Psychology and Christianity* 11 (1992): 157.

41. Mauger et al., "The Measurement of Forgiveness," *Journal of Psychology and Christianity,* 170–180; Michael J. Subkoviak, Robert D. Enright, and Ching-Ru Wu, "Current Developments Related to Measuring Forgiveness," paper presented at the annual meeting of the Mid-Western Educational Research Association, Chicago, October 1992; Michael J. Subkoviak, Robert D. Enright, Ching-Ru Wu, Elizabeth A. Gassin, Suzanne Freedman, Leanne M. Olson, and Issidoros Sarinopoulos, "Measuring Interpersonal Forgiveness," paper presented at the annual meetings of the American Educational Research Association, San Francisco, April 1992; S. H. Wade, "The Development of a Scale to Measure Forgiveness," Ph.D. diss., Fuller Theological Seminary, 1989.

42. John H. Hebl and Robert D. Enright, "Forgiveness as a Psychotherapeutic Goal with Elderly Females," *Psychotherapy* 30 (1993): 658–667.

43. Benson, "Forgiveness," *Journal of Psychology and Christianity,* 79; John Gartner, "The Capacity to Forgive: An Object Relations Perspective," *Journal of Religion and Health* 27 (1988): 313–320.

Chapter 8: Redemption

1. I believe this standard is appropriate for all therapists, regardless of their religious orientation. Though it is not common practice, I believe agnostic or atheistic counselors should also make their religious values known prior to starting counseling relationships. Even nonreligious people have religious values that potentially affect counseling process and outcome.

2. This description is admittedly a cognitive therapist's slant on object-relations theory. See Anthony Ryle, *Cognitive-Analytic Therapy: Active Participation in Change* (New York: Wiley, 1990), 96–118.

3. Stanley R. Graham, "Desire, Belief, and Grace: A Psychotherapeutic Paradigm," *Psychotherapy: Theory, Research, and Practice* 17 (1980): 371.

4. Condensed from R. John Huber, "Psychotherapy: A Graceful Activity," *Individual Psychology* 43 (1987): 439.

5. The connection between Adlerian methods and grace is described well in Huber, "A Graceful Activity," *Individual Psychology,* 437–443.

6. For two excellent books illustrating the changes taking place in cognitive therapy, see Richard C. Bedrosian and George D. Bozicas, *Treating Family of Origin Problems: A Cognitive Approach* (New York: Guilford, 1994); Jeremy D. Safran and Zindel V. Segal, *Interpersonal Process in Cognitive Therapy* (New York: Basic Books, 1990).

7. Kenneth S. Pope and Shirley Feldman-Summers, "National Survey of Psychologists' Sexual and Physical Abuse History and Their Evaluation of Training and Competence in These Areas," *Professional Psychology: Research and Practice* 23 (1992): 353–361.

8. Francis J. McConnell, "Redemption," *The International Standard Bible Encyclopedia,* ed. James Orr et al., 2541–2544.

9. A relational Christian theology has implications for counseling practice. See James H. Olthuis, "God-With-Us: Toward a Relational Psychotherapeutic Model," *Journal of Psychology and Christianity* 13 (1994): 37–49.

10. J. Stuart Holden published many of his sermons in *Redeeming Vision* (London: Robert Scott, 1908). This quotation is from page 87.

11. Wesley's views on religious affections can be found in Gregory Scott Clapper, "John Wesley on Religious Affections: His Views on Experience and Emotion and Their Role in the Christian Life and Theology," (Ph.D. diss., Emory University, 1985), 211.

12. Jonathan Edwards, "Excerpts from *Religious Affections,*" in *Devotional Classics,* ed. Richard J. Foster and James Bryan Smith, (San Francisco: HarperCollins, 1993), 20.

13. Richard J. Foster, *Celebration of Discipline: The Path to Spiritual Growth* (San Francisco: HarperCollins, 1988), 144.

14. Andrew Murray, *Humility* (Old Tappan, N. J.: Fleming H. Revell, 1895), 19.

15. Hendrika Vande Kemp, "Psychotherapy and Redemption: A Tribute to a 'Dying Mom,'" presented at the 98th annual convention of the American Psychological Association, Boston, August 1990.

16. Terese A. Hall, "Spiritual Effects of Childhood Sexual Abuse in Adult Christian Women," *Journal of Psychology and Theology* 23 (1995): 129–134.

17. It is often difficult to see any spiritual value during times when God seems distant, but people of faith throughout history have found these to be times of important spiritual growth. This theme is frequently seen in the Psalms and also in the writings of Saint John of the Cross, as discussed in chapter 6.

18. American Psychological Association, "Guidelines for Providers of Psychological Services to Ethnic, Linguistic, and Culturally Diverse Populations," *American Psychologist* 48 (1993): 45–48.

19. See Hendrika Vande Kemp, "Psychotherapy as a Religious Process: A Historical Heritage," *Psychotherapy and the Religiously Committed Patient,* ed. E. Mark Stern (New York: Haworth Press, 1985), 135–146.

20. Dick Westley, *Redemptive Intimacy* (Mystic, Conn.: Twenty-Third Publications, 1981), quote from back cover.

21. Joel Weinberger, "Common Factors Aren't So Common: The Common Factors Dilemma," *Clinical Psychology: Science and Practice* 2 (1995): 45.

22. Ibid., 61.

BIBLIOGRAPHY

AAMFT Code of Ethics. Washington, D.C.: American Association of Marriage
and Family Therapy, 1991.

Abramson, Lyn Y., Martin E. P. Seligman, and John D. Teasdale. "Learned
Helplessness in Humans: Critique and Reformulation." *Journal of Abnormal
Psychology* 87 (1978): 49–70.

Adams, Jay E. *Competent to Counsel.* Grand Rapids: Baker, 1970.

——— The Christian Counselor's Manual. Grand Rapids: Baker, 1973.

Adams, Samuel A. "Spiritual Well-being, Religiosity, and Demographic
Variables as Predictors of the Use of Christian Counseling Techniques."
Poster presented at the annual meetings of the American Psychological
Association, Los Angeles. August 1994.

Allport, Gordon. *Pattern and Growth in Personality.* New York: Holt, Rinehart
and Winston, 1961.

American Psychiatric Association. *Diagnostic and Statistical Manual of Mental
Disorders,* 4th ed. Washington, D.C.: American Psychiatric Association, 1994.

American Psychological Association. "Ethical Principles of Psychologists and
Code of Conduct." *American Psychologist* 47 (1992): 1597–1611.

——— "Guidelines for Providers of Psychological Services to Ethnic,
Linguistic, and Culturally Diverse Populations." *American Psychologist* 48
(1993): 45–48.

Augsburger, David. *Caring Enough to Forgive.* Ventura, Calif.: Regal Books, 1981.

Augustine. "The Confessions of St. Augustine." In *The Treasury of Christian
Spiritual Classics.* Nashville: Thomas Nelson, 1994.

Ball, Robert A., and Rodney K. Goodyear. "Self-reported Professional
Practices of Christian Psychotherapists." In *Psychotherapy and Religious
Values,* edited by Everett L. Worthington, Jr., Grand Rapids: Baker, 1993.

Bandura, Albert. "Self-efficacy Mechanism in Human Agency." *American
Psychologist* 37 (1982): 122–147.

Barr, Charles R. "Panic Disorder: 'The Fear of Feelings.'" *Journal of Psychology
and Christianity* 14 (1995): 112–125.

Bass, Ellen, and Laura Davis. *The Courage to Heal: A Guide for Women Survivors of
Child Sexual Abuse.* New York: HarperCollins, 1992.

Beck, Aaron T., Arthur Freeman, & Associates. *Cognitive Therapy of Personality Disorders.* New York: Guilford, 1990.

Bedrosian, Richard C., and George D. Bozicas. *Treating Family of Origin Problems: A Cognitive Approach.* New York: Guilford, 1994.

Belgum, David. *Guilt: Where Psychology and Religion Meet.* Englewood Cliffs, N.J.: Prentice-Hall, 1963.

Benedict of Nursia, "Excerpts from *The Rule.*" In *Devotional Classics,* edited by Richard J. Foster and James Bryan Smith. San Francisco: HarperCollins, 1993.

Benson, Colleen K. "Forgiveness and the Psychotherapeutic Process." *Journal of Psychology and Christianity* 11 (1992): 76–81.

Beougher, Timothy, and Lyle Dorsett, eds. *Account of a Campus Revival: Wheaton College 1995.* Wheaton, Ill.: Harold Shaw Publishers, 1995.

Bergin, Allen E. "Psychotherapy and Religious Values." *Journal of Consulting and Clinical Psychology* 48 (1980): 95–105.

——— "Religiosity and Mental Health: A Critical Reevaluation and Meta-analysis." *Professional Psychology: Research and Practice* 14 (1983): 170–184.

——— "Values and Religious Issues in Psychotherapy and Mental Health." *American Psychologist* 46 (1991): 394–403.

Bergin, Allen E., Randy D. Stinchfield, Thomas A. Gaskin, Kevin S. Masters, and Clyde E. Sullivan. "Religious Life-styles and Mental Health: An Exploratory Study." *Journal of Consulting and Clinical Psychology* 35 (1988): 91–98.

Bieler, Ludwig. *The Works of St. Patrick.* New York: Newman Press, 1953.

Bloom, Anthony. *Beginning to Pray.* New York: Paulist Press, 1970.

Bonar, Cyde A. "Personality Theories and Asking Forgiveness." *Journal of Psychology and Christianity* 8 (1989): 45–51.

Bonhoeffer, Dietrich. *The Cost of Discipleship.* New York: Macmillan, 1959.

Bulkley, Ed. *Why Christians Can't Trust Psychology.* Eugene, Ore.: Harvest House, 1993.

Calvin, John. "Book 1: On the Knowledge of God the Creator." In *John Calvin on the Christian Faith,* edited by John T. McNeill. New York: The Liberal Arts Press, 1957.

——— *Institutes of the Christian Religion.* Edited by John T. McNeill. Philadelphia: Westminster Press, 1960.

Capps, Donald. "The Deadly Sins and Saving Virtues: How They Are Viewed by Clergy." *Pastoral Psychology* 40 (1992): 209–233.

Carlson, Charles R., Panayiota E. Bacaseta, and Dexter A. Simantona. "A Controlled Evaluation of Devotional Meditation and Progressive Relaxation." *Journal of Psychology and Theology* 16 (1988): 362–368.

Carter, Del Myra. "An Integrated Approach to Pastoral Therapy." *Journal of Psychology and Theology* 14 (1986): 146–154.

Carter, Emily F., Michael E. McCullough, Steven J. Sandage, and Everett L. Worthington, Jr. "What Happens When People Forgive? Theories, Speculations, and Implications for Individual and Marital Therapy." Paper presented at the meetings of the American Psychological Association, Los Angeles. August 1994.

Carter, John D. "Psychopathology, Sin and the DSM: Convergence and Divergence." *Journal of Psychology and Theology* 22 (1994): 277–285.

Cavanagh, Michael E. "The Concept of Sin in Pastoral Counseling." *Pastoral Psychology* 41 (1992): 81–87.

Clapper, Gregory Scott. "John Wesley on Religious Affections: His Views on Experience and Emotion and Their Role in the Christian Life and Theology." Ph.D. diss., Emory University, 1985.

Clark, David K. "Interpreting the Biblical Words for the Self." *Journal of Psychology and Theology* 18 (1990): 309–317.

Cloke, Kenneth. "Revenge, Forgiveness, and the Magic of Mediation." *Mediation Quarterly* 11 (1993): 67–78.

Code of Ethics of the National Association of Social Workers. Washington, D.C.: National Association of Social Workers, 1993.

Collins, Gary R. *Christian Counseling: A Comprehensive Guide.* Waco, Tex.: Word, 1980.

——— "Moving through the Jungle: A Decade of Integration." *Journal of Psychology and Theology* 11 (1983): 2–7.

——— The Biblical Basis of Christian Counseling for People Helpers. Colorado Springs, Colo.: NavPress, 1993.

——— "The Puzzle of Popular Spirituality." *Christian Counseling Today* (winter 1994): 10–14.

Crabb, Lawrence J., Jr. *Effective Biblical Counseling: A Model of Helping Caring Christians Become Capable Counselors.* Grand Rapids: Zondervan, 1977.

Craigie, Frederic C., and Siang-Yang Tan. "Changing Resistant Assumptions in Christian Cognitive-Behavioral Therapy." *Journal of Psychology and Theology* 17 (1989): 93–100.

Crocker, Sylvia Fleming. "Prayer as a Model of Communication." *Pastoral Psychology* 33 (1984): 83–92.

Cunningham, Bobby B. "The Will to Forgive: A Pastoral Theological View of Forgiving." *The Journal of Pastoral Care* 39 (1985): 141–149.

Davenport, Donna S. "The Functions of Anger and Forgiveness: Guidelines for Psychotherapy with Victims." *Psychotherapy* 28 (1991): 140–144.

DiBlasio, Frederick A. "Forgiveness in Psychotherapy: Comparison of Older and Younger Therapists." *Journal of Psychology and Christianity* 11 (1992): 181–187.

——— "The Role of Social Workers' Religious Beliefs in Helping Family Members Forgive." *Families in Society: The Journal of Contemporary Human Services* (March 1993): 163–170.

DiBlasio, Frederick A., and Brent B. Benda. "Practitioners, Religion, and the Use of Forgiveness in the Clinical Setting." *Journal of Psychology and Christianity* 10 (1991): 166–172.

DiBlasio, Frederick A., and Judith Harris Proctor. "Therapists and the Clinical Use of Forgiveness." *The American Journal of Family Therapy* 21 (1993): 175–184.

DiGiuseppe, Raymond A., Mitchell W. Robin, and Wendy Dryden. "On the Compatibility of Rational-Emotive Therapy and Judeo-Christian Philosophy: A Focus on Clinical Strategies." *Journal of Cognitive Psychotherapy: An International Quarterly* 4 (1990): 355–368.

Donahue, Michael J. "Intrinsic and Extrinsic Religiousness: Review and Meta-analysis." *Journal of Personality and Social Psychology* 48 (1985): 400–419.

Dreelin, Elizabeth DesPortes, and H. Newt Malony. "Religious Functioning and Forgiveness." Paper presented at the meetings of the American Psychological Association, Los Angeles. August 1994.

Driskill, Joseph D. "Meditation as a Therapeutic Technique." *Pastoral Psychology* 38 (1989): 83–103.

Educational Psychology Study Group. "Must a Christian Require Repentance before Forgiving?" *Journal of Psychology and Christianity* 9 (1990): 16–19.

Edwards, Jonathan. "Excerpts from *Religious Affections.*" In *Devotional Classics,* edited by Richard J. Foster and James Bryan Smith. San Francisco: HarperCollins, 1993.

Ellis, Albert. "There Is No Place for the Concept of Sin in Psychotherapy." *Journal of Counseling Psychology* 7 (1960): 188–192.

——— The Case against Religion: A Psychotherapist's View. New York: Institute for Rational Living, 1971.

——— "Psychotherapy and Atheistic Values: A Response to A. E. Bergin's 'Psychotherapy and Religious Values.'" *Journal of Consulting and Clinical Psychology* 48 (1980): 635–639.

——— The Case against Religiosity. New York: Institute for Rational Living, 1983.

——— "Do I Really Hold That Religiousness Is Irrational and Equivalent to Emotional Disturbance?" *American Psychologist* 47 (1992): 428–429.

——— "My Current Views of Rational-Emotive Therapy (RET) and Religiousness." *Journal of Rational-Emotive & Cognitive-Behavior Therapy* 10 (1992): 37–40.

——— "The Advantages and Disadvantages of Self-help Therapy Materials." *Professional Psychology: Research and Practice* 24 (1993): 335–339.

Ellis, Albert, and Eugene Schoenfeld. "Divine Intervention and the Treatment of Chemical Dependency." *Journal of Substance Abuse* 2 (1990): 459–468.

Enright, Robert D. "Piaget on the Moral Development of Forgiveness: Identity or Reciprocity?" *Human Development* 37 (1994): 63–80.

Enright, Robert D., and Robert L. Zell. "Problems Encountered When We Forgive One Another." *Journal of Psychology and Christianity* 8 (1989): 52–60.

Enright, Robert D., David L. Eastin, Sandra Golden, Issidoros Sarinopoulos, and Suzanne Freedman. "Interpersonal Forgiveness within the Helping Professions: An Attempt to Resolve Differences of Opinion." *Counseling and Values* 36 (1992): 84–103.

Erickson, Millard J. *Christian Theology*. Grand Rapids: Baker, 1985.

Erickson, Richard C. "Morality and the Practice of Psychotherapy." *Pastoral Psychology* 43 (1994): 81–91.

Erikson, Erik H. *Childhood and Society*. New York: Norton, 1963.

"Ethical Principles of Psychologists and Code of Conduct." *American Psychologist* 47 (1992): 1597–1611.

Ethical Standards. Alexandria, Va.: American Counseling Association, 1988.

Finney, John R., and H. Newton Malony. "An Empirical Study of Contemplative Prayer as an Adjunct to Psychotherapy." *Journal of Psychology and Theology* 13 (1985): 284–290.

Foster, Richard J. *Celebration of Discipline: The Path to Spiritual Growth*. San Francisco: HarperCollins, 1988.

——— Prayer: Finding the Heart's True Home. San Francisco: HarperCollins, 1992.

Foster, Richard J., and James Bryan Smith, eds. *Devotional Classics*. San Francisco: HarperCollins, 1993.

Frank, Jerome D. "Therapeutic Factors in Psychotherapy." *American Journal of Psychotherapy* 25 (1971): 350–361.

——— "Psychotherapy: The Restoration of Morale." *American Journal of Psychiatry* 131 (1974): 271–274.

Friesen, Will, and Al Dueck. "Whatever Happened to Law?" *Journal of Psychology and Christianity* 7 (1988): 13–22.

Galanter, Marc, David Larson, and Elizabeth Rubenstone. "Christian Psychiatry: The Impact of Evangelical Belief on Clinical Practice." *American Journal of Psychiatry* 148 (1991): 90–95.

Gartner, John. "The Capacity to Forgive: An Object Relations Perspective." *Journal of Religion and Health* 27 (1988): 313–320.

Gassin, Elizabeth A., and Robert D. Enright. "The Will to Meaning in the Process of Forgiveness." Journal of Psychology and Christianity 14 (1995): 38–49.

Gladson, Jerry A. "Higher than the Heavens: Forgiveness in the Old Testament." *Journal of Psychology and Christianity* 11 (1992): 125–135.

Gladson, Jerry, and Charles Plott. "Unholy Wedlock? The Peril and Promise of Applying Psychology to the Bible." *Journal of Psychology and Christianity* 10 (1991): 54–64.

Graham, Stanley R. "Desire, Belief, and Grace: A Psychotherapeutic
Paradigm." *Psychotherapy: Theory, Research, and Practice* 17 (1980): 370–371.

Gramzow, Richard, and June Price Tangney. "Proneness to Shame and the
Narcissistic Personality." *Personality and Social Psychology* Bulletin 18 (1992):
369–376.

Gruber, Louis N. "True and False Spirituality: A Framework for Christian
Behavioral Medicine." *Journal of Psychology and Christianity* 14 (1995):
133–140.

Hales, Shawn W., Randall Sorenson, Joan Jones, and John Coe.
"Psychotherapists and the Religious Disciplines: Personal Beliefs and
Professional Practice." Paper presented at the conference of the Christian
Association for Psychological Studies, Virginia Beach. April 1995.

Hall, Terese A. "Spiritual Effects of Childhood Sexual Abuse in Adult Christian
Women." *Journal of Psychology and Theology* 23 (1995): 129–134.

Hallesby, Ole (translated by Clarence J. Carlsen). *Prayer.* Minneapolis: Augsburg
Publishing House, 1931.

Harris, Thomas A. *I'm OK—You're OK: A Practical Guide to Transactional
Analysis.* New York: Harper & Row, 1967.

Hauck, Paul. *Reason in Pastoral Counseling.* Philadelphia: Westminster, 1972.

——— "Religion and RET: Friends or Foes?" In *Clinical Applications of
Rational-Emotive Therapy,* edited by Albert Ellis and M. E. Bernard. New
York: Plenum Press, 1985.

Hazard, D. *A Day in Your Presence: A 40-Day Journey in the Company of Francis of
Assisi.* Minneapolis: Bethany House, 1992.

Hebl, John H., and Robert D. Enright, "Forgiveness as a Psychotherapeutic
Goal with Elderly Females." *Psychotherapy* 30 (1993): 658–667.

Henry, William P., Hans H. Strupp, Thomas E. Schacht, and Louise Gaston.
"Psychodynamic Approaches." In *Handbook of Psychotherapy and Behavior
Change,* 4th ed., edited by Allen E. Bergin and Sol L. Garfield. New York:
Wiley, 1994.

Holden, J. Stuart. *Redeeming Vision.* London: Robert Scott, 1908.

Holling, David W. "Pastoral Psychotherapy: Is it Unique?" *Counseling and Values*
34 (1990): 96–102.

Hood, Ralph W., Jr., Ronald J. Morris, and P. J. Watson. "Religious Orientation
and Prayer Experience." *Psychological Reports* 60 (1987): 1201–1202.

Hope, Donald. "The Healing Paradox of Forgiveness." *Psychotherapy* 24 (1987):
240–244.

Horrigan, Bonnie. "Christiane Northrup, MD: Medical Practice as a Spiritual
Journey." *Alternative Therapies in Health and Medicine* 1 (1995): 64–71.

Huber, R. John. "Psychotherapy: A Graceful Activity." *Individual Psychology* 43
(1987): 437–443.

Human Development Study Group. "Five Points on the Construct of Forgiveness within Psychotherapy." *Psychotherapy* 28 (1991): 493–496.

Hunt, Dave, and T. A. McMahon. *The Seduction of Christianity.* Eugene, Ore.: Harvest House, 1985.

Hurding, Roger. *The Bible and Counselling.* London: Hodder & Stoughton, 1992.

Hybels, Bill. *Too Busy Not to Pray: Slowing Down to Be with God.* Downers Grove, Ill.: InterVarsity Press, 1988.

Hymer, Sharon. *Confessions in Psychotherapy.* New York: Gardner Press, 1988.

Jacobs, H. E. "Confession." In *The International Standard Bible Encyclopedia,* edited by James Orr, John L. Nuelsen, Edgar Y. Mullins, Morris O. Evans, and Melvin Grove Kyle. Grand Rapids: Eerdmans, 1956.

Jagers, J. Lee. "Putting Humpty Together Again: Reconciling the Post-Affair Marriage." *Journal of Psychology and Christianity* 8 (1989): 63–72.

John of the Cross. "Excerpts from *The Dark Night of the Soul.*" In *Devotional Classics,* edited by Richard J. Foster and James Bryan Smith. San Francisco: HarperCollins, 1993.

Johnson, Eric L. "A Place for the Bible within Psychological Science." *Journal of Psychology and Theology* 20 (1992): 346–355.

Johnson, W. Brad. "Rational-Emotive Therapy and Religiousness: A Review." *Journal of Rational-Emotive & Cognitive-Behavioral Therapy* 10 (1992): 21–35.

——— "Christian Rational-Emotive Therapy: A Treatment Protocol." *Journal of Psychology and Christianity* 12 (1993): 254–261.

——— "Outcome Research and Religious Psychotherapies: Where Are We and Where Are We Going?" *Journal of Psychology and Theology* 21 (1993) 297–308.

Johnson, W. Brad, and Charles R. Ridley. "Brief Christian and Non-Christian Rational-Emotive Therapy with Depressed Christian Clients: An Exploratory Study." *Counseling and Values* 36 (1992): 220–229.

Johnson, W. Brad, Ronald DeVries, Charles R. Ridley, Donald Pettorini, and Deland R. Peterson. "The Comparative Efficacy of Christian and Secular Rational-Emotive Therapy with Christian Clients." *Journal of Psychology and Theology* 22 (1994): 130–140.

Jones, Enrico E., and Steven M. Pulos. "Comparing the Process in Psychodynamic and Cognitive-behavioral Therapies." *Journal of Consulting and Clinical Psychology* 61 (1993): 306–316.

Jones, Stanton L. "A Constructive Relationship for Religion with the Science and Profession of Psychology: Perhaps the Boldest Model Yet." *American Psychologist* 49 (1994): 184–199.

——— "Tentative Reflections on the Role of Scripture in Counseling." Presentation made to psychology graduate students at Wheaton College, April 1994.

Jones, Stanton L., and Richard E. Butman. *Modern Psychotherapies: A Comprehensive Christian Appraisal*. Downers Grove, Ill.: InterVarsity Press, 1991.

Jones-Haldeman, Madelynn. "Implications from Selected Literary Devices for a New Testament Theology of Grace and Forgiveness." *Journal of Psychology and Christianity* 11 (1992): 136–146.

Jung, Carl G. "On the Psychology of the Unconscious." In *Two Essays on Analytical Psychology*. Princeton, N.J.: Princeton University Press, 1972.

Kelly, Timothy A., and Hans H. Strupp. "Patient and Therapist Values in Psychotherapy: Perceived Changes, Assimilation, Similarity, and Outcome." *Journal of Consulting and Clinical Psychology* 60 (1992): 34–40.

Kelsey, David H. *The Uses of Scripture in Recent Theology*. Philadelphia: Fortress Press, 1975.

à Kempis, Thomas. "The Imitation of Christ." In *The Treasury of Christian Spiritual Classics*. Nashville: Thomas Nelson, 1994.

Koenig, Harold G., Lucille B. Bearon, and Richard Dayringer. "Physician Perspectives on the Role of Religion in the Physician–Older Patient Relationship." *The Journal of Family Practice* 28 (1989): 441–448.

Lambert, J. C. "Prayer." In *The International Standard Bible Encyclopedia*, edited by James Orr, John L. Nuelsen, Edgar Y. Mullins, Morris O. Evans, and Melvin Grove Kyle. Grand Rapids: Eerdmans, 1956.

Lambert, Michael J. "Psychotherapy Outcome Research: Implications for Integrative and Eclectic Therapists." In *Handbook of Psychotherapy Integration*, edited by John C. Norcross and Marvin R. Goldfried. New York: Basic Books, 1992.

Lambert, Michael J., and Allen E. Bergin. "The Effectiveness of Psychotherapy." In *Handbook of Psychotherapy and Behavior Change* (4th ed.), edited by Allen E. Bergin and Sol L. Garfield. New York: Wiley, 1986.

Lawrence, Constance. "Rational-Emotive Therapy and the Religious Client." *Journal of Rational-Emotive Therapy* 5 (1987): 13–20.

Lawrence, Constance, and Charles H. Huber. "Strange Bedfellows?: Rational-Emotive Therapy and Pastoral Counseling." *The Personnel and Guidance Journal* 61 (1982): 210–212.

Lederer, Richard. *Anguished English*. New York: Dell Publishing, 1987.

Lewis, C. S. *Mere Christianity*. New York: Macmillan, 1952.

Lindsay-Hartz, Janice. "Contrasting Experiences of Shame and Guilt." *American Behavioral Scientist* 27 (1984): 689–704.

Linehan, Marsha M., *Cognitive-behavioral Treatment of Borderline Personality Disorder*. New York: Guilford, 1993.

Martinez, Frank I. "Therapist-Client Convergence and Similarity of Religious Values: Their Effect on Client Improvement." *Journal of Psychology and Christianity* 10 (1991): 137–143.

Maslow, Abraham H. *Religions, Values, and Peak-Experiences.* New York: The Viking Press, 1964.

Mauger, Paul A., Tom Freeman, Alicia G. McBride, Jacqueline Escano Perry, Dianne C. Grove, and Kathleen E. McKinney. "The Measurement of Forgiveness: Preliminary Research." *Journal of Psychology and Christianity* 11 (1992): 170–180.

McConnell, Francis J. "Redemption." In *The International Standard Bible Encyclopedia,* edited by James Orr, John L. Nuelsen, Edgar Y. Mullins, Morris O. Evans, and Melvin Grove Kyle. Grand Rapids: Eerdmans, 1956.

McCullough, Michael E. "Prayer and Health: Conceptual Issues, Research Review, and Research Agenda." *Journal of Psychology and Theology* 23 (1995): 15–29.

McCullough, Michael E., and Everett L. Worthington, Jr. "Models of Interpersonal Forgiveness and Their Applications to Counseling." *Counseling and Values* 39 (1994): 2–14.

———— "Encouraging Clients to Forgive People Who Have Hurt Them: Review, Critique, and Research Prospectus." *Journal of Psychology and Theology* 22 (1994): 3–20.

McMinn, Mark R. "Religious Values and Client-Therapist Matching in Psychotherapy." *Journal of Psychology and Theology* 12 (1984): 24–33.

———— "Religious Values, Sexist Language, and Perceptions of a Therapist." *Journal of Psychology and Christianity* 10 (1991): 132–136.

———— Cognitive Therapy Techniques in Christian Counseling. Waco, Tex.: Word.

———— "RET, Constructivism, and Christianity: A Hermeneutic for Christian Cognitive Therapy." *Journal of Psychology and Christianity* 13 (1994): 342–355.

McMinn, Mark R., and Gordon N. McMinn. "Complete Yet Inadequate: The Role of Learned Helplessness and Self-Attribution from the Writings of Paul." *Journal of Psychology and Theology* 11 (1983): 303–310.

McMinn, Mark R., and Katheryn Rhoads Meek. "Training Programs." In *Ethics and the Christian Mental Health Professional,* edited by Randolph Saunders. Downers Grove, Ill.: InterVarsity Press.

———— "Ethics Among Christian Counselors: A Survey of Beliefs and Behaviors." *Journal of Psychology and Theology.*

McMinn, Mark R., and Nathaniel G. Wade. "Beliefs about the Prevalence of Dissociative Identity Disorder, Sexual Abuse, and Ritual Abuse among Religious and Non-religious Therapists." *Professional Psychology: Research and Practice* 26 (1995): 257–261.

McMinn, Mark. R., and James C. Wilhoit. "Psychology, Theology, and Spirituality: Challenges for Spiritually Sensitive Psychotherapy." *Christian Counseling Today* (winter 1996).

Meek, Katheryn Rhoads, Jeanne S. Albright, and Mark R. McMinn. "Religious Orientation, Guilt, Confession, and Forgiveness." *Journal of Psychology and Theology* (fall 1995).

Meek, Katheryn Rhoads, and Mark R. McMinn, "Forgiveness: More than a Therapeutic Technique." *Journal of Psychology and Christianity* (in press).

Menninger, Karl. *Whatever Became of Sin?* New York: Hawthorne Books, 1973.

Merton, Thomas. *Praying the Psalms.* Collegeville, Minn.: Liturgical Press, 1956.

——— *Life and Holiness.* New York: Herder and Herder, 1963.

Miller, Alice. *Banished Knowledge.* New York: Doubleday, 1990.

Moon, Gary W. "Spiritual Directors, Christian Counselors: Where Do They Overlap?" *Christian Counseling Today* (winter 1994), 29–33.

Moon, Gary W., Judy W. Bailey, John C. Kwasny, and Dale E. Willis. "Training in the Use of Christian Disciplines as Counseling Techniques within Christian Graduate Training Programs." In *Psychotherapy and Religious Values,* edited by Everett L. Worthington, Jr. Grand Rapids: Baker, 1993.

Mowrer, O. Hobart. "'Sin,' the Lesser of Two Evils." *American Psychologist* 15 (1960): 301–304.

——— "Integrity Groups: Basic Principles and Objective." *The Counseling Psychologist* 3 (1972): 7–32.

Mowrer, O. Hobart, and A. V. Veszelovszky. "There May Indeed Be a 'Right Way': Response to James D. Smrtic." *Psychotherapy: Theory, Research, and Practice* 17 (1980): 440–447.

Murray, Andrew. *Humility.* Old Tappan, N.J.: Fleming H. Revell, 1895.

Myers, David G., and Malcolm A. Jeeves. *Psychology through the Eyes of Faith.* San Francisco: Harper & Row, 1987.

Narramore, S. Bruce. *No Condemnation.* Grand Rapids: Zondervan, 1984.

Olthuis, James H. "God-With-Us: Toward a Relational Psychotherapeutic Model." *Journal of Psychology and Christianity* 13 (1994): 37–49.

Orlinsky, David E., Klaus Grawe, and Barbara K. Parks. "Process and Outcome in Psychotherapy—Noch Einmal." In *Handbook of Psychotherapy and Behavior Change,* 4th ed., edited by Allen E. Bergin and Sol L. Garfield. New York: Wiley, (1994): 270–376.

Pascal, Blaise. *Pensées.* New York: Viking Penguin, 1966 translation.

Pecheur, David Richard, and Keith J. Edwards. "A Comparison of Secular and Religious Versions of Cognitive Therapy with Depressed Christian College Students." *Journal of Psychology and Theology* 12 (1984): 45–54.

Pennebaker, James W., Cheryl F. Hughes, and Robin C. O'Heeron. "The Psychophysiology of Confession: Linking Inhibitory and Psychosomatic Processes." *Journal of Personality and Social Psychology* 52 (1987): 781–793.

Peterson, Eugene H. *A Long Obedience in the Same Direction: Discipleship in an Instant Society.* Downers Grove, Ill.: InterVarsity Press, 1980.

Pingleton, Jared P. "The Role and Function of Forgiveness in the Psychotherapeutic Process." *Journal of Psychology and Christianity* 17 (1989): 27–35.

Poloma, Maraget M., and George H. Gallup, Jr. *Varieties of Prayer: A Survey Report.* Philadelphia: Trinity Press International, 1991.

Pope, Kenneth S., and Jacqueline C. Bouhoutsos. *Sexual Intimacy between Therapists and Patients.* New York: Praeger, 1986.

Pope, Kenneth S., Barbara G. Tabachnick, and Patricia Keith-Spiegel. "Ethics of Practice: The Beliefs and Behaviors of Psychologists as Therapists." *American Psychologist* 42 (1987): 993–1006.

Pope, Kenneth S., and Shirley Feldman-Summers. "National Survey of Psychologists' Sexual and Physical Abuse History and Their Evaluation of Training and Competence in These Areas." *Professional Psychology: Research and Practice* 23 (1992): 353–361.

Pope, Kenneth S., Janet L. Sonne, and Jean Holroyd. *Sexual Feelings in Psychotherapy.* Washington, D.C.: American Psychological Association, 1993.

Postema, Don. *Space for God: The Study and Practice of Prayer and Spirituality.* Grand Rapids: CRC Publications, 1983.

Powell, John. *Fully Human, Fully Alive.* Niles, Ill.: Argus, 1976.

Propst, L. Rebecca. "The Comparative Efficacy of Religious and Non-religious Imagery for the Treatment of Mild Depression in Religious Individuals." *Cognitive Therapy and Research* 4 (1980): 167–178.

Propst, L. Rebecca, Richard Ostrom, Philip Watkins, Terri Dean, and David Mashburn. "Comparative Efficacy of Religious and Nonreligious Cognitive-behavioral Therapy for the Treatment of Clinical Depression in Religious Individuals." *Journal of Consulting and Clinical Psychology* 60 (1992): 94–103.

Quackenbos, Stephen, Gayle Privette, and Bonnel Klentz. "Psychotherapy: Sacred or Secular?" *Journal of Counseling and Development* 63 (1985): 290–293.

Rapee, Ronald, and David Barlow. "Panic Disorder: Cognitive-behavioral Treatment." *Psychiatric Annals* 18 (1988): 473–477.

Reisner, Andrew D., and Peter Lawson. "Psychotherapy, Sin, and Mental Health." *Pastoral Psychology* 40 (1992): 303–311.

Richards, P. Scott. "Religious Devoutness in College Students: Relations with Emotional Adjustment and Psychological Separation from Parents." *Journal of Counseling Psychology* 38 (1991): 189–196.

Riodan, Richard J., and Diane Simone. "Codependent Christians: Some Issues for Church-Based Recovery Groups." *Journal of Psychology and Theology* 21 (1993): 158–164.

Rosenak, Charlotte M., and G. Mack Harnden. "Forgiveness in the Psychotherapeutic Process: Clinical Applications." *Journal of Psychology and Christianity* 11 (1992): 188–197.

Ryle, Anthony. *Cognitive-Analytic Therapy: Active Participation in Change.* New York: Wiley, 1990.

Safran, Jeremy D., and Zindel V. Segal. *Interpersonal Process in Cognitive Therapy.* New York: Basic Books, 1990.

Sandage, Steven J., Everett L. Worthington, Jr., and William Smith. "Seeking Forgiveness: Toward an Integration of Psychology and Theology." Paper presented at the annual meetings of the Christian Association for Psychological Studies, Virginia Beach. April 1995.

Sanford, Agnes. *The Healing Light.* New York: Ballantine Books, 1972.

Schneider, Susanne, and Robert Kastenbaum. "Patterns and Meanings of Prayer in Hospice Caregivers: An Exploratory Study." *Death Studies* 17 (1993): 471–485.

Seamands, David A. *Healing of Memories.* Wheaton, Ill.: Victor Books, 1985.

Smedes, Lewis B. *Forgive and Forget: Healing the Hurts We Don't Deserve.* San Francisco: Harper & Row, 1984.

Smith, M. Brewster. "Selfhood at Risk: Postmodern Perils and the Perils of Postmodernism." *American Psychologist* 49 (1994): 405–411.

Smith, Mary Lee, G. V. Glass, and R. L. Miller. *The Benefits of Psychotherapy.* Baltimore: Johns Hopkins Press, 1980.

Smrtic, James D. "Time to Remove Our Theoretical Blinders: Integrity Therapy May Be the Right Way." *Psychotherapy: Theory, Research, and Practice* 16 (1979): 185–189.

Somberg, Daniel R., Gerald L. Stone, and Charles D. Claiborn. "Informed Consent: Therapists' Beliefs and Practices." *Professional Psychology: Research and Practice* 24 (1993): 153–159.

Stover, Elaine D., and Mark Stover. "Biblical Storytelling as a Form of Child Therapy." *Journal of Psychology and Christianity* 13 (1994): 28–36.

Strupp, Hans H. "The Psychotherapist's Skills Revisited." *Clinical Psychology* 2 (1995): 70–74.

Subkoviak, Michael J., Robert D. Enright, Ching-Ru Wu, Elizabeth A. Gassin, Suzanne Freedman, Leanne M. Olson, and Issidoros Sarinopoulos. "Measuring Interpersonal Forgiveness." Paper presented at the annual meetings of the American Educational Research Association, San Francisco. April 1992.

Subkoviak, Michael J., Robert D. Enright, and Ching-Ru Wu. "Current Developments Related to Measuring Forgiveness." Paper presented at the annual meeting of the Mid-Western Educational Research Association, Chicago. October 1992.

Sullivan, Harry S. *Conceptions of Modern Psychiatry.* New York: Norton, 1953.

Sullivan, Therese, William Martin, Jr., and Mitchel M. Handelsman. "Practical Benefits of an Informed-consent Procedure: An Empirical Investigation." *Professional Psychology: Research and Practice* 24 (1993): 160–163.

Sweeney, Daniel S., and Garry Landreth. "Healing a Child's Spirit through Play Therapy: A Scriptural Approach to Treating Children." *Journal of Psychology and Christianity* 12 (1993): 351–356.

Tan, Siang-Yang. "Cognitive-Behavior Therapy: A Biblical Approach." *Journal of Psychology and Theology* 15 (1987): 103–112.

———— "Religious Values and Interventions in Lay Christian Counseling." *Journal of Psychology and Christianity* 10 (1991): 173–182.

———— "Ethical Considerations in Religious Psychotherapy: Potential Pitfalls and Unique Resources." *Journal of Psychology and Theology* 22 (1994): 389–394.

Tangney, June Price. "Moral Affect: The Good, the Bad, and the Ugly." *Journal of Personality and Social Psychology* 61 (1991): 598–607.

Tangney, June Price, Patricia Wagner, Carey Fletcher, and Richard Gramzow. "Shamed into Anger? The Relation of Shame and Guilt to Anger and Self-Reported Aggression." *Journal of Personality and Social Psychology* 62 (1992): 669–675.

Tangney, June Price, Patricia E. Wagner, and Richard Gramzow. "Proneness to Shame, Proneness to Guilt, and Psychopathology." *Journal of Abnormal Psychology* 103 (1992): 469–478.

Task Force on Promotion and Dissemination of Psychological Procedures. "Training in and Dissemination of Empirically Validated Psychological Treatments: Report and Recommendations. *The Clinical Psychologist* 48 (1995): 3–23.

Theologia Germanica. In *Devotional Classics,* edited by Richard J. Foster and James Bryan Smith. San Francisco: HarperCollins, 1993, 147–153.

Tjeltveit, Alan C. "The Ethics of Value Conversion in Psychotherapy: Appropriate and Inappropriate Therapist Influence on Client Values." *Clinical Psychology Review* 6 (1986): 515–537.

Todd, Elizabeth. "The Value of Confession and Forgiveness according to Jung." *Journal of Religion and Health* 24 (1985): 39–48.

Tozer, A. W. *The Pursuit of God.* Camp Hill, Penn.: Christian Publications, 1993.

Vachon, Dominic O., and Albert A. Agresti. "A Training Proposal to Help Mental Health Professionals Clarify and Manage Implicit Values in the Counseling Process." *Professional Psychology: Research and Practice* 23 (1992): 509–514.

Vande Kemp, Hendrika. "Psychotherapy as a Religious Process: A Historical Heritage." In *Psychotherapy and the Religiously Committed Patient,* edited by E. Mark Stern. New York: Haworth Press, 1985.

———— "Psychotherapy and Redemption: A Tribute to a 'Dying Mom.'" Presented at the 98th Annual Convention of the American Psychological Association, Boston. August 1990.

Veenstra, Glenn. "Psychological Concepts of Forgiveness." *Journal of Psychology and Christianity* 11 (1992): 160–169.

Vitz, Paul C. *Psychology as Religion: The Cult of Self-Worship.* Grand Rapids: Eerdmans, 1977.

Wade, S. H. "The Development of a Scale to Measure Forgiveness." Ph.D. diss., Fuller Theological Seminary, 1989.

Walls, Gary B. "Values and Psychotherapy: A Comment on 'Psychotherapy and Religious Values.'" *Journal of Consulting and Clinical Psychology* 48 (1980): 640–641.

Warnock, Sandra D. M. "Rational-Emotive Therapy and the Christian Client." *Journal of Rational-Emotive & Cognitive-Behavior Therapy* 7 (1989): 263–274.

Weinberger, Joel. "Common Factors Aren't So Common: The Common Factors Dilemma." *Clinical Psychology: Science and Practice* 2 (1995): 45–69.

Weiner, Bernard. "On Sin Versus Sickness: A Theory of Perceived Responsibility and Social Motivation." *American Psychologist* 48 (1993): 957–965.

Weiner, Bernard, Sandra Graham, Oli Peter, and Mary Zmuidinas. "Public Confession and Forgiveness." *Journal of Personality* 59 (1991): 281–312.

Westley, Dick. *Redemptive Intimacy.* Mystic, Conn.: Twenty-Third Publications, 1981.

Whiston, Susan C., and Thomas L. Sexton. "An Overview of Psychotherapy Outcome Research: Implications for Practice." *Professional Psychology* 24 (1993): 43–51.

Willard, Dallas. *The Spirit of the Disciplines.* San Francisco: HarperCollins, 1988.

Woodward, Kenneth L. "What Ever Happened to Sin?" *Newsweek* (6 February, 1995): 23.

Worthen, Valerie. "Psychotherapy and Catholic Confession." *Journal of Religion and Health* 13 (1974): 275–284.

Worthington, Everett L., Jr. "Religious Counseling: A Review of Published Empirical Research." *Journal of Counseling and Development* 64 (1986): 421–431.

———— ed. *Psychotherapy and Religious Values.* Grand Rapids: Baker, 1993.

———— "A Blueprint for Intradisciplinary Integration." *Journal of Psychology and Theology* 22 (1994): 79–86.

Worthington, Everett L., Jr., Philip D. Dupont, James T. Berry, and Loretta A. Duncan. "Christian Therapists and Clients' Perceptions of Religious Psychotherapy in Private and Agency Settings." *Journal of Psychology and Theology* 16 (1988) 282–293.

Worthington, Everett L., Jr., and Frederick A. DiBlasio. "Promoting Mutual Forgiveness within the Fractured Relationship." *Psychotherapy* 27 (1990): 219–223.

Young, Jeffrey E. *Cognitive Therapy for Personality Disorders: A Schema-focused Approach,* rev. ed. Sarasota, Fla.: Professional Resource Press, 1994.

Zackrison, Edwin. "A Theology of Sin, Grace, and Forgiveness." *Journal of Psychology and Theology* 11 (1992): 147–159.

ABOUT THE AUTHOR

Mark R. McMinn, Ph.D., is a professor of psychology at Wheaton College Graduate School in Wheaton, Illinois, where he directs and teaches in the Doctor of Psychology program. A diplomate in Clinical Psychology of the American Board of Professional Psychology, McMinn has thirteen years of postdoctoral experience in counseling, psychotherapy, and psychological testing. McMinn is the author of *Making the Best of Stress: How Life's Hassles Can Form the Fruit of the Spirit; The Jekyll/Hyde Syndrome: Controlling Inner Conflict through Authentic Living; Cognitive Therapy Techniques in Christian Counseling;* and *Christians in the Crossfire* (written with James D. Foster). He and his wife, Lisa, have three daughters, Danielle, Sarah, and Megan.